Results May Vary

Results May Vary
Christian Women Reflect on Post-College Life

Edited by Linda Beail and Sylvia Cortez

POINT LOMA
PRESS

Results May Vary: Christian Women Reflect on Post-College Life

Point Loma Press Series

Point Loma Press
3900 Lomaland Dr.
San Diego, CA 92106

Wipf and Stock Publishers
199 W. 8th Ave., Suite 3
Eugene, OR 97401

www.wipfandstock.com

ISBN 13: 978-1-62032-930-6

Credits

Director of the Wesleyan Center: Mark Mann
Managing Editor, Point Loma Press: Sharon Bowles
Assistant Editor and Layout Coodinators: Kaitlin Barr Nadal and Lydia Heberling

Results May Vary

III. Wholeness and Holiness: Living an Embodied Life • 171

Foreword for Point Loma Press Series

Point Loma Press was founded in 1992 to provide a publishing outlet for faculty and to serve the distinct theological mission of Point Loma Nazarene University (San Diego, CA). Over time the press has grown to publish authors from a wider range of institutional backgrounds, but its core mission remains the same: to encourage and extend a distinctly Wesleyan theological perspective on various topics and issues for the church today. Most Point Loma Press books are theological in scope, though many are quite practical in their focus, and some address non-theological topics but from a Wesleyan theological perspective. All Point Loma Press books are written with a broad audience in mind, intended to contribute effectively to contemporary scholarship while also being accessible to pastors, laypersons, and students alike. Our hope is that our new collaboration with Wipf & Stock Publishers will continue to allow us to expand our audience for the important topics and perspective of our work.

Point Loma Press welcomes any submissions that meet these criteria. Inquiries should be directed to PointLomaPress@pointloma.edu or 619-849-2359. When submitting, please provide rationale for how your work supports the mission of the Point Loma Nazarene University Wesleyan Center to articulate distinctly Wesleyan themes and trajectories.

Acknowledgments

The editors would like to thank Point Loma Nazarene University, particularly the Office of Spiritual Development and the Margaret Stevenson Center for Women's Studies, for supporting the development of the Women's Forum program that led to this book. We are grateful to everyone at Point Loma Press who helped to inspire and sustain this project. Thank you to Maxine Walker for the idea of turning these conversations into a book and never taking "no" for an answer; to Sam Powell for careful reading of the first draft and helpful suggestions, and changing the shape of the project in a more fruitful way; to Mark Mann, for enthusiastically believing in this project and seeing it through; and to Kaitlin Barr Nadal, Sharon Bowles, and Lydia Heberling for their invaluable assistance in copyediting and laying out the book. Thanks as well to the PLNU Wesleyan Center for a summer grant that enabled the editing of this volume.

We are indebted to all of our students who have attended the Senior Women's Forum over the years. Thank you for letting us share in your journeys, and for all of the rich conversations that have ensued. We are enormously grateful for each of the many women faculty, staff, alumni and friends who have shared their stories and experiences at Women's Forum. Without you, this book would not exist. Lauren Winner, thank you for inspiring these conversations with your writing, and for participating in our first Women's Forum. We are so glad to have had you as a friend of this project from the very beginning. Huge thanks to Kelly Bennett, for suggesting the fabulous title. Most of all, we want to thank each of the contributors to this volume who have shared so insightfully and generously their own hard-won wisdom. Their faithfulness and commitment in their own journeys inspire us all to move forward with a greater sense of hope and courage.

Linda would like to thank Sylvia, for the deep friendship that has grown from the work of Women's Forum and this book. It has been a delight and a privilege to partner with someone so creative, thoughtful, passionate, and trustworthy. You have made all the hard work more fun than I could have imagined. Thank you for caring about the details, and for all of the many hours of conversation and writing in just about every coffee shop in San Diego (and now a few in Kiev, too). I am profoundly grateful for your presence in my life. Thanks to Mom and Dad for always supporting me in whatever I take on. Caroline and Joshua, thank you for all of the ways you have contributed to this project—from letting me share the parts of my story that are also yours, to literally attending the Women's Forum in my arms and being patient while I was writing and editing with Sylvia. More importantly, thank you for being the amazing people you are and for the joy it is to be your mom. Eric—you make my life possible in more ways than I can count. Thank you for the richness of our life together, for making me laugh more than anyone else can, for braving the adventure of parenting with me, and for your unwavering love. Sylvia and I are particularly grateful for all the tangible things you contributed to this project, from many hours of holding down the fort while I was gone, to the endless supply of snacks and coffee that kept us both going. Thanks for the cookies! I love you.

Sylvia feels great gratitude to Linda, who all those years ago was willing to partner together on a program she had no idea would lead to this book! Her knowledge, insight and reflections on these many topics have given a firm foundation to the Women's Forum and this book. It would not have been as challenging or fun without her courage, passion for women's studies, hard work, and faithful friendship. Thank you to Mom, for your effortless and unwavering love; to Liz, Cyndi & Judy, my three amazing sisters, because you humble me with your love and support especially now that I'm thousands of miles away; and to Dad, for your quiet and tender presence in my life. Mary Paul—you made work even more rewarding than I imagined. Thank you for your tenacity, laughter, long conversations and our pedicure runs. I'm grateful to Café Calabria coffee house for letting me linger after closing time so I could write. Finally, deep thanks to Vova, for walking alongside me in friendship for 18 years; and for asking me to walk the rest of my years with you in marriage. я тебя люблю, очень сильно

Introduction:
Illumination on the Path

Here is the world. Beautiful and terrible things will happen. Do not be afraid![1]
—Frederick Buechner

Graduation can be such a gratifying achievement, but it's also like standing at the edge of the known world and peering into the abyss, not knowing what life will really be like after that momentous event happens. As with any big life transition—getting married, finding a new job, expecting a baby, entering retirement—you joyfully anticipate the date on the calendar that you've looked forward to for so long, but also view the unknown future with some trepidation. It can be such an amazing feeling of both exhilaration and fear.

The idea for this book, written specifically for young women in their early twenties very much standing at the edge of the unknown, presented itself following a series of forums held at Point Loma Nazarene University. The Senior Women's Forum was a response to the growing need not only to train and mentor young women in their chosen fields of study, but to prepare them for the whole journey of life. We discovered in our work with university students that there was a huge need to provide a space where women could share honestly with their younger counterparts a fuller truth about vocation, ambition, faith, money, marriage, sexuality, and friendships. "If you do not tell the truth about yourself you cannot tell it about other people," wrote Virginia Woolf.[2] One of the goals for the

---

1   Frederick Buechner, *Wishful Thinking: A Seeker's ABC* (New York: HarperCollins, 1993), 39.

2   Virginia Woolf, *The Moment, and Other Essays* (London: Hogarth Press, 1952), 121.

Women's Forum was to tell the truths we ourselves had learned surrounding the complexity of each of these topics. This is not as simple as it sounds. It is always a challenge to be vulnerable, to present choices we might have made differently with more knowledge and insight. We came back again and again to the many silent truths or, more insidiously, *half-truths* that had been presented to us about life, and the many *myths* we had imbibed that shattered in the realities of our own experiences. Much of what we hope to do in this book is to demystify the perceptions surrounding these topics. We wish to do this particularly through the lens of our own varied experiences as they have been and continue to be illuminated by our Christian faith, convictions, and practices.

As we continue to engage university students in discussions about these transitions, we discover over and over that many of them still are given only half-truths about marriage, motherhood, parenting, friendships, vocation, ambition, and finances. And we never cease to be alarmed that many of the myths we had fallen prey to in our day are still alive and well in their world. The "ring by spring" aspiration prevalent when we were college students still persists among many young women in colleges across the nation, all too often leading some of them to despair at the pressure of this expectation. What a relief it has been for many young women to hear us say that it is an unnecessary pressure to expect that one should be engaged, and at least attached, by the time one graduates. How reassuring for them to discover that not all of us knew exactly what career we wanted to pursue for the rest of our lives when we graduated college, or that the journey would end up quite different than anticipated.

For women, and perhaps for Christian women in particular, there are multiple messages within our culture that should be questioned: that there is one best course (education, then career, then marriage, then motherhood), or that there is a single right set of expectations for our lives. Such messages cause misguided anguish for not being on course or not having yet arrived. Even worse, women put their lives on hold, waiting for these momentous events to occur before life can begin. Without realizing it, we can often be stifled by an unnecessary expectation that damages or hinders our true sense of identity. Mixed in with this message is the insidious promise that if we just do everything "right," life will all work out perfectly the way we expect—we'll be happy, get married, have healthy kids, and have a job we love. Though many women over the course of time have silently or unknowingly lived with these expectations, when we look around at the many godly women in our own lives, we see a beautifully diverse group of women whose lives did not necessarily reflect one course or path. Rather, life circumstances, dreams, choices, jobs, relationships, and a host of other factors led them in so many different, unexpected, and wonderful directions—thus the title for this book.

Among the many truths we discovered in our conversations was the reality that women are incredibly creative in the midst of challenges, and that the choices they make can vary greatly. Of the many women who share in these essays, some have married, others have not. Some have borne children, others have not. Some chose to stay at home to rear their children before beginning or returning to their careers, and others remained in their careers, balancing marriage, motherhood, and work. These differing voices and choices provide young women with a more accurate picture of the diversity of experiences and many directions that in turn shatter the myths of our societal expectations.

The great enemy of the truth is very often not the lie—deliberate, contrived, and
dishonest—but the myth—persistent, persuasive, and unrealistic.
—John F. Kennedy[3]

In order to grow, we must sometimes be willing to let go of the notions and beliefs that no longer sustain the complex circumstances and systems society offers. Ignorance attempts to keep us fastened to easy platitudes and black and white answers. But experience shapes us in ways we would never have imagined. "You learn by living," said Eleanor Roosevelt.[4] We simply found ourselves trying to be faithful to what we had learned in our living, and to share this truth. Why had it been so hard for others to tell us the whole truth? Why had it been so difficult for us to begin to tell the truths we had learned? Perhaps it is the breakdown of extended kinship networks in this highly mobile era, which has made it harder for us to see these whole truths lived out and passed down from one generation of women to another. Perhaps also it's because we feel the whole truth might seem too daunting and scary in the midst of all the excitement of graduation and optimism about various life choices and the future in general.

We trust that all young women, despite the hardships we know they'll face, will make it. Just as they have learned in college to move forward in their careers with knowledge, skill development, and thoughtful reflection,

---

3   John F. Kennedy, Yale Commencement Address, 11 June 1962. Found at http://millercenter.org/scripps/archive/speeches/detail/3370

4   Eleanor Roosevelt, *You Learn by Living: Eleven Keys for a More Fulfilling Life* (Louisville, KY: Westminster John Knox Press, 2004).

we desire for women to make time for thoughtful reflection in all areas of their lives, to develop good discernment that empowers them to move forward mindfully rather than simply reacting to life's unexpected and challenging dimensions. The ability to recognize this creative work of making strong choices that fit the circumstances of our present journey is cause for celebration. What continues to engage us in these conversations is our understanding of what poet Adrienne Rich said so well: "When a woman tells the truth she is creating the possibility for more truth around her."[5] Not only is a woman's own life enlightened by the truth—others around her are witnesses to that truth, and have the opportunity to be impacted and strengthened by that truth.

Content and Layout

The diverse women who share their experiences here are deeply connected to various Christian universities, from recent college grads to women retired from their lifelong careers, single and married, mothers and not, with many different interests, personalities, and ambitions. Most of these authors are professors in Christian universities across the United States and Canada. Though varied in ages and life experiences, they are united in their commitment to Christ and to the flourishing of other women. Their voices, rather than being in competition with one another, make up a rich conversation about the realities of Christian womanhood. There is no one single way to live out our callings, or one cookie-cutter ideal that we should all aspire to. In these writers' attempts to live faithfully, and reflect honestly on what they've learned, we discover that, indeed, results may vary. Rather than feeling defensive about our choices or judging other women because they are unlike us, we hope the juxtaposition of these narratives will cause us to feel affirmed, to learn from what is new or challenging, and to support each other more fully in living out what God calls each of us, in our own unique circumstances and gifts, to do.

In trying to capture the broad array of issues women face, we have divided these wide-ranging essays into three main sections. The first, "Love, Laughter, and Loss: Living in Relationships," provides reflections on friendship, dating, being married, being single, and parenthood. One theme heard in many women's stories is the importance of women's friendships throughout their lives, even as those friendships are complicated by changes

---

5   Adrienne Rich, *Women and Honor: Some Notes on Lying* (Berkeley, CA: Cleis Press, 1990), 191.

in values, geography, or family circumstances. Sometimes we are taken by surprise at which friendships deepen over time, which end, and where we discover new ones. How does marriage change things? From women in long-lived marriages, we get honest glimpses of struggles and success. Others examine cross-cultural partnerships, divorce, and identity crises. What about dating in the post-college years? It can be difficult, exhilarating, and surprising, while being single can be demanding and joyful—not just a holding pattern while waiting for "real life" to begin. Even motherhood can come about in unexpected ways, or rock our identities with unanticipated realizations. Over and over again, women discover grace, wrestle with deep questions, and find life is far more different than they originally expected.

Our second section, "Between Calling and Commerce: Living in Faithful Vocation," tackles issues of ambition, careers, vocation, and money. We face so many choices of how to spend our time and our money. How do we decide? Women at all stages of their professions—from first jobs to retirement and everything in between—talk about how they made their choices and found their callings. Some were serendipitous, others more straightforward; some found work they loved, while others are finding the workplace more challenging than they expected. Some discuss candidly the pressures and rewards, especially within a Christian community, of combining professional work and mothering. Running throughout these different choices and stories are themes of power, responsibility, and faithfulness. How do ideals of Christian womanhood make space for God's callings to serve the church and the world, or fit with the economic realities women face today? How do we reflect theologically on making and spending money? What are the nitty-gritty realities of paying rent and buying groceries on your own for the first time?

In "Wholeness and Holiness: Living an Embodied Life," women speak about sexuality, health, and spiritual formation. Jesus tells us to love God with all of our mind, soul, heart, and strength. How do we practice that? For women in particular, our bodies are so frequently subjected to scrutiny, deemed imperfect, manipulated or malnourished, even misused sexually. Often we internalize and reproduce this pressure or hatred of our physical selves. But as embodied beings created in the image of God, who calls his creation good, we need a different set of expectations and practices. In these essays we hear women speaking about disordered eating, sexual exploitation, emotional stress, and spiritual struggle. As Christians, they find theological resources and redemptive hope in the gospel to combat some of these cultural messages and practices that can be so damaging. From creative arts, to learning to cook healthy food, to finding biblical foremothers, or following the rhythms of the liturgical year, we hear practical and profound re-visioning of how to be whole—and holy—throughout the journey of our lives.

While these stories reflect many different women's experiences, they cannot capture all the myriad realities Christian women live. We do not claim to be exhaustive, or to have included every significant issue faithful women face. Nor is this a self-help book to be read as set of rules or advice to follow. Rather, we hope the truthfulness, insight, and generosity with which these women share their narratives serve as a catalyst for even more honest reflection and conversation about the realities of women's lives.

Illumination

Every Sunday morning in many churches throughout the world, people offer up a "prayer for illumination." In that prayer we ask God to open our hearts and minds to hear with joy the truth God has for us on that day— even in the Scriptures that we may have heard dozens of times before, we ask for a fresh understanding of their meaning and relevance to our lives. As we put together this book, we have thought a lot about illumination. As we have worked with young women in their twenties, stepping into their adult lives with all the promise and uncertainty, we have prayed with them for light to see the path ahead. Sometimes there is only enough light to illuminate the next step; sometimes there is enough brilliance to see and celebrate the big picture of how their talents and experiences are weaving together in a purposeful way. In either case, we have prayed for enough illumination to keep moving forward and to see God's grace at work in all our lives.

This metaphor of light permeates the essays in this anthology. Our purpose in gathering these stories is threefold. First, each of these narratives is a testament to the ways in which women whose lives are illuminated by their faith in Christ live out this faith. As they face a variety of issues and make life choices, each grounds her decisions and practices in her commitment to know and glorify God. While results may vary in the complexities of their life circumstances and choices, they bear witness to the constancy of God's grace and love. Second, we hope that these stories help to illuminate some of the issues, choices, and complexities with which women in their twenties grapple. From a range of ages, life experiences, and perspectives, these narratives are intended to bring more light to topics that may sometimes seem shrouded in mystery, partial truths, or silence.

Third, we hope that by sharing our own hard-earned wisdom—of myths that turned out not to be true, or mistakes we made, or things that we have learned with joy—these essays contribute in some small way to you, our readers, in letting your own lights shine. We hope that they encourage, comfort, reassure, challenge, and inspire you to live your lives brightly and without fear.

Often when she speaks on the topic of faithful living, Sylvia lights the "Christ candle" and leaves it burning throughout her talk to remind us of Christ's presence with us all the time. We know that Jesus is the light of the world, and that light is the unwavering point around which we orient our whole lives. His light and love give us our purpose and meaning, and guides the ways in which we spend our time and energies.

Just after Easter a few years ago, Linda's three-year-old daughter decided to play church. She assembled her dolls and stuffed animals, and started "preaching" to them. And when Linda asked her what she was preaching, she simply yelled exuberantly, "Resurrection! Resurrection! Resurrection!"

How true. There is the whole gospel, wrapped up in one simple word. That is Christianity in a nutshell: light, life, hope, and love where once there was darkness, death, despair, and hate. The triumph of the Resurrection is what makes our faith possible. We take note that the very first news of the miracle of resurrection was entrusted to a woman. There is Mary, the first evangelist, preaching the gospel of Christ's triumph over death to the disciples. As women, we too are the light of Christ to the dark places of the world.

Because we as women fully bear the image of Christ, our hearts break when women are oppressed and devalued, whether right here in our community or when we see it in headlines from around the globe. When women are reduced to merely bodies or sexuality, assaulted, demeaned, and dismissed, it breaks God's heart, too. God, who created us in God's own image, wants us to flourish. God loves our strength, our intelligence, our nurturing, and all the unique experiences and gifts we bring to the world as women.

We also think of the light that other women have brought to illuminate our paths, and we hope these essays share some of that light. There are the older women who have been our mentors and role models—our mothers and grandmothers, and other women who have pointed the way. During Linda's first year of college, she had a class that began at eight in the morning with an impressive young female instructor. On the first day, she asked the class to please wait for her if she was ever a few minutes late to class. She explained that she would surely be on her way, but that she had to wait for the caregiver for her two preschool sons to arrive before heading to campus. Later in the semester, she gave the class a research day, explaining that she would be out of town, walking in the graduation ceremony to receive her Ph.D. in literature. The next week she brought in photos, and Linda remembers marveling at this lovely, brilliant young woman with a professor husband and two sweet little boys, aglow with the triumph of earning her doctorate. She was a great teacher, but even more than that, she was an incredible role model. Even though Linda sat in the back of the class, too shy to speak or to go talk to her during her office hours, this professor made a huge difference in her life. Linda recalls, "She made me believe, as I progressed through college, that someone like me could do that too. She made me feel like it would be possible to be a scholar, to be passionate about learning and teaching, and to be happily married and have children. She was the person I wanted to grow up to become. I could never diminish the importance of my male mentors and professors who worked with me and encouraged me to continue my education. But none of them *embodied* the things I hoped for in my own life; none of them looked like me. It was this woman who made the difference—who made it seem *not* impossible, but actually probable, to do what I do now, because I'd seen her do it first. Her life, even though she didn't realize it at the time, was the light that helped me see my own future."

There are women all around us, throughout all of our lives, young and old, who project a kind of light in both large and small ways, sometimes boldly and sometimes hidden. They embody the courage to see dreams into existence, and in doing so create a kind of space for us to imagine the possibilities in our own lives. There are the peers, friends, and roommates who walk beside us in tears and in laughter, supporting us with friendship and love. Together we banish the darkness along the way. And of course, there are the young women who come behind us. We feel a responsibility to you, our readers. We hope in these chapters that we have been able to shed some light on the thorny and joyful dilemmas of life, to demystify and illuminate the path ahead. We hope we have made that darkness a little less scary for you than it was for us.

Finally, as we write, we think of *your* light, the beautiful and unique spark that shines in each one of you. We hope that you know how lovely and gifted you are, and that you are ready for the road ahead, even if you don't always feel confident and prepared. Don't be afraid to let your light shine! We desperately need the glow of your work, your insight, and your love. The world would be a darker place without it. Each one of you has something to give that no one else can give. We pray that through these essays, and through the conversations we have with one another, that Christ's light will burn brightly in each of us, and that we may light the way for each other as women—not isolated and alone, but as those called to bring God's love and hope to the world. Amen.

—Linda Beail and Sylvia Cortez

Love, Laughter, and Loss: Living in Relationships

So many new experiences and life transitions can occur in our twenties: graduating from college, beginning a career, moving to a new apartment or even a new city, getting married, learning to live on one's own, and taking on new financial responsibilities. All of these opportunities allow us to explore who we are and force us to make strong decisions about our lives. Ideally, we engage these questions and challenges in community. Life is meant to be lived in community and indeed is made richer by those relationships in our lives that we all long for and need. The people in our lives strengthen us with joy, laughter, comfort, courage, and wisdom. But relationships can also be difficult, broken, and confusing. How do we find new friends in adulthood, or maintain old ones in the midst of so many life changes? How do we find a spouse, or create a family? What happens when a marriage fails, or a friendship ends? When the realities of our friendships, romances, or families turn out differently than we might have expected, it can challenge our faith and our sense of self. How do we cope with changes in our relationships even as our own identities are shifting and growing?

Making, Breaking, and Keeping Friendships

Melissa Tucker

As soon as we hit kindergarten, each of us began the search for our lifelines—our "group," or at the very least, someone to eat lunch with. Away from the shelter of family for the first time, we were taught explicitly *how* to have friends. We learned that to have a friend is to be one, right along with lessons on the four food groups and the importance of exercise. We actually had to be directed about these most basic urges. Our kindergarten teachers grasped that the longing for companionship is as natural as the drive for food. But any desire needs refining.

In childhood socialization, the main concern for anyone is *making* friends. Around junior high, the new and painful process of friendship-*breaking* emerges. In adulthood, when the gifts of maturity and experience equip us better for the cycle of friendships, the challenge is actually *keeping* them. For as much as friends shape our young lives and identities, it is fascinating (and sad) how easily the priority of friendship can downshift in adulthood. The inevitable responsibilities of growing up demand our time and energies and, suddenly, we're consumed. It takes intentional care to nurture friendship as we age.

The specific people who populate the journey will come and go over the years. Nurturing friendships is an overall commitment to maintaining the influence of friendship and not necessarily preserving the specific friends of the present moment. This distinction was a hard-learned lesson of my stubborn twenties. I now acknowledge that I need community, but that I don't need particular people to comprise that community. The *art* of making, breaking, and keeping friends is to figure out how to do so with open hands, to give others the space to be welcome—and the freedom to leave—without clinging. The *science* of friendship is that we are wired for

23

it. And though it takes work and practice, the beauty and gift is absolutely worth the effort.

Making

The adjective "life-giving" has become a compass for me and my friends as we discern what is holy or best and how to live; I make friends because friends are life-giving. Everything that happens in my days is made more real, more alive by their accompaniment. Joys are brighter, and pain, transition, and the mundane are more tolerable. My community feels sacred to me and is so vital to my conception of faith that I can't separate the two. Our primary command as Christians is to love God and love neighbor. The "and" connecting the two makes them simultaneous. Friendship is the backbone of my life. It aligns me, supports me, and holds the pieces of my life together and in this way serves as a physical representation of God at work in my life in a great and mysterious way. My friends are a reflection of the compassionate attributes of God. They are also direct answers to my prayers.

I am the most extroverted person I know. In early childhood, unbeknownst to my parents, I would lay in the fetal position at the end of the hall an hour after bedtime, eager to hear their conversations or even just the hum of their voices. I come from a family of introverts who take their downtime seriously, so I relished the two-week summer vacations to San Diego to be with Grandma Betty. Grandma Betty can talk. And she just starts over again if she runs out of things to say. Some of my best memories growing up are of the two of us, up before my sister, eating English muffins with butter and peanut butter, chit-chatting like old friends.

The summer between my seventh and eighth grade years, my parents announced to my sister and me that we were moving. It felt like a death sentence. I had made it through elementary school with a good little group of friends in my pocket—and now everything was going to change. I went into a long, dark period of inner rebellion. Because I had grown up in a very unique environment (my parents worked at a children's home where we also lived), I refused to adjust to our new home in hopes that my parents would see my sadness and move us back. In my stubbornness, I dug in my heels. For four long years, I hid inside myself, unwilling to make friends. I grew shyer and less confident as high school rolled on.

Eventually, I settled in with a group of kind girls when the loneliness became too intense, but I left for college not long afterward. My extroverted self was desperate for friendship. I had dismissed my need for connection long enough. To this day, the most earnest prayer I have ever prayed, through tears and fists, was "God, help me find friends. Pleeeeeeease." To sum up a lot of life in between that plea and today, I can say, surer than I can say most anything else, that God answered my prayer. My net is full. I have inspirational, fun, deep, interesting people for friends. They are my spiritual companions, fellow party-throwers, sanity preservers, personal comedians, and anchors.

Gaining these friends was certainly not an overnight miracle. God has graced my life with these beautiful people, but it took honest self-evaluation and good doses of openness and courage to earn them. Additionally, many of my friendships are deepening as only the passage of time can allow. It's been a gradual process. I didn't anticipate that my prayer for genuine, deep friendships would require a change in me before a change in my circumstances. My prayers led me into reflection. I had to admit that those years of sulking produced weeds that grew up and around my personality. My natural extroversion and activism were barely visible. Eventually, my prayer expanded to include, "Help me get back to myself." Hiding away inside myself meant hiding away from everyone else, too. College was a blessed chance to break out. In the first year of college, everyone seems to be scrambling to fall in with a comfortable set of friends while attempting to appear absolutely unconcerned about it. I felt inferior, nerdy, and rusty at making friends, but I pushed myself to the edge of security and tried out for a musical/drama travel group that performed original scripts and songs for churches and youth gatherings. I had always attended high school plays and musicals, wishing to trade places with the actresses on stage. I felt compelled to give myself the chance, though it felt like the longest shot ever. I'm baffled I made the group, because I was honestly the least talented member musically. When they asked me to harmonize in my audition, I simply sang an octave lower.

Thank God I somehow made the cut, because that group saved me. Weekly practices with twenty-five other students offered me a way back to my authentic self. I experimented with saying the things I had always held back in high school and jumped at the chance to coordinate our travel schedule. I was (finally) the loud, take-charge, busy person I was born to be. I spent three years traveling in this group, and I thrived. Obeying my curiosity about joining a performing group was the diving board into a pool of friendships I wouldn't have made otherwise. Sure, I may have found people to spend time with, but these people were spending their time in ways I valued, and that shared mission bonded us. It gave us more to work with.

Over the years, I'm constantly surprised at the medley of people who have become my closest confidants. I'm a white, straight, unmarried, thirty-three-year-old Christian female. I'm grateful many of my friends don't fit this description. Cultivating a sense of openness about who I meet and how/where/when I meet them is critical to the process. Even more fundamental, however, is extending that openness and welcome to myself. Openness to myself leads me to moments that require courage—the courage to introduce myself, to extend a hand, to invite, and, sometimes, to audition.

Breaking

College is a bumpy time—maybe even more so than junior high. The launch toward independence is a shaky ride of instability and confidence, maturing and regressing. My early college girlfriends and I called ourselves "sisters" from the start. In many ways, we had no idea how accurate this sentiment would be. As in familial sister relationships, growing up together isn't easy. My sister and I experienced rivalries, enmeshment, and the struggle for individuality on our way to developing an adult relationship. My girlfriends and I went through similar processes. Some friendships survived the changes, several did not, and a few bounced back after years of distance. As much as I hate to admit it, change in friendship is unavoidable.

A lovely gift of growing older is the recognition of boundaries. I'm limited by a twenty-four-hour day, an aging body, money, responsibilities, and energy. I've worked to become better over time at figuring out how to make the most of what I have to give. Taking a step back every now and then to observe the landscape of friendships in my life is a regular practice. It allows me to see where unhealthy dynamics might be creeping in, to assess the mutuality of my friendships, and to check my sense of boundaries so my community and I can lead healthy, productive lives.

Or, at least, that's my goal.

Ignoring boundaries is my sad vice. It doesn't help that I persevere to a fault and think that anything good should never have to change. I caused myself extra pain in the confusion of changing relationships because I simply couldn't let people go. For legitimate reasons, people move in and out of our lives. At times I've been guilty of taking these departures too personally and ruining some relationships by attempting to hold on too tightly.

Some of my friendships begged for change because they were actually dysfunctional. In college, my girlfriends and I learned to lean on each other in some of our weakest, lowest moments. This, obviously, is a benefit of friendship, but the way we did it began patterns of co-dependence that lasted beyond college. Certain friends noticed this more quickly than I did and intentionally pulled away from me in order to analyze our situations better. Other friends went through personal tragedies, and they pushed the intimacy of our friendship away. My longest friendship, born in childhood, crumbled when we realized we couldn't be honest with each other, for fear of hurting the other. We protected each other so much that we reinforced a false reality that conflicted with the real events happening between us.

I interpreted all these losses as my fault. *If I had only . . . If I were more . . . If only . . .* But when I tried even harder to repair them, they got worse. A few cut off contact altogether, unsure of how to proceed. This may not be the best remedy for an ailing friendship, but I can't place the blame fully on them—or on me—for any of these scenarios. It took me a long time to understand that friendships have their own lifespan. Some truly will stand the test of time, and some will fade like seasons.

Learning how to read friendships and their longevity involves watching out for dysfunction in the forms of toxic people, unhealthy dynamics, and unfair expectations. These things usually surprise us, but thankfully tend to be more rare. A more common factor contributing to the life expectancy of a friendship is how connected two people can remain over time. Even the best of friends grow apart. It's inevitable that some friendships won't be able to bend with the changes of adult life. Moving, work, marriage, motherhood, acquiring new friends, and sickness are all potential circumstances that can transition a friendship. I've also experienced growing apart from friends because of shifts in what were once shared worldviews. Our opinions and convictions are shaped and changed by family influences, global events, continued education, and vocational experience. The strongest, most long-lasting friendships I have are the ones built up over years on a common vision for the way life should be lived, how to spend money, what quality time looks like, and the purpose of life. I gradually see less of friends with whom values have diverged over time, as we have fewer ways to relate to each other. Sometimes we directly address these changes, but usually it's an unspoken wait-and-see process. I'm learning to be patient in moving through new phases with friends. Most importantly, I'm better at *expecting* the changes.

Keeping

For me, keeping friendships means sustaining community in my life. In one sense, it is nurturing current friendships with genuine care and generous time. In another sense, it is allowing current friendships to fade if necessary and trusting that new community, with effort, will replenish itself. Moving forward through life with friends is a dance that requires faith in God's provision, confidence that we have important things to contribute to each other, and honesty about our needs and limitations.

In college, it's easy to see friends often. Life together doesn't have to end when we no longer live in a dorm or eat in a cafeteria three times a day. And it doesn't have to be relegated to having roommates (though well-chosen ones make good travel partners for the journey). With loads of flexibility and intention, my community and I stay connected in an amazingly consistent way. Post-college life, with its independence, busyness, travel, romances, and domestic responsibilities, can trap anyone into self-absorption. All these components of adult life will demand attention and, yes, in the midst of it all, it is work to create space for friends. Even so, we don't need friendships *in spite* of all that's going on, but *because* of all that's going on. It is precisely because we fight with our bosses, go on wonderful or horrific dates, backpack through South America, suffer heartbreak, lose a parent, or get sick that we need the comfort and companionship of others.

The logistics of adult friendships change, but connection with good friends can absolutely remain solid. My friend Melissa and I have been close since the day we met in college. She was married early on in our friendship, and life with *her* has been life with *them*. She and Justin are masterful at opening space in their home for others; we actually lived together for a year. Melissa is the kind of friend I could catch up with every day on the phone (and I hate talking on the phone). We used to teach in adjacent classrooms and spent hours together each week in long, lingering dinners.

After they adopted their first child, we found that leisurely dinners and late-night phone conversations were difficult to manage with an infant in the mix. The circumstances of our friendship, in order to keep our tight bond, had to adjust. It continues to adjust with the adoption of two more children—this time a six-year-old and a baby. So, we mostly hang out at their house. I learn the family routines and pitch in where I can. I babysit so they can still go on dates. We share big life moments over email, and she catches up when she can, which is usually during the quiet moments of naptime. We still need to know what's going on in each others' lives, and we plan in advance for weekend getaways and coffee dates. Our friendship can't be spontaneous, as it concerns four other people at all times. That's just reality. We're committed to each other, and this means we're committed to working out the details of each new reality either of us faces.

My friendship with Melissa and Justin exemplifies the best we can offer and receive from friends as we grow older: openness and respect. I cherish the wide-open window I get into their family life. Not only does it help preserve our long-standing friendship, but it teaches me so much about life stages I have yet to experience. They don't treat me as though I can't relate simply because I'm single. They also recognize that they are unable to completely fulfill each other within the goodness of their bond. Healthy couples will turn outward to life-giving friends who can fill in the gaps that even the best marriage relationship has. Genuine openness and respect between me and the couples in my life make such a difference in the longevity and strength of our friendships with each other.

I have to be open-minded and respectful in return. I could be bitter that my friends keep having babies. I could resent each conversation about wedding dresses. I could simply refuse to go to another shower or house-warming, and gravitate toward my also-single friends who eat late dinners out on Friday nights. The older I get, the easier it is to slip into comparisons, but this is a quick route to excluding others, feeling unnecessarily bad about myself, and selfish introspection. With a genuine joy for the developments in others' lives, I invite the same kind of response in my direction. Generosity is reciprocal. Maintaining enthusiasm and interest in friends' moves, work, dates, marriages, kids, and spiritual and personal growth is essential, regardless of whose life changes.

With each friend I've kept over the years, I've definitely had to be creative. The same formula doesn't work for each person's unique configuration of lifestyle and demands. With flexibility, ingenuity, effort, cooperation, and empathy, my friends and I keep moving forward together. Sometimes we move in stops and starts. The path can be fairly winding. Certain transitions are harder to adjust to depending on where I am in my own life. My friends who work from home as mothers can see each other throughout the day. They can swap childcare and discuss the latest parenting issues. I can't fully participate in or relate to these things—which is honestly okay. Many of them can't relate to my work travel throughout Baja, México, or know what it's like to consider internet dating. Certain circumstances of life determine who we see, why we see them, and how much time we can spend together. Being honest about this enables us to manage our lives together with grace and realistic expectations.

The story of Jesus in the Garden of Gethsemane is a favorite section of scripture for me. It's a small, but rich passage. Jesus' pending betrayal and arrest drive him to the solace and quiet of the Garden for prayer and focus. Everything about this scene—the withdrawal from the city, the intimacy of prayer, the gravity of the circumstances—implies solitude and isolation. Yet it is significant that Jesus brings his friends. He asks them to just be, to sit while he grieves in prayer. Instead, they fall asleep. His disappointment is clear. These are his last minutes as a free man, and he is in need. He doesn't ask them to protect him, to listen for the coming crowd, to console him, or to pray with him, even. In his desperation, he simply wants *them*. He wants companionship. The presence, familiarity, and solidarity of his friends is so important to him that he interrupts his pleading prayers three times to wake them up. Christ's life is marked by dynamic exchanges with his community. From simple common meals to suffering through loss together, Jesus embodies commitment to those closest to him.

Jesus calls out to his friends in the Garden because he values togetherness. Life is fuller and more authentic when shared. Though each friendship has a life of its own, and circumstances of life dictate certain realities that affect our friendships, my community full of diverse perspectives and gifts has guided and sustained me. The more I live, the more I value and rely on the people who have known me through tragedy, transitions, and time. And so, I open up my hands, welcoming in old and new relationships, giving all a free space to just be.

Three Strikes and You're ... In: Learning to Date

Coleen Montgomery

When Bobby pulled my huge 1989 earrings out of my ears with a magnet, I should have realized he was flirting, but I was so busy bemoaning Mike's lack of interest in me that I ignored Bobby. I deemed myself un-datable because the popular guy I liked didn't like me.

And so the myth began. I believed I would always be a non-dater because I was not one of those serial daters who always had someone to date and ten other people eager to be next. Instead, I would be the "friend girl" who would listen to everyone's relationship problems, jealously watch the "datable" girls having fun, and pout.

This myth took hold so easily because I didn't know myself very well. As a result, I continued to pursue the same guys that everyone else found most attractive, and my insecurity never allowed me to admit interest in someone whom my peers might have snubbed. I wanted acceptance from friends more than I wanted a date with a really nice but magnet-wielding science geek like Bobby.

I missed many dating opportunities because I withdrew and waited for those all-star guys to come to me. Thankfully, over time I learned that the most "datable" (and attractive) girls are those who are the most confident in themselves. But I really am getting ahead of myself.

When I was a college junior, I came across a survey I had filled out during my freshman year asking me to rate my priorities for choosing a small Christian college. Out of the twelve options (which included "being involved in a ministry" or "learning more about faith"), my top three were:

1. Get an education.
2. Make new friends.
3. Date.

I was horrified, mostly because I had actually submitted that superficial and truthful list to the college. Even more horrific . . . I *still* wasn't dating. I always expected that I would have some fairytale romance and would be married right out of college. Of course, everyone expected that. But my two college dates—the guy I met at driving school (who got into a horrible car accident the next week) and the guy who wanted to rule Iceland one day (seriously)—didn't look like they were going to work out.

Nothing hastened my dating desperation like realizing that soon I was leaving college, what I considered the prime place to hook a husband. But I did my best to project a confident and independent image. In the eyes of my friends and family, I was the free-spirited traveler who was going to teach overseas and embrace my singleness. In reality, I was trying to avoid "settling down" alone for as long as possible. I didn't want to be the nice girl who ends up married to her teaching job.

Those seven years of post-college singleness, however, were an absolutely necessary (albeit difficult) part of my journey. I got to travel, learned to live on my own, and even did "marry" my job for awhile. I learned a little bit more about living a balanced and healthy life. I can't imagine what my life would be like if I had found my spouse when I was in college. I have evolved so much since then.

The good news: Waiting to meet or marry a mate is really normal. In fact, the average marrying age for women in the U.S. in 2006 was twenty-six—though this may not seem like reality when your roommates are visiting reception sites during finals week.

While some people might be ready for marriage just out of college (both my sisters had June weddings right after graduation), most of us can look forward to exploring God's refining plans for us within the context of singleness.

That refining can be painful, awkward, and lonely. The principal at my new job asked if he should introduce me to the staff as "single and looking," and family friends inevitably wanted to know: "When will we be dancing at *your* wedding?"

Of course, the awkward comments and questions alone didn't do much to refine me, but my reactions to them began that process. Should I pity myself as much as grandma's cousin seems to pity me? Should I abandon my wedding magazine clippings, and with them the hope that I would walk down the aisle? Should I allow myself to consider that God might have some crazy, non-traditional plan for my life?

I just wanted to skip to the last page of my life's novel and *know*. If I knew what the ending would be, then I could brace myself and plan. And I like a plan.

But living with that tension of uncertainty is what stretched me. I realized that God would care for me, regardless of what the next chapter might bring. I bought a house and a Kitchen-Aid mixer and understood that I would survive (and even thrive) without a husband or a wedding registry. And when people asked me when I was going to meet Mr. Right, I was able to laugh and say, "Maybe never!"

I still hoped to meet someone, but I made a decision not to become desperate.

Meanwhile, as the possibility that I could end up a spinster schoolmarm emerged, my married friends and family became desperate for me. Friends arranged dates with East Coast doctors, recently widowed computer teachers, and a husband's-sister's-friend from 200 miles away. My mom cried over her Olive Garden dinner, telling me that she just hoped I'd meet somebody who wasn't divorced. Even my dad came home talking about the semi-professional arm wrestler he had met at the irrigation pipe store.

So that was settled. We all wanted me to get married.

As a college student and as a single twenty-something, I believed what so many people told me: that although I (apparently) wasn't the kind of girl whom guys wanted to date, someday I would meet The One, and it would just be IT.

Now that I thought about it, the once-romantic idea seemed like a recipe for desperation, not to mention an extremely unhealthy way to start a relationship. I didn't want to be the girl whom some guy would "settle down with" but wouldn't enjoy dating. I also didn't want to feel pressured to glom onto the first guy to come along. I imagined myself introducing a new boyfriend to my family and having them immediately start making wedding plans.

I simply wanted to date, not commit my life to someone, and I was ready to do something about it. Suddenly, it didn't seem so silly to flirt with the barista at the local coffee shop. I thought about going to the movies with the cute bagger at the grocery store who didn't fit my perfect-mate profile. I was even willing to troll single-but-hopeful groups at local churches, hoping they wouldn't be overrun with balding computer geeks. It's hard to explain why, but I used to think I was somehow "above" these things. Maybe I thought I shouldn't have to try so hard to meet someone. Maybe I subconsciously held on to some of that knight-in-shining-armor fairytale. In any case, I decided I would let down my guard, open my mind, and see what would happen.

That didn't mean I was ready to settle for a half-baked version of my dream. I knew myself well enough to realize that I would rather be single than poorly matched. (It's easy to fantasize about long evenings with someone until you realize that person is boring, controlling, or doesn't like theme parties.) I braced myself for the weight of dealing with emotional baggage, and I gave myself permission to be picky.

That didn't mean the dates started pouring in. I was still that friend of yours who really should be dating someone. But I wasn't, and I settled into a life where I scanned the coffee shop for datable guys every time I looked up from my pile of essays and begged my guy friends to take me to the prom (which I was supposed to chaperone). I traveled every summer and haunted the living rooms of my married friends. I wasn't desperate (except when pleading for prom dates), but honestly, I wasn't satisfied.

So how does it happen that I now find myself at age thirty-five to be one of *them*—one of the women who has crossed to the other side and is happily married with two crazy children? That happened fast. Until age twenty-eight I was a single English teacher . . . with a cat (okay . . . I'll admit it, two cats). I'd never even had a boyfriend.

I decided to try the internet dating scene, not because I was desperate to find The One (although I had a slim hope), but because I knew I needed some practice. I posted a silly picture of myself, wrote a light-hearted and sincere profile, and made no apologies about looking for a smart, funny Christian guy. Never having identified myself as a dater, I was shocked and complimented by the number of responses I received. And although most of them were obviously bad fits, I ended up meeting some really interesting and quirky people who helped me narrow and define my essentials and negotiables for a lasting relationship. And spending so many evenings on dates also reminded me that I had other needs and other goals to pursue. I needed nights when I could make dinner with friends, read a good novel, or plan my summer vacation. I tried to find balance.

In so many ways, the whirlwind of internet dating helped prepare me for when I did meet my husband. When he sent me his profile, I didn't rush out to buy a wedding magazine, but I thought that he might be fun to meet. And as we continued our relationship, I dated him because I genuinely liked him, not because I feared he might be the only guy to come along.

And let's face it, I was picky. Even though I knew I wouldn't find someone perfect, I wasn't willing to overlook (what I considered) major red flags. So when I did join the dating scene, I implemented a simple three-strikes rule. Some guys didn't get even three chances.

Some examples: Speedo guy, nicknamed such because of his strike one: He was also a strict vegan. He was also short. (Sorry, that's three.) National Spelling Bee guy: He admitted he sometimes beats people up in bars. (Strikes one-two-three. Over-share.) Or how about the I-once-picketed-a-Mormon-church guy (What?): His last name was Van Foeken. (A strike for any teacher.)

And then five months into my dating adventure, I met my future husband, Stefan: piercings (strike one), recovering alcoholic and drug addict (strike two), and tattoos of Kermit the Frog and the monster from *Where the Wild Things Are* (strike three). But he was the coolest date that I'd had yet, and I went home to tell my roommate that I thought he'd even go to the prom with me.

Even though I didn't expect to meet someone *perfect*, I ended up with someone whom I would have considered a walking red flag. Thankfully, he overlooks what he considers my three potential deal-breakers: I won't ride his motorcycle, won't play video games, and can't stand math.

When I did bring Stefan home to meet the family, he was definitely not the Prince Charming they had imagined. After all, he wasn't the kind of guy *I* had expected to meet, either. They also didn't anticipate that (despite my best intentions to be level-headed and balanced) I would turn into a giddy schoolgirl who wanted to spend all of my time with my new boyfriend. That just wasn't me. At least not the "me" they had known for twenty-eight years. All of a sudden, I was eating "weird" food, dividing my time between my family and his, and seeing movies that previously I would have overlooked on the rental shelf. Basically, they felt like I was changing, and they didn't approve.

I grew up trying to please my parents (and everybody else), so it was very difficult for me to move forward in my relationship without their enthusiastic blessing. But I knew myself, and I decided to trust my instincts and see what would happen. I used good friends as a sounding board and made a conscious effort to pursue my own goals and attend all family functions. It didn't take long for my family to see that I was still the same person. I had just been stretched a bit. And within a few months, they all accepted Stefan as well. What isn't to like? He cooks holiday dinners, entertains all the kids, and makes me very happy.

We'll celebrate our seventh anniversary this November, and my life has changed dramatically in that time. No more cats (he's allergic). No more students (I'm staying at home with our son and daughter). And no more looking for rings on the hands of the firemen who walk into Starbucks.

In an abstract way, though, life has hardly changed at all.

I'm still determined not to be desperate (as suburban housewives have been known to be). I still struggle with balance, insecurities, and reminding myself that it's not healthy to expect a fairytale. I still want to please people and need to take time to pursue my own goals and dreams. I have to intentionally make time for family and friends. I wish I knew the ending of my children's stories so I could be assured that they will be okay. And I still have to give all of these things to God and trust that he will give me peace.

It's the same story; it's my story—just a new chapter.

Singleness: More Than a Holding Pattern

Jamie Noling

My parents did not allow me to start dating officially until I was sixteen, which felt shamefully late at the time. One of my greatest sources of anxiety in the three years before I was allowed to date was that I would be asked out by a cute boy for whom I had feelings of infatuation, and then I would need to have the most awkward and humbling conversation imaginable with him. Fortunately, most of the young men I found interesting at the time were equally terrified at having these kinds of conversations and were just as happy for us to flirt in the hallways between classes, to sit next to each other in youth group, or to have lengthy phone conversations at night.

I can safely say that I have been in the world of dating for sixteen years now, which means I have been actively or inactively dating for as much of my life as I have not. But there comes a point in one's dating life when the term "single" no longer denotes a lack of boyfriend, but instead marks one's lack of spouse. In this new phase, one can literally be dating and still be "single." And this designation becomes as defining and permanent-feeling as "adult" or "American," and even becomes a category for how one is ministered to at church. (For our purposes, I will separate the terms, using "dating" as the actual practice of going on dates and fraternizing with the opposite sex, and the term "single" to discuss the lifestyle of the unmarried status.)

In the year that I moved across the country to begin my dream job, a dear friend of mine celebrated her wedding to a sweet man she adored. At the wedding festivities, a friendly acquaintance approached me. "So Jamie, what's going on with you?"

With excitement about the new events of my life, I told her of my new job, highlights of my cross-country relocation road trip, and my doctoral research, which was well underway. When I finished, she gave me a condescending look of tolerance. "No Jamie, that's not what I meant."

Then she raised her eyebrows, and again repeated the question with a more hushed tone. "What's going on with you?"

A little embarrassed, I turned apologetic. "Well." I hesitated. "I just moved, so I don't really know anyone yet. I'm not dating anyone, if that's what you mean."

Then, her unforgettable next sentence: "Well, Jamie, you better hurry up—before it's too late." And there it was—the true measure of my life.

My sixteen years of dating have come with incredible blessings and a few tremendous inconveniences. I have been confronted with some unfortunate myths, like the one that was subtly communicated to me by the well-intentioned acquaintance at the wedding—a woman isn't complete without a spouse, or, there may come a moment in a woman's life when she finds that time is up, and she is no longer eligible for love or marriage or parenthood. But the most important thing I have learned about both dating and singleness in these last sixteen years is this: Any circumstance in which I find myself is a context in which to live out my discipleship as a follower of Jesus.

In my post-college life, there has not been another context that has been as formational for my discipleship as has dating and singleness. The character and work of the Living God are true anchors for one's soul and identity, no matter the circumstances. For me it has been essential to remember who God is and how God feels about me, especially during the times when my Christian communities have extolled Christian marriage and family to the point that I felt left out of something important and essential to the Christian faith. It was through wrestling with some common myths and engaging true questions of my soul that I realized dating and singleness, with all of their blessings and inconveniences, are both opportunities to live out my discipleship. I have been thinking lately about four distinct areas of stewardship: work, home, soul, and community.

Stewardship of Work

On the morning of my birthday, my mom called to tell me that she had been praying for me as I started a new year and that while she had been praying for me, she got the sense that it was going to be a big year for me. My mom can usually be trusted in these kinds of things, so I listened closely for more, but that was it. *Why was it going to be a big year? Was I going to marry my current boyfriend? Would I get the job that I was waiting to hear about? Could it be related to the completion of my master's degree scheduled for later that year?* She wished me a happy birthday and left me to wonder for the rest of that day (and that year) why it was going to be such a big year.

As I look back on that unusual birthday phone call, I realize that she was exactly right. That year was a defining year in my life, but not because of events. It was the choices I made that became so defining for me.

My wonderful boyfriend and I came to a heartbreaking point in our relationship when we realized, about a year into our dating, that our professional dreams were not compatible and our real-life expectations were not similar. We each needed something from the other that neither of us could, or wanted, to be. As we evaluated the rift that threatened our relationship, we took time for prayer together, met with mentors, and assessed whether the necessary changes could be made without compromising our own unique gifts and callings. We decided that they could not.

I confronted some of the questions and messages that I had picked up along the way. In conversations with some of my single girlfriends during this period, we were all thinking about the same question. We were ambitious, adventurous women who also hoped to have families. And, whether we were dating someone at the time, had an unrequited interest in a male friend, or had no love interest to speak of, the question was the same for each of us: How much of my life do I plan when I don't know the outcome of my love life? What if I move to the other side of the country and then find out that the man of my dreams was interested in me as well? What if I move to another continent, and then I don't meet anyone? Should I plan my life around the *hope* of love?

In my life, this question, *How much of my life do I plan when I don't know the outcome of my love life?*, surfaced because I was nearing the end of my graduate degree. If my boyfriend and I continued to date, I would want to live in the not-too-distant vicinity, and would need to consider local jobs. But my dream jobs were located, in truth, in far-off destinations, and pursuing them would mean a big move that I would certainly make if the circumstances of my love life were different.

These kinds of decisions cannot be simplified or made formulaic. But it was really helpful for both my boyfriend and me to discuss what kinds of jobs I was interested in applying for and where. It was helpful for me to see my own excitement and not to suppress the joy that goes with the use of my gifts. It was helpful for him to have clarity about what my dreams and goals were so that we could evaluate whether we could really support each other and empower each other's giftedness. Though we were not able to support each other as we might have hoped, I know that, for me, those conversations helped to bring clarity and passion to the way that I minister to the world around me.

I began to think that year about the myth that a man's work is more valuable than a woman's. No one said this to me directly, but over the years there had been subtle comments that led me to this unfortunate conclusion. When I was younger, I had numerous people in my church say to me, "You are so gifted for ministry. Maybe one day you'll marry someone like Billy Graham." Such statements implied that my pastoral gifts would help make me a great pastor's wife, rather than a great pastor.

In that year, I wondered if God might be leading me to surrender my calling to enable the work of this man in my life. I wondered aloud about this one afternoon on a walk with my long-time friend Dan. Dan is a good and patient listener, and when I talked about surrendering my call to ministry, his response was kind and immediate. "Jamie, let me ask you a question. Did God call you to ministry?"

"Yes"—I was confident about that.

"Then Jamie, that's not optional. That's a command. Anything else that you do needs to fit with that, not the other way around."

I began to see that an issue about stewardship was tangled up in the myth of men's work being more valuable than women's. God had created me. With intention, God put each gift inside of me to be used for His glory. At that time in my life, I had people say things to me like, "Maybe God doesn't want you to use all of your gifts." *What?—Not want me to use my gifts! How could that be?* The parable of the talents, in Matthew 25:14–31, indicates that burying a gift in the ground is not pleasing to the Master. Subsequently, God had not only given me unique gifts but had also nurtured their growth through education, experiences, and mentorship.

At the end of that year, I gained greater clarity about my calling. I was confident that God had called me to, and gifted me for, ministry. I knew that any future dating relationships I found myself in would need to include supporting and helping one another to be the part of the body of Christ that God had designed each of us to be. I could not wait until marriage to serve God, so I continued serving God in the place where He had put me, and then, after I graduated from my master's program, I moved across the country to work with college students and began my doctorate so that I would be well-equipped to minister to the people I sensed God was leading me to serve. I was beginning to think that living as a disciple of Jesus meant carefully attending to, and stewarding, the gifts that He had put in me so that His name and His story could be told through my life.

Stewardship of Home

When I left for my senior year of college, my parents packed up some of their kitchen extras to assist me in my first year of off-campus apartment living. Each pot, pan, and dish that I used that year held sweet memories of my childhood. My blankets and towels were hand-me-downs, too. When I graduated from college, those same beloved hand-me-downs stayed with me. It wasn't until about five years after graduation that I started saying things like, "I really would like to get some dishes of my own." Or, "I'd love to get some new towels." After all, these belongings had had an entire lifespan before they came to me, and now, even I had owned them for more than six years. And, from too many people to identify, I heard this response: "Oh Jamie, don't do that. You will get married some day! Just hold out!"

What they were saying made sense financially: Why buy new things if I am going to receive those very things as gifts in the near future? The problem was, there was no indication that bridal showers would be in the near future for me. Though I took their advice and waited, at some point a few years later, I got tired. I got tired of not having enough dishes for my dinner parties and needing to use paper plates. I got tired of sleeping in sheets that had holes in them. I got tired of towels that were discolored, frayed, and coarse. Most of all, I got tired of feeling like my household was not my own, a hand-me-down extension of my parents' home. When I decided to make a very meager investment in some household items and received some of these things for Christmas presents, some of my friends understood. Others said things like, "Jamie, don't lose hope. You're not too old to get married."

All of this caused me to wonder why unmarried people don't need plates and towels as much as married people. After all, unmarried people eat and shower, too. I wondered about the cultural associations and fears that were represented by these household items. Was it that an unmarried woman with an equipped home might appear selfish, or hopeless, or worst of all, self-sufficient? I also wondered why marriage justified so much consumerism, a practice that surely does not help young couples get their marriages off to a selfless and simplistic start (two key values of the Christ-centered life). Wedding gifts should be an expression of love for a couple.

Wedding gifts are among the first things that are jointly owned by both people, and among the first things the couple takes care of together. There is beauty in a gift that encourages sharing and symbolizes the start of a new home and family. But in many cases, wedding gifts have become an expectation and a rite of passage into adulthood.

The myths I encountered in those days were that in order to have a successful marriage, the couple needs stuff, and that singleness is just a waiting place, like a bus stop, en route to a real destination, not a lifestyle that is respectable enough to warrant towels from the current decade. I have a hard time with the concept of Christian marriage justifying consumption and materialism. I love the joyful generosity that surfaces in the hearts of loved ones around the time of a wedding. But in Jesus' teachings there is no mention of needing "stuff" in order to follow Him, whether one is married or not. And, because I did not want to spend my life waiting in expectancy for gifts that would supposedly accompany the love of a spouse, I decided to go ahead and buy dishes on which I could serve meals to my students and towels that hadn't been used at one point to dry off our family dog after her bath.

What I came to believe was that though, as my friends suggested, it might be more financially responsible not to "waste" money on things that could later be gifts at a wedding, it was more expensive to my self-esteem and to my discipleship not to equip myself with the tools for living. If I treated my home like it was in-waiting for something, it was hard for me to find emotional rest there. It meant that I was embarrassed to use my home for Christian hospitality because I didn't have enough chairs, coffee mugs, or sheets for my guests.

I once heard a speaker at a conference talking about consumerism. She explained that if I have the gift of hospitality, then using some money on plates was actually good stewardship because it is equipping myself for the work of the kingdom, just like a musician buying a musical instrument, or a pastor attending seminary. Of course it can be easy to lose sight of good stewardship in this culture of materialism. In my own singleness, I came to the conclusion that it was healthy for me to make a few additions to my household. Now, when I invite students over to my house for dinner and discussion, I have enough place settings of hodge-podge silverware that they are all able to eat without prongs of plastic forks snapping off in their chicken and enough dishes that knives no longer tear through paper plates. Now, I am able to joyfully and frequently share my home with others.

Stewardship of the Soul

In the early years of my professional life, I quickly learned that an easy way to move forward in one's career is to overwork—even in the Christian workplace. Working weekends, sending middle-of-the-night emails, answering the phone after 9 p.m., and creating programs and opportunities that are outside the scope of one's work will gain one favor with employers and colleagues. The values of American professionalism are quick responses, innovative ideas, going above and beyond the call of duty, thinking outside of the box, and having a commitment to one's place of work. My single colleagues would comment, "I'm going to work hard now. After all, I'm single, and I can do that" or "It's easier for me to work late hours than it is for my colleagues, because I don't have a family." From married professionals, I heard, "I don't understand why I have to stay late. I have a family. Can't my coworker stay late? I mean, what does she have to do anyway? She doesn't have a family; she has more spare time than I do."

There seems to be a subtle, or not so subtle, expectation in many workplaces that single people should work longer hours than those who are married and who have children. Some workplaces are great at respecting the life of the unmarried employee, seeing their familial relationships, friendships, and personal well-being as equally important as those with families. However, that is not the case in all workplaces.

The unfortunate underlying myth communicated by this expectation, that unmarriedness means a greater capacity for professional contribution, is that the personal well-being of the unmarried woman needs not be honored or respected. I grew up in a context in which spiritual and physical well-being were high values, and with that came an understanding that rest, exercise, meaningful relationships, and spiritual community are vital to the soul. Even in my years of unmarriedness, I have not been able to dismiss what I know to be important: My soul needs to be cared for and nourished. It is not good for me to over-stay at the office, no matter how meaningful my work, how great my students, no matter how much I love teaching, or studying, or preaching, no matter how great the crisis, or how incredible the projected guilt. I have little to offer if I don't create time for my soul to rest in God's presence—for physical rest, opportunity for leisure, enjoying the world and the relationships that God has provided. I am a hard worker, and I love my work. As a pastor, I cannot afford to offer my students the model of a life of frenzy without time for Sabbath. How can my employer respect my need for rest and personal care if I don't?

In my early professional life, one friend told me that her supervisor said to her, "I will never send you home. If you want to overwork, its fine with me, so just make sure to take care of yourself. If it's 9 p.m. and you need to go home, you will need to figure that out for yourself because I'm never going to tell you to go or encourage you to take a vacation day."

As bleak as her supervisor's sentiment sounds, I've thought of it again and again. The responsibility to determine my limits is my own. Many women are nurtured to believe that they should please everyone around them. Most workplaces will exploit that. It is my job to protect my boundaries and not treat my own life like it's not valuable just because I don't have a husband or children. I am a disciple of Jesus and that means that my work is important, but so is setting aside time to be in the Divine Presence of the Living God and to nurture God's work within me.

Stewardship of Community

When I moved across the country and knew not a soul, I came into contact with a wonderful couple who were my age, came from my home state, and had just moved to the area for graduate school. We became fast friends. I was incredibly blessed that these friends did not discount our friendship because I was not "a couple." Both the husband and the wife befriended me. They would pick me up on Sunday mornings and we would make the thirty-minute trek to church, giving each other life updates as we drove. We would have lunch afterward and talk about our reflections on the scripture and the sermon. They would invite me over to their home for a weekly television show and holiday meals. I would invite them for evening walks around the campus and over to my house for weeknight quesadillas. Their expressions of love and hospitality were significant to me. Too often there is a social divide between those who are married and those who are not, a divide that, sadly, is often reinforced in worshipping congregations.

Within true Christian community, there are no singles. As 1 Corinthians 12 describes, we are a body. We are a family. It grieves me when I walk into a church and get the sense that the only way unmarried people can fit into the life of the church is either through participation in a singles group or through care for the youth. Singleness is not something that is isolated to one age group. Some singles are in their early twenties; others are widows; others are survivors of difficult marriages. To assume that all singles should be relegated into a group where they should remain until they meet someone to legitimize their participation in the life of the congregation shows disregard for an important theological premise: God is the one who legitimizes our participation in the congregation, not a spouse, nor anyone else.

Singles should not be treated like, or act like, victims. Being married does not validate discipleship in any way, and to insinuate that it does is to overlook the practical examples of many significant biblical figures, including Jesus. There can certainly be loneliness associated with singleness, but in my own experience, the most pertinent reason for that was the sense I had that my life was not enough, that it was missing something, that it was not complete, and that I wouldn't really be able to belong to a church community until I came as a family. Those realities are lonely. But they are also culturally constructed realities that dismiss God's truth. Singleness, dating, marriage, as well as any other life circumstances are just contexts in which to live out Christian discipleship.

Conclusion

Dan's wife, Leanne, said to me on New Year's Eve, "I do not simply want to be advancing the narrative of my own life. My life is God's. That is the narrative that I want to be advancing." When I surrendered my life to God at a young age, I gave every part of my life to God. This means that anything that God entrusts to me, whether that be a set of skills, new or used possessions, meaningful work, or the care of a person, all of these are contexts in which I am to carry out the values of Jesus.

If I think about my dating life as a context for living out the convictions of my faith, and not simply a means for personal happiness, then the questions and the motives of dating change. The relationship takes on a culture of honoring one another above oneself, extending thoughtful and caring hospitality to the other, and empowering the use of one another's gifts toward the healthy functioning of the body of Christ. Likewise, if I think about my singleness as a context for living out the convictions of my faith, and not simply a means for personal gain or a temporary holding place on the way to a different life, then the lifestyle changes. The choices become deliberate. The use of money and time are not just for frivolity; everything matters. The soul is important enough to guard with rest and personal health. The unmarried life is not a temporary holding place in which one is waiting for life to start. Real life begins when one meets the Living God, and, in that case, no matter the blessings, inconveniences, myths, or circumstances, life has already begun.

Beyond Picture Perfect

Linda Beail

If you were to come to my home, you would see some beautiful framed photos scattered about: a bride and groom smiling radiantly, a mother cradling a newborn baby, two adorable kids grinning at Disneyland, a picture-perfect family on vacation by a waterfall at Yosemite. Those pictures reflect my reality, the marriage and family I hoped and prayed for since I was a girl. One might look at them and think, "How typical. How lovely. How trite. How simple." But those pictures capture only moments, the surface of reality, and mask the long, tumultuous journey going on before and between those moments. My story is unique, but I think not unusual: under the surface of almost all of our family photos or three-sentence biographies is a more complicated tale of heartbreak, joy, courage, and unexpected twists in the road. Let me share the complex story behind those simple photos–the not-so-beautiful images, the things I have learned the hard way about marriage and relationships.

Lesson #1: Love is not enough, or if you flunk out of premarital counseling, maybe you shouldn't get married.

Fresh out of college, I fell madly in love with a cute, quiet boy from my church back home. We had one of those intense, romantic courtships; soon we were engaged. So off we dutifully went to have some premarital counseling before our lovely June wedding. And after several stormy, tearful sessions, the warm, older gentleman in the local pastoral counseling office looked at us kindly and said, "I can see that you each have strong feelings for the other, and that you seem to really love each other, but—you really don't have anything in common. From money to career ambitions to family plans, you don't see any of it the same way. I really don't know how you will be able to make a marriage work."

Well. You might think that we could take a hint, that when he stopped just short of screaming, "Please don't get married!" we might have listened. Oh, no. We simply decided that we were the poster children for the idea that opposites attract, that our strong chemistry and deep feelings of love would be enough to weather any storm and solve any problem. And we didn't even hesitate as we walked—nearly ran—down the aisle on a sunny summer afternoon to say "I do," careening headlong into the biggest mistake of our young lives.

I can see now that I was set up for this failure. When we started dating, I had just moved to a new city, where I knew no one, to begin a graduate program. Only a few people in my family had even attended college, and no one had been to graduate school, so I had few role models and felt like a fish out of water. I was excited, yes, but also scared, lonely, and insecure about my own abilities now that I was surrounded by so many successful, high-powered scholars. I clung to this new romantic relationship like a lifeline. From it I got the affirmation, love, and companionship that were in short supply in all other aspects of my life. And I had few friends or family around to help me keep this relationship in perspective, to notice the flaws as well as the positive facets of this blossoming romance. The support system that had kept me grounded and given me valuable reality checks was suddenly far away. I was on my own—and in over my head.

I wanted to get married. Not only would that stave off my fear of ending up alone, but I also thought it would prove to my family, friends, and even myself that I was now truly an adult. I wanted to start my own little family, to erase the problems of the family I grew up in by starting afresh, with a relationship all my own. And I was in love, which in my mind meant the automatic next step was to get married. In the church, I'd heard all my life about the importance of commitment and making love last for a lifetime. No one ever talked about love that might not stand the test of time. Finally, he sure was handsome, my guy. We had some amazing chemistry. I was a nice evangelical girl, intent on saving myself for marriage—a laudable goal, to be sure. But now I *really* wanted to have sex. With him. As soon as possible. So like many a Christian young woman, a lot in love, a little bit in lust, I got married.

Five years later, he walked out the door (slamming it hard on his way). Marriage had just been too difficult for us. Five years of anger, frustration, loneliness, and betrayal had driven us too far apart. We'd walked down the aisle promising that no matter what happened, "We'll make it work."

Love would be enough to see us through whatever challenges lay ahead. We cared for each other and would refuse to give up.

But feelings of love—no matter how strong or real they are—are no match for compatibility. We thought we'd grow together, but as we grew up throughout our twenties, we grew very much apart, discovering different expectations ingrained in each of us about what adulthood should look like. It was exhausting trying to constantly overcome those differences. I always felt like I wasn't a good wife, that I couldn't be who he needed me to be, and even the trying made me feel alien and unhappy with myself. I'm sure he felt the same way. We ended up angry, worn out, and lonely. For despite my relief at getting married, thinking that I had eluded being alone, what I'd discovered was this: There is no place lonelier than inside an unhappy marriage.

Of course, many people in our society have gone through divorces. There's even a term for the increasingly common short first marriages of people in their twenties: starter marriages. But I never, ever considered that it might happen to me. I believed in the sacredness of marriage. I thought I was loyal, loving, and committed to him 'til death us do part. When my ex-husband left, I was devastated. I was sick with grief and failure. I lost faith in my own judgment, and I was frightened by the thought of being single and of never being able to have the children I so desperately wanted. I felt like perhaps I had wasted those years and been cheated out of the happy ending I deserved and expected. Which brings me to . . .

Lesson #2: You are not entitled to a husband, children, and "happily ever after", or, you can feel cheated, or you can make choices.

When I was a little girl and people asked me what I wanted to be when I grew up, I never failed to answer, "A mommy!" As I got older and other interests and ambitions were added to the picture, the desire to be a mother strengthened as well. I was happy to put off having babies until I had finished my graduate degree, found a job, became more financially solvent, and put my rocky marriage on more solid footing. But I fully expected this postponement to be short and looked forward to plunging into parenthood. Instead, as I turned thirty—that invisible deadline in the heads of women in my generation, the moment when most of my friends quickly became pregnant with their first babies—I was unexpectedly divorced and pretty sure I might have lost my opportunity to have children at all. I was not happy about this—to put it mildly.

I was furious. I felt betrayed by my ex. I felt stupid for ever trusting him and loving him in the first place. I railed at him, at God, at life in general. "It's not fair!" screamed every cell in my body. I wanted to be a wife and a mother, to build a life with someone, to create a home and family. How in the world could I be alone instead? Flailing about bitterly, I wondered how my life could have gone so horribly awry.

Slowly, in the midst of my anger and panic, I realized that no one has the checklist-perfect life. God does not guarantee any of us all the accoutrements we think we need in life—the perfect spouse, the great job, unfailing health, the house with the white picket fence, or 2.3 adorable children. When God promises to give us "the desires of our hearts," it is not a blank check for health and wealth; God will fulfill our desires *when those desires rightly come from the Creator who shaped us in the first place*. We are created to yearn for relationship with God, to long for righteousness, to live justly and love mercy. When those fundamentally human, God-given desires are what our hearts seek, guess what? They will be fulfilled. But all the other extraneous symbols of success, or relationships and emotions we are sure would fill our loneliness if only we could find them, are doomed to fail at making us truly whole. They aren't what we ultimately want, or need. And we certainly aren't promised the fairytale, with Prince Charming (and a castle full of cute kids), as our birthright. So I could be mad that things didn't work out the way I naïvely had planned. Or I could grow up, stop feeling cheated by things that were not under my control, and make choices about what to do with the life I had.

Being suddenly single again gave me a lot of freedom. Rather than moaning about what I *didn't* have, I could make choices about what to do with the time, money, and energies I did have. I realized that I could now travel the world, an opportunity I'd never had before, and I loved the experiences I had around the globe. I was able to invest in friendships, and in the lives of my students, in ways that I could not have if I'd had my own family to care for. Caring for them filled a deep desire to nurture, creating emotional connections that were different from spouse and kids, but fun and fulfilling in ways I couldn't have imagined. I dated interesting, successful men whom I never would have met back in college. Whenever I felt envious of my married, mothering friends, I reminded myself how much they might want to trade places with me sometimes, too. I realized that if I wanted to be a parent, I could think of ways to accomplish that without feeling dependent on, or betrayed by, my ex-husband. I promised myself that when I was thirty-five, I'd revisit my feelings about motherhood. If

I wasn't married by then, I could consider other options, like adopting a child. Until then, I would choose not to panic or wait for my "real life" to start, but to enjoy the life I had.

By giving myself some space, I was able to feel some measure of control and responsibility for my own life instead of careening out of control, sure that someone else was to blame for my unhappiness. I wasn't dependent on someone or something else (Prince Charming's kiss, perhaps?) to give my life joy or meaning; I would play the cards I was dealt, and turn them into a winning hand one way or another. Nobody has unlimited options to create the perfect life out of a vacuum. We all have to work within the context of our family situations, our economic circumstances, etc. Recognizing that life had taken certain twists and turns enabled me to let go of my anger and desperation as I had to make decisions about how to react to those changes. I regained a better sense of myself, and of my worth, as I made positive choices about how to live my life rather than wallowing in regret and sorrow. I began to experience redemption, hope, and freedom. I began to see that my life hadn't ended with the mistake of a marriage, or the devastation of a divorce.

Let me be clear: I will always be profoundly saddened that I broke a vow I fully intended to keep for the rest of my life. Even though the circumstances were complicated, and I wasn't the one who walked out first, I did eventually walk away from the wreck of our relationship and move on with my life as well. God has brought me healing, hope, wisdom, and joy. I am relieved not to be in that turbulent, violent, debilitating relationship anymore. I am safer, healthier, and happier now. But I don't take my divorce lightly. I will always feel sorrow for the damage we did to each other, and for breaking that sacred promise, even when it became impossible to keep. But I am glad to have moved on. And when I learned to let go of the fairytale I'd blithely assumed to be my due, and to make choices with the life I'd been given, well, what do you know? After a while, a really good guy came along and surprised me.

I was definitely not going to pursue anybody. I was pretty content with my life, open to the possibility of romance but not starved for it. Eric fell in love with me pretty quickly, while I was more suspicious of all those fluttery feelings. I'd been burned by that before! But as the months went by, I realized that I deeply trusted him. I knew I could rely on him; he was kind, he was honest, he was full of integrity, and he cared for me in a way I'd never experienced.

Lesson #3: It's great to marry a grown-up and it's hard to marry a grown-up.

There are a lot of advantages to getting married a little later in life, but there are some drawbacks, too. One great thing about getting married in your thirties is that your spouse is a known quantity; he's got a track record. You know if he's going to be a responsible adult, because he already is one. This time around, I wasn't hoping that the guy I married would grow up into someone I would still love and respect. When I married Eric, I knew exactly what I was getting—and the same went for him. I knew he was financially stable, cared about his work, and put family first. He knew that I was passionate about my work, too, and wasn't going to turn into June Cleaver someday. We were able to discuss realistically our hopes and expectations for our life together, and find agreement.

(In a nice corollary to lesson #1: If you ace your premarital counseling, it might be a sign you were meant to be together.) When Eric and I got engaged, the clergywoman who was going to marry us had us each take an extensive survey as part of our marriage preparation. She sent it off through her church to be scored, and when it came back, the senior pastor handed it over to her saying, "I don't know who these people are, but tell them they should definitely get married. I've never seen results like this. They are the most compatible couple I've ever heard of!"

It is an amazing relief to marry someone who shares your worldview. It is definitely less exhausting than struggling and arguing over everything in life, from the big decisions to the small reactions to everyday events. But there was some difficulty in marrying someone who was already a fully-formed adult, too. We both already had our own careers and households, and there were a lot of hard choices to make about how to combine our lives. I don't mean things like which microwave or sofa to keep. Eric lived on the East Coast, and I was in California. Which of us was going to give up our current job and home? What was going to be fair to each of us, and how could we keep from resenting each other later over these choices and compromises? Eric decided his job was more portable than mine, and he was happy to come live in sunny San Diego—but there are still moments when I worry that he sacrificed too much of his career for mine, or that he will regret that decision someday. And even in the small things, there were compromises to be made. We each had our own ways of doing things, and we were pretty set in those ways. (Eric *still* thinks I load the dishwasher wrong, and has been known to reload it after I leave the kitchen . . .)

But we both have more perspective now, and we can let the small stuff go. It's really not worth having a fight over every little thing. Sadly, we both have brought a lot more baggage into this relationship than we had when we were twenty. Both of us have had our hearts broken and have scars to prove it. But we also have more wisdom, grace, and gratitude at finding someone trustworthy to share our lives with. We know that the deep, underlying love we have for one another is worth more than some exasperating quirks. And we have a different perspective now on the purpose of marriage. It's not about falling in love, or romance, or even companionship or self-fulfillment. While we were dating, we came across this line by Henri Nouwen:

> The basis of marriage is not mutual affection or feelings of emotion and passions that we associate with love, but a vocation, a being elected to build together a house for God in this world, to be like the cherubs whose outstretched wings sheltered the Ark of the Covenant and created a space where Yahweh could be present.[1]

When Eric proposed to me, he didn't ask me to become his wife; he asked me if I would be his partner in helping him build that kind of life, to create a place in the world where God's grace and love could be manifest. At our wedding, our treasured friend and minister blessed our union with a prayer for our marriage to be a witness of God's gracious work in the world. We are partners, not just for each other, but for a larger purpose.

Eric is a great partner. He respects, loves, and supports me in all that I do. We have embarked on an amazing project of co-parenting our two children. Our life is a constant re-negotiation of roles, working together to keep our home running, our careers on track, and our kids well nurtured. Each of us sees the other's time as equally valuable, and we trade off things like who cooks or takes the kids to the doctor, or who can work late on a big project. It's a life that is sometimes messy, always in flux, bursting at the seams with joy and challenge.

Lesson #4: Two may become one but they are also still two.

Marriage is a wonderful, mysterious union. But even though we're building a great life together, Eric and I are still two very different individuals. In my first marriage, I was young and insecure enough to worry constantly about how my ex-husband's choices and behavior reflected on

---

1　Henri Nouwen, *Clowning in Rome* (New York: Image, 2000), 44.

me, and was always trying to get him to be more like me—like an extension of my identity. With Eric, I've realized that I can give him the space to be the unique individual he is. We don't have to be exactly alike to prove our love and commitment to one another.

I've learned that I still really need my women friends. Eric isn't my "everything," and it would be totally unrealistic and an unfair burden to expect him to be. He is my partner, my love, the father of my children, the one I love and trust more than any other person on earth. But some of the things that interest me—like shopping for shoes, or discussing a best-selling novel, or dissecting the latest parenting trends—just don't interest him that much. And some of my fears and experiences as a woman just boggle his mind (How in the world can you think you're fat? You're beautiful!). I need my women friends to compare notes on relationships, mothering, aging, being female in the workplace, and countless other topics. I need their support, and laughter, and shoulders to cry on, in ways that don't diminish my relationship with my husband, but complement and enrich it.

I have a strong marriage—but not a perfect one. Though secure in our underlying commitment to stay together, we have our moments of anxiety and conflict. Life has thrown us some difficult curve balls.

Over the past few years, Eric and I have lost two very wanted pregnancies to miscarriage. After a healthy, easy pregnancy with our daughter, we were taken totally by surprise by the sudden end of our plans and dreams for another baby. Though up to half of all women experience a miscarriage at some point in their lives, it's not something most people talk about experiencing, so it was a shock when it happened to me. Both times, I ended up in the emergency room having unexpected hemorrhaging and surgery in the middle of the night. Our grief and loss did draw us closer together; we alone had eagerly anticipated those births, and we were the only two who felt and mourned their loss so keenly. Yet we also experienced that grief quite differently. Eric, who had seen me hysterical with pain and cramping during the first miscarriage, and passed out cold with the second, was scared to death of what was happening to his beloved wife. He wanted to make sure my life wasn't in danger; he didn't want to lose me, or to become a single parent to the child we already had. Afterward, he wasn't sure he wanted to try again to have another baby. He was frightened for my health, and he felt like my focus on getting pregnant again wasn't fair to the beautiful daughter we already had. Why couldn't we be grateful for her, instead of feeling so bereft of another child?

I, on the other hand, felt like my body had betrayed me. I felt defective as a woman, and I wanted to get pregnant again as soon as possible, to "fix" what had gone wrong by sustaining a healthy pregnancy. I couldn't understand his reluctance. And I wanted to talk about the miscarriages, over and over, as if by talking about them I could somehow make sense of what had happened. Miscarriage is such an invisible loss. We lost our pregnancies at ten and seven weeks—early enough that very few people had even known I was expecting. When people did know, they said sympathetic but cruel things like, "Oh well, you can always try again," or "Well, it's probably better this way—it's nature's way of correcting a mistake, and you wouldn't have wanted a baby with severe problems, would you?"

But that did not seem to be the point. That's not what I had imagined when I found out I was pregnant—losing the baby, or having a child with a myriad of health problems. I had wanted and planned for these pregnancies, and each time I'd already begun to imagine that tiny spark of life growing into my own baby, perfect and sweet, and to love it. I needed to remember those potential lives—though it seemed like wallowing in grief to Eric—because if I didn't remember them, who would? The love and hopes we had for them would be forgotten completely. This incredibly painful experience would mean nothing—and I needed it to mean something, to turn into some redemptive wisdom or truth. He couldn't understand why I felt like I had failed as a woman, when the doctors told us that there was nothing I'd done physically to cause the miscarriages. They occurred for two different reasons, both "flukes," and no one was to blame. I was sad that our dreamed-of family, with two children spaced three years apart, was never going to be as I'd planned. It was hard not to be in control, and to let go of my own expectations.

One of my dear friends, who is also a therapist, told me something that helped us tremendously in the midst of all this. She said that although many people might think that what they needed was to be alone together in their grief—consoling each other because they alone understood the loss they both had suffered—we actually might not be the best at comforting each other. "You've both just experienced a huge loss, and you're both hurting," she said. "You may be too wounded to help each other. You may need some space and some other people to talk to in order to heal."

She was right. We had both gone through these losses, but we had each experienced them differently. Her words allowed us to give one another the space to grieve separately as well as together, to begin healing, and to move forward in our relationship. With joy and trepidation, we learned that we were expecting another child, and welcomed our precious son into our family.

Lesson # 5: There is no "happily ever after", or, marriage is full of joy and sorrow all at the same time.

This past summer, Eric and I planned to celebrate our 10th wedding anniversary in Hawaii, where we had honeymooned. We were looking forward to the trip immensely, an oasis in the midst of busy lives where we could really renew and celebrate our relationship. It felt like we were approaching a huge, joyous milestone. Then, the week before we were to leave, my beloved 92-year-old grandmother passed away. We canceled our trip so that I could be with my family and attend her funeral. Just days later, Eric got the unexpected news that his dad had been hospitalized for some tests. This was surprising, because his dad was the most vital, healthy person you'd ever want to meet—always hiking, eating healthy, outgoing and friendly, quick with a joke and an encouraging word—an incredibly warm, witty, loving man who was really the heart and soul of Eric's family. The tests showed he had malignant melanoma that had metastasized to his brain. We were stunned.

The next few months were the hardest of our marriage. Eric spent part of almost every week or weekend of the fall traveling 1000 miles to where his parents lived, to help care for his dad as he underwent treatment and his health failed. His dad was his role model, his hero, and his dear friend, and he was emotionally devastated by the sense of grief and loss he was experiencing. His mom also has some serious, chronic health issues, so Eric became the person in charge of their legal, financial, and medical decisions—a heavy and time-consuming burden. Even when he was home, he wasn't really present mentally or emotionally; he was dealing with paperwork or on the phone to doctors, insurance companies, or his siblings scattered across the country, keeping them updated on Dad's health. Yet how could I be critical or resentful? He was going through a huge loss, and I wanted to be supportive. I ached for him and the pain that he was experiencing. But I also wanted my husband back. I was single-parenting my kids most of the time—and our household is definitely a partnership, so it was not a pretty picture to have me trying to pick up all the slack, still do my job, and try to be there for Eric. The pressure felt relentless, and his dad's prognosis grew more and more grim.

In the midst of all of this, one of my dearest friends got married. Her wedding was a beautiful, joyful celebration. I felt such happiness for her and her new husband, at the very same time that I felt surrounded by darkness, despair and difficulty in my own family. At the wedding, I remember thinking how I did truly wish that their current emotions—that giddiness and excitement of making that commitment, the euphoria of being with the person you love —would last for a long, long time. I hoped that they would have many more moments of happiness than of sorrow in their life together.

That part was easy to say, in the midst of the congratulatory hugs and smiling pictures. The part that was harder—that I couldn't quite put into words, and that seemed too depressing for the occasion, and yet the part that I wished for her in my deepest heart, the part I was learning ten years in—was this. Loss and sorrow will come in life. They aren't the exception. They aren't rare. The richness of life is that the happiness and the sadness come all mixed together. You can celebrate your anniversary in between two funerals. And the best gifts of marriage are to have a partner who is true, and trustworthy, and who will weather the storms with you. I wished for my dear friend to find in her marriage what I have found: the sweetness of fidelity in the midst of the most bitter circumstances; the preciousness of loving and being loved not at our best, but in our utter vulnerability and pain.

My life, and my marriage, and my family are so far from perfect, no matter what the pictures look like. We are not living "happily ever after." It's so much more complicated than that. We are picking up the pieces after losing his dad, trying to comfort our children in the greatest loss they've experienced in their young lives. We're celebrating their triumphs in math tests and soccer games, laughing at silly jokes at the dinner table and crying with them at bedtime when they are sad and scared. We are exhausted and irritated sometimes, and grateful to hold one another close at others. We are re-planning that anniversary trip to Hawaii. It won't be as simply blissful as our honeymoon, but will be even more treasured.

A Foreign Affair: The Adaptive Journey of Intercultural Marriage

Melissa Gentzkow Lázaro

I'm not quite sure when exactly I became attracted to other cultures, but this attraction has long been a part of my story. I would deliberately engage in conversation with people who talked and acted differently than me. Just like I always wanted to have braces when I had naturally straight teeth, I wanted to have more culture in my blood than my white blended makeup. I wanted to hear, understand, and experience something that was not my own. I remember enrolling in seventh-grade Spanish and thinking this was my first step to understanding another culture. The more languages I could learn, the more people I could communicate with and share with. I had no idea how this small choice at age twelve would greatly influence my journey. I suppose it's important never to underestimate the dreams of our youth, the small choices that lead to big experiences and the passion that never leaves us.

The same year I started learning Spanish, I met a Mexican man (then a boy) who would eventually become my first love. We were friends through junior high and high school and dated in college, but it was an eight-year relational cycle of bliss and broken hearts. And finally it ended, during my junior year of college. My dreams of a junior-high sweetheart love story were shattered. I know it sounds ridiculous, but I had visions that after college, I would marry him and move to San Francisco. I would take a helicopter to my towering corporate office and travel the world with the wave of my magic bank account. When that relationship died, so did my dreams. I was a planner, and my plan had failed. That relationship endured some of the most formative years of my life, and perhaps that is why its end was so devastating. So much of my parent-separated identity had been entangled in this relationship. He shared my history, my tears of growth, and my dreams of life after college. He challenged me to become more independent, yet his words anchored on my heart. I felt like a piece of me was gone, and I had to create a new plan. That plan was to fly far away. I had to redefine who I was and what I wanted—alone.

My friends and family worried that I would never return. They were not too far off from God's greater plan. I decided to move to Madrid and further pursue my goal of learning Spanish. I knew that if I wanted a career in Southern California someday, it would benefit me to speak the language. Three months after graduation, I was living in a small flat blocks from the Palace. I knew no one. I loved it. I would take long walks in the city, soak up the architecture and art, people-watch, and eat delicious food.

I spent a year working as an au pair and attending the university. I studied with students from all over the world, taking classes in Spanish language and conversation, film, art, architecture, history, literature, and economics. When school was finished, I taught English to executives, rented a summer flat, and toured southern Europe and England. I was redefining "me" and creating a new version of wholeness in being single and depending solely on God for comfort, understanding, and companionship.

I remember vividly one evening—I can even see the sunset behind the Palace as I walked through the Plaza de Opera toward the royal gardens— God spoke to me. I replied back, "Lord, I know you're here. Thank you for this time. Thank you for this moment. I now realize that I would rather be alone than in a relationship that is not of your will."

This was a critical turning point in my post-college identity. God revealed to me that people may go away (permanently or temporarily), but God is always constant. As long as my identity was in Him, then the actions and decisions of others could not shake me. This proved essential in marriage.

A month after that turning point, along came a bird. A bird? Yes, "un pájaro." I found myself at a Spanish culture exchange party. I was talking to a man in Spanish and couldn't think of how to say the word "bird." So another man leaned over and said, "Pájaro." We exchanged smiles and later engaged in a night-long discussion. That man was Oscar, my future husband. Oscar and I courted for nine months before I boarded a plane, once again, and moved back to the States to attend graduate school. We didn't know if the relationship could endure 8,000 miles, but we committed to staying in touch.

For two years, Oscar and I defied all odds of a trans-Atlantic relationship. Long-distance relationships (inter or mono-cultural) usually work well for two busy people. We both could have our own lives, and when we were together, we were focused on us as a unit. But the benefit of growing together slowly through mediated communication was offset with the romanticized nature of the relationship. When we were together, we ignored the annoyances because we were so happy to finally be together. We didn't experience the day-to-day interactions and conflicts like most same-location couples. Most of our conflicts erupted from the frustration of not being together and were constrained by calling plans and email (there was no such thing as video conferencing). I couldn't see the importance of the day-to-day interaction until after we were married.

We were engaged shortly after my graduate work was finished. Ten days after we announced our engagement, we faced a crisis many married couples never face—Oscar had cancer. While he contemplated his own mortality and fear of never having children, I set aside (or ignored) my own concerns and pretended like everything was still normal. This was a pebble in the road, not a boulder. I somehow thought that once we were married, everything would be normal and easier.

On February 10, 2001, we were married. Oscar's family and friends flew out for the ceremony, and it was a beautiful winter day. Some days I reflect on that first year as a wonderful time of cable-free discussions and secure silence, untainted and easier. Some newlyweds will fulfill the ideals of a year-long honeymoon, while others confess to it being the hardest year of their marriage. For us, the romanticized story of "finding love abroad" (a tall, dark, and handsome Spaniard, no less) was not as Disney illustrated. We had to rewrite our own "in a land far away" fairytale.

Like many young married couples, there were so many levels of change we hadn't anticipated. We were both just trying to survive—independently and cohesively. Our first year involved Oscar recovering from radiation treatments, cultural shock, and the dissolution of an IT career—the market had collapsed. He was unemployed with no friends or family, except me. In many ways he was completely dependent on me—the antithesis of our customary long-distance relationship. He was forced to find an unskilled job because ignorant Americans mistook his broken English for lower intelligence. I had to find a job that could support both of us. I struggled with the reality that I had married a wonderful man who was culturally accustomed to his mom taking care of him. I had to teach him U.S. cultural and social norms, including the practicalities of writing a check, doing laundry, etc. He wanted me to correct his grammar publicly, but I felt disrespectful in doing so.

While I enjoyed being a modern woman, there was a part of me that wished I didn't have to take care of him. I had been on my own since I was eighteen. I had gone away to college and put myself through school. I had had the experience of living with different people and had learned to adjust to their norms and personalities. I had had the adult responsibilities of paying for rent, a car payment, and health insurance, and balancing this with social commitments.

Oscar did not enter our relationship with these advantages. He went straight from living at home, and his mom taking care of all his basic needs, into marriage. He never shared a room, let alone a house, or a bank account. I found myself frustrated in helping him instead of being grateful he wanted to learn. Oscar had fewer doubts. His British mom and his Spanish dad had an intercultural marriage that worked. So while there was the sadness of missing friends, family, and work, for him there was more hope, fewer questions.

Yet, I pondered. Why did I think something magical would happen once we were living in the same place—that everything would be easy? What if he wanted to move back to Spain? Could I do what he had done— leave all my family and friends permanently? What if we had children and unforeseen circumstances occurred, like I died or we got divorced? Could he take our children away to his country? In the case of death, our children would be separated from my extended family and their home culture. How would this detrimentally impact their lives? If divorced, I might never see them again.

At twenty-five, I had not considered the vastness of our lifelong decision. I was in love, focused on the present and a blurry, optimistic future. I had fallen in love with him because of his spirit, his intellect, his sense of humor, his attractiveness, his optimism, and his respectfulness. I ignored that our cultures' subtle and big differences could negatively impact our relationship as much as it made it flourish.

Sarah Donovan's unpublished thesis discusses the stress and coping mechanisms that intercultural couples face:

> Couples revealed common stressors from family and society disapproval, language barriers, logistics, cultural barriers and traditions, and children. Coping resources included humor, learning about the other's culture, support, communication, personal preparation, working to-

wards common goals, and religion. These couples were found to have attitudes of commitment to their marriage and each other, and a belief that they were not that different from their partner. [1]

Our experiences have been similar. We face all those stressors, and cope with mounds of laughter. We are committed to our marriage in spite of and because of our intercultural differences. We may be from two different sides of the world, but our childhoods were similar. We both grew up in the middle class. Both of our sets of parents had been married for more than twenty-five years. We each had two siblings and cherished our friendships. We have different hobbies but similar interests. We are not that much different. Yes, his eyes are brown and mine are green. He has brown hair and mine is blonde, but our interests and the passion for our family is the same. Most of all, our foundation is in Christ.

The first stressor that we approached was my family's acceptance of Oscar. My extended family embraced him, but my mother and father created obstacles and vocalized concern all the way down the aisle (literally). Their biggest concern was his faith. Oscar was baptized in the Anglican Church (Episcopal) and went to Catholic school. Christianity was a part of his life and belief system, but it was certainly not the evangelical Christianity that I grew up in. My father was an evangelist, not the norm. My parents could not understand how someone could be a Christian and yet be unable to recite a favorite Bible verse or any scripture. This was our first cultural (perhaps subcultural) difference. Oscar lived the values and believed what I believed, but how we expressed this through religious rites was different.

My parents also couldn't understand his English. They had no idea who this person was beyond their initial three-month interaction. They had never been to Spain or experienced his culture. They basically were having to trust God that I had made the right choice.

It was difficult to engage in marriage with the resistance of my own family. We needed their encouragement and support entering marriage, arguably more than a monocultural couple did. Thankfully, a year later they recognized Oscar's deep faith beyond his words and culture, by how he lived his life. Our common Christian values are the foundation that supersedes any intercultural beliefs. My parents now love Oscar like a son, but it was a long journey for them. In retrospect, I can see their concerns; marriage is the biggest decision in one's life and not to be taken lightly. Like

---

1   Sarah Donovan, "Stress and coping techniques in successful intercultural marriages" (M.A. thesis, Virginia Polytechnic Institute and State University, 2004), ii.

parenting a child, there are many things you cannot anticipate or foresee until you experience it.

Communication and language created more of a challenge than a barrier. Oscar and I don't take communication for granted. We consider the intention of the message first before actual words (something all relationships could benefit from). Some words directly translated sound harsh, and the heart gets lost in translation. Out of necessity, we are more resourceful in our communication because sometimes the words don't translate at all. We always beat our friends at Charades and Pictionary because we've grown accustomed to depending on multilingual channels of nonverbal communication to compensate for our lack of words. We find meaning together.

We also find our miscommunications entertaining (even if after an hour-long debate, we realize we're arguing for the same outcome). It's important to have a good sense of humor if you marry someone from a different culture, and you have to be able to laugh at yourself. This is true in any relationship, whether friendship or marriage. Our miscommunications occur on a daily basis—in words, actions, and intent. Humor can be the saving grace in those heated moments of conflict. Sometimes we talk in the language that feels most comfortable, even if it means he talks in Spanish while I respond in English. When we're in public I find it amusing. Oscar speaks only Spanish when the children are around, and I primarily speak in English. We get the strangest looks from people because we will hold complete conversations in both languages. Our children respond to both and consequently speak more Spanglish than Spanish.

Because I speak and understand Spanish, I didn't feel left out when interacting with his family and friends. I also lived in his country, so I can pull from that experience and try to relate. I don't know everything about his culture—how could I? But I am eager to learn. It's not just a desire that I have in my soul to understand my husband's culture better, but the respect owed to him for absorbing himself completely and humbly in mine. I think that mystery, the things we don't know yet, keeps our relationship alive in ways that we *do* take for granted.

As Donovan expressed, there were some logistical nuances that eroded the bliss of finally being together—forever. Immigration paperwork was one. We couldn't leave the country for our honeymoon because he didn't have the "right" to travel. There is this myth surrounding intercultural marriages that once you get married, your non-citizen partner automatically becomes a citizen. This couldn't be further from the truth. We faced years of immigration processing and exorbitant attorney fees. This is the norm in the United States. Seven years after we were married, Oscar became a U.S. citizen (while happily retaining dual citizenship in his home country of Spain). He now had the same rights as our children and me.

We continually deal with finding the financial means to visit Oscar's family and friends every other year. It is a part of our life, a necessity for our budget, and yet we can't afford to visit them as often as we'd like. Initially, we committed to sharing every other Christmas with his family, but logistically this did not work out—between my job, Madrid's weather, holiday times, and children being born. We have been blessed to see his family about every nine months, but this has become more complicated over the years. We have two children now, so that's two more plane tickets and 15 hours on a plane with two small children. And while it's difficult to put a price tag on family, the reality is that we don't come from wealthy families who can assist us.

Oscar has acclimated wonderfully to this country, but there is nothing like being "home." Even in my small stints living abroad, I've discovered there is something about the comfort of being in your home city, where things are familiar and it doesn't take effort to orientate or communicate. It is as if your whole body, soul, and mind can sigh in relief. There are days that Oscar feels (and rightly so) that he gave up everything to live here with me, so I am granted little grace to complain on any grounds. For Oscar, these days are few, but other couples, whose foreign (or non-native) spouses have not accepted the new location as their new home, may experience more conflict. Some monocultural couples coming from different regions or states may have similar conflicts.

Although it might be easy to conclude that intercultural marriages have a higher divorce rate because they have additional stressors or amplified stressors, there are no conclusive published studies to prove this. In fact, it might be argued that intercultural marriages have a lower to normal divorce rate because there is a conscious effort to find commonality and bonding, and an awareness of differences that need to be communicated and worked out. Monocultural couples may assume norms and commonality when they actually exist only minimally.

Oscar and I are likely to be more creative in how we approach decisions, because we benefit from being educated by two different cultural and educational systems. The trick is in being equally fascinated to learn more about our partner's heritage and understanding. We are also more flexible out of necessity. There are more compromises: handling holidays and vacations, communicating religion, consumerism vs. conservationism, food, language, dress, rituals, and parenting.

We bring together diverse backgrounds to share and enjoy. Our children are blessed to have multiple cultures influencing their lives. Not only do they have the benefit of learning two languages from birth, but they are exposed to a variety of foods, music, art, and ways of thinking. We celebrate both countries' holidays. Some are the same, so we incorporate Spanish (and other cultural) traditions with the common holidays. My ancestors are German, so for Christmas we do Advent and hide the pickle ornament on Christmas Eve. We also celebrate Los Reyes (The Three Kings) and remember the gifts they brought Jesus. We exchange gifts on December 25 and once again on January 6 to keep this Spanish tradition alive. Oscar and I want to have our own family traditions, too, not just culturally bound ones.

Our children's lives are richer because of this exposure, not more complicated. For our situation, it is a positive experience because both our families embrace our marriage. My parents enjoy being the American grandparents, and his parents embrace their unique names ("abuelo" and "abuela") as the Spanish/British grandparents. On either side, there is not an attitude of one culture being better than the other, and I think that makes all the difference. I realize not all intercultural couples are blessed by this inclusion, and there is potential for children to feel pulled one way or another or desperate to create their own culture. Some intercultural couples may feel left out when their children have the physical appearance of a more dominant gene pool. I love that our children reflect both; they are a physical embodiment of our cultural fusion. As in any marriage, similarities help us stay together too. Oscar and I have our own hobbies and interests, but we've made a concerted effort to maintain similar interests and develop hobbies together. For the past six years, we have been buying, fixing up, and selling homes. We both participate in the location and negotiation of the home buying/selling, and we love designing and creating something together.

The downside has been that we have lived in the mess. There are a few major stressors that most marriages don't survive—major illness, remodeling, and death in the family. In less than eight years of marriage, we've had all three. Our hobby can be stressful and tiring. But it is something that bonds us—something we can talk about (besides our children and work)—a project we can work on together.

We've had a large learning curve compared to most monoculture couples, but the struggles have given us an incredible bond. We work very hard at our relationship. We value it more than anything. We recognize how remarkable it is that God brought us together despite being 8,000 miles apart. It warms our hearts that future generations will look back at their ancestors (us) and find something special about our story. We hope it will give them the courage to face their relational giants. And while I have tried to plan and map out my course, I learned (and am still learning) along the way that "Many are the plans of a person's heart, but it is the Lord's purpose that prevails" (Proverbs 19:21, NIV). From seventh grade to more than seven years of marriage, what a journey God has guided. I can't imagine my life any different. I cherish the miracle of our two children, when doctors told us it might be impossible post-cancer. I am proud that our family is first-generation American and first-generation Spanish. We wouldn't want it any other way.

Sailing On: A Mid-Life Look at a Medical Marriage

Allyson Jule

I have been married for twenty-five years this year. This fact boggles my mind. How do any two people, often from vastly different backgrounds, reach this milestone? Millions do it all the time, of course, but it still amazes me that two people can find a way to make life meaningful and joyful while journeying through the various passages of time with the inevitable shifts of focus and desires.

What I wanted and needed at twenty is not what I want and need now at forty-five. My husband and I have both changed. This fact is not mentioned very clearly or perhaps not heard very well when launching the marriage boat. Like most people, we made the decision to marry because of how things looked on one side of the ocean, and then found the winds and waves along the way to be surprisingly upsetting. Marriage is a like a round-the-world sailing trip for two. What has bewildered me the most, what has shaken our shared boat most drastically, is our current mid-life adjustment to our new realities. The metaphor still holds: A sailing trip starts off calmly, sun shining, the lure of adventure beckoning, and it can take some time for a real ocean storm to set in.

My husband, Marvin, was in medical school when we married—entering his first year. Our first child arrived within the year and our second about eighteen months after that. By twenty-one, I was the mother of two and the wife of a man I barely saw because the demands of medical school consumed his time and attention. I think my youthful and naïve optimism was what helped in these early days of de-facto single parenthood. I didn't know what marriage was supposed to feel like, so Marvin's absence simply became a part of the experience. Marvin was rarely home; when he was, he dropped off his laundry and slept through the day or night. His internship and residency were brutal and part of a dying tradition to have young doctors experience a boot camp of sorts: every third night at home, with all other days and nights at the hospital. I see now that a deep loneliness was setting in; storm clouds were forming. But I was quite a capable and plucky person, and I had watched enough television medical dramas to know that the life of a doctor in training was tough and that this phase would be worth it, of course, because the vocation was mighty and noble and important. People said it would pay well, but this was never a draw to me, and I still have little interest in the money.

I had grown up with the average admiration for medical doctors: They were set apart, special people cut from a certain cloth whose jobs meant they faced life-and-death decisions on a daily basis. They were admired so deeply because they were often so admirable: smart, brave, focused, self-sacrificing. Most are very intelligent, altruistic, professional, calm, able, and good with other people's pain. My mother was a full-time nurse throughout my childhood. Because of this, I had spent much time in city hospitals meeting her after school and thus had an awareness of the lifestyle concerning the twenty-four-hour need for medical services.

More importantly, though, I was deeply in love at eighteen and felt that Marvin was a divine gift to me and to the whole world. My hope was that I would be part of his vocational calling by being supportive and encouraging and able to manage all things on the home front. My contributions would include raising our children, keeping house, writing all Christmas cards, and arranging for family memories as part of what I saw as a shared vocational calling to medicine. I would be his helpmeet. Besides, I had my own career as a teacher and later as an academic. As such, I would need little and give much. I had convinced myself that, as a grateful and humble Christian woman, I would not need or ask for anything for myself. I would be the Proverbs 31 woman who managed the household affairs with great competence, joy, and wisdom. My own career would not make many demands on my marriage; rather, it would add to my own sense of self. It certainly paid the bills in the early days—hence it had purpose. Did this mean that my aspirations were small? I think I genuinely felt capable of managing the career without it demanding anything from my marriage or family life regarding time or support. Being independent would be the model.

The years of medical training dragged on; the children grew bigger and started school. Eventually, Marvin bought a medical practice, but this meant moving across the country for us, and I didn't want to leave the East Coast. Life on the West Coast suited him quite well, but I did not feel at home there and I grew quiet—still determined but not quite as naïve about where my happiness and joy would come from. He grew into a very happy, successful person who went on to specialize in OB/GYN work, which meant that the "on-call" training of medical school actually morphed into our everyday lifestyle for many years. Marvin was on twenty-four-hour call for all his maternity patients, seven days a week, and he thrived. His lifestyle became our regular family structure—there was consistently the very real possibility that he would be called away to the hospital to deliver a baby or to tend to an emergency of another sort. There were few family holidays, and most special occasions were interrupted and superseded by the needs of others.

I immersed myself in the children and my own emerging academic life. What this choice of being fostered was an increasingly separate-sphere marriage. His career consumed him, and my career consumed me. I spent years focusing on graduate work and lecturing overseas, and he built a successful family/maternity practice. We were friendly people on the same metaphorical boat, with shared space, but we had many solitary, unshared thoughts.

I have little doubt that many marriages develop this pattern of coping with life: dual-career marriages where both partners coexist with little overt stress, managing high-powered or demanding careers, supporting the nature of each other's vocations, but growing independently. Marvin and I had married young and had children early on. The immediate needs of those early years set a pattern that necessitated a low-maintenance marriage. Our occasional disagreements or arguments were rare and they usually were resolved in the same way: I'd complain; he'd defend himself; I'd retreat; he would too. We went on like this for years. Then this medical marriage hit mid-life: The kids left home, a serious health crisis occurred (an earlier cancer returned and was managed), and I found myself fighting off a deepening depression. My life felt hollow, in spite of a dynamic Christian faith that I shared with Marvin. We had developed terrific friends and a vibrant church life together, yet I felt so very lonely.

I went digging for some help, reading up on the subject and searching for some ways to manage the storms that now ravaged our little sailboat.

What I found in the extensive literature on medical marriages was ever-more depressing.

Medical marriages have a much higher risk of stress and unhappiness because of the high demand of the job, the driven and focused people who enter medicine in the first place, and how this vocation intensifies the self-sacrificing or helping-others elements of that personality. I had known Marvin as a teenager, but our worlds and their interests meant a diverging set of concerns: His were medical, and mine were academic. We shared conversations about our lives, sure, but our deepest and most-connected conversations were with others. This seems to be common among functioning medical marriages (Rout, 1996).

Esther Nitzberg (1991) writes about doctor's wives in particular in *Hippocrates' Handmaidens*. Her research includes interviews with hundreds of doctors' wives across the United States and the troubling mental health concerns, which include a heavy dependence on alcohol and pain medication and higher suicide rate, among such women. Nitzberg cites several lifestyle issues contributing to their diminished health and well-being. A doctor's wife will get a full night's sleep only one-third to one-half of the time due to his schedule; she will spend most of her married life "waiting, accommodating, adjusting and handling alone the responsibilities of the home and children," and her self-esteem will plummet as she is "asked to be a wife to the profession" and "always come last" in her husband's list of priorities (5).

Wives of doctors with a high female patient load (like GPs who do maternity care) must also deal with the elevated status of their husbands in the eyes of other women. The non-medical wives in medical marriages express deep frustration at societal expectations that they should be filled with gratitude and related support for their "highly respected" husbands, and that they must exemplify "tact, discretion, and reduced curiosity" about their husband's work while requiring little attention themselves. Other rules also seem to apply: "make a good impression for his patients, don't interfere, don't talk about patients, don't nag, don't be jealous" (21). That doctors' wives will cite unusually low levels of self-esteem might align with the unusual demands for disconnectedness, including from her husband and other women. It is not surprising, then, that such wives build and reinforce walls around themselves. Needless to say, more and more doctors are not male, are not married, or are in nontraditional relationships. Even so, power differences make an impact. More recent research (Rout, 1996) suggests that it is the male doctor/female non-doctor marriage in particular that suffers most because of the gender imbalances already in place between many men and women. Most often the men make the greater amount of money, which also adds to power imbalance and related life choices. Life can be full and wonderful when one or both spouses are engaged in very meaningful and productive work that benefits the world. But the reality is that it is usually the wives who take the more supporting role to their husbands' high-powered careers, especially after children come along. This scenario is not limited to medical marriages. Many women may find themselves in a situation similar to mine, married to ambitious professional men but feeling lonely and unprepared for the high cost paid for his success. But medical marriages seem to be especially vulnerable.

I found that I wasn't alone or unique in experiencing a nagging sense of disillusionment, jealousy, and invisibility. On several occasions, it became evident that my own emotional needs could not compete with a patient for my husband's intense attention, even in a health crisis of my own. I also began to feel aware of my aging body. Most of his days are spent with younger and younger women, as they are cared for through pregnancy and delivery, or with staff and nurses, who share so much of his daily life and drama. This is his job. But it was bothering me more and more. Reading about the inevitability of loneliness among doctors' wives left me feeling hopeless. Twenty-five years is a long time not to explore such deep and intimate realities. What took us so long to reach a breaking point?

In the end, all it took was a small annoyance (a flirting nurse at a Christmas party) to tip me over the edge and land us in a counselor's office for six months. I cried for weeks on end, couldn't eat, couldn't sleep. I watched an awful lot of daytime TV and barely coped with my teaching and research. I felt defeated by my life. How had a functioning Christian marriage so derailed? How had we found ourselves so off-course? James Hollis (1993) in *The Middle Passage: From Misery to Meaning in Midlife* says, "Life is unsparing in asking us to grow up and take responsibility for our lives. As simplistic as it may sound, growing up is really the inescapable demand of the Middle Passage" (42). We had to grow up.

I am so proud of my husband, a very popular and successful doctor who finds his work incredibly rewarding. But as I entered mid-life, I felt a growing sense of need for him myself. The children were gone, the house was empty, we were both growing older, and the younger habits didn't seem to make as much sense anymore. Carl Jung (1965) would point to something about the "persona-shadow dialogue": To the degree we have identified with our "persona" (or our socialized self), so will we suffer anxiety at being pulled away from this "adaptation" at some point to address the reality of our inner needs. After years of playing the roles that others, and even myself, thought I was "supposed" to play, I could no longer deny my deeper need for connection and purpose. Who, exactly, was I? What, exactly, did I need? These were now the crucial questions I began to ask myself.

My demands for more of his time transformed from hysterical-sounding to calmer proclamations. Through counseling, I learned to be clear, to myself first of all, that I wasn't being hard on him for making these demands at mid-life but was rather honoring the truth of our experience. Did he hear this? Not at first. It took some painful months and professional help to clarify our needs: We both craved more time together; he needed less time on call and more boundaries; we needed more holidays together. The process has not been easy, and it has been hard to explain to the others in our shared worlds who often don't understand what the wife of a popular Christian doctor could possibly complain about or who feel that I should leave the marriage if I'm not happy. I was determined to hold on. We had both worked so hard that it seemed like a failure of sorts and a betrayal of an early belief that things would always get better.

Slowly, it has. Marvin has cut back on his hours. He is home for dinner with me each evening. We watch television together and take evening walks. We travel. We talk about our daily lives and our deepest hopes and fears. We read the same books. We laugh together and stay up late to talk over something that matters. In other words, we have entered each other's lives in a fuller way. After twenty-five years of marriage, I feel more married—I want more of him, and I can see that he wants more of me, too.

It appears that this sailing trip has weathered some dark days and rough seas at the midway point. What we've learned so far (our mid-life inventory):

- No matter how prepared we thought we were for marriage, the reality for us was lonelier than we imagined it would be. Our primary task in intimacy is to form and protect a deep companionship. My mid-life depression turned out to be a gift, in that it caused us to work on and strengthen our intimacy and reliance on each other.
- Spouses need to be a priority: Patients, students, clients, or customers are vitally important to our vocations, but we are sacred

territory as spouses. Neglect of a spouse is too costly. We need each other.

- Our children are a great blessing, and they filled the house with joy and noise. They required all our attention and care for many crucial years of child-rearing, but they also served as kind buffers to us as a couple. The empty nest can be painful, even if everyone is doing well and is happy with new successes. It was a major life adjustment that caught us off guard.

- Money and in-laws were often our "issues," but at mid-life these appear to have shrunk away to nothing of concern. I can sense now that they were never the problem. Control or freedom, loyalty or misplaced attachments were the problems. Nothing can replace the complete connection of marriage. To protect this for each other and ourselves, other demands (including other people) must be put in their rightful places.

- Health crises are upsetting and can be isolating. We coped in solitude with such realities, unable to reach out to the one who needed us most. Calling out for our spouse, even if he is a busy doctor, is always the right and appropriate thing to do. I had to acknowledge and give voice to my own deepest needs, honor them, and trust them to him as my spouse.

My midpoint has been painful, but it has provided an unparalleled opportunity to take a new view of marriage. Great losses often occur at midlife: Children move away; health can fail; marriages can dissolve if they can't be rebuilt; despair and disappointment can set in. The experiences have been existentially terrifying because of a loss of a certain developed identity. I had worn a mask of competence and independence throughout most of my marriage that eventually had to melt away so I could discover my more authentic self for both myself and my husband.

Not only had I depended on a certain "persona" that couldn't hold up—to my surprise, he was doing the same. Acknowledging this has given us as a couple possibilities for greater intimacy. I need my husband's actual presence and attention to be fully known; I didn't understand this until midlife. Now as we lay claim to an authentic, maturing marriage, we can sail into the horizon treasuring each other as much-loved companions.

References

Hollis, James. 1993. *The Middle Passage: From Misery to Meaning in Midlife.* Toronto: Inner City Books.

Jung, Carl. 1965. *Memories, Dreams, Reflections.* Translated by R. & C. Winston. New York: Vintage Books.

Nitzberg, Esther. 1991. *Hippocrates' Handmaidens: Women Married to Physicians.* Binghampton, NY: Haworth Press.

Rout, U. 1996. "Stress among General Practitioners and Their Spouses: A Qualitative Study." *British Journal of General Practice,* 46: pp. 157–60.

Smith, Cynthia S. 1980. *Doctors' Wives: The Truth about Medical Marriages.* New York: Seaview Books.

"Equal Opportunity Kitchen": A Dual-Career Family in Christian Ministry

Mary Rearick Paul

T wenty-five years ago, when my husband and I married, we were young, relatively naïve, and deeply in love. We each had received the gift of being raised by parents who had good marriages—not perfect, but good. From these marriages, we had learned some basic characteristics of a healthy marriage. The marriages of our parents expressed strong mutual support and respect. There was a solid sense of commitment and care in good and bad times. These marriages and families grew within the context of the Christian faith and church.

And yet there were some aspects we set out to do differently. Our parents had fairly traditional patterns of male/female roles. The women had initially stayed home, raised children, and then eventually earned graduate degrees and moved into professions. True, our mothers were engaged in professional development in ways that differed from their peers. Nevertheless, the working assumption was that the husband's career was primary.

Before our wedding, among other details, Bruce and I were talking about the imminent name change. My suggestion was that we each take my last name as our shared middle name. Bruce pondered this and then suggested that if the name change was up for discussion, so should be the place of our wedding (I assumed it would be in my hometown). Ultimately, he kept his name and I kept my hometown wedding. Not a deeply reflective decision, but sometimes immediacy and pragmatism rule the day.

My mother laughed when I said that our plan was to each cook three nights a week and go out for dinner one night a week. She announced the plan to my aunts, who each had seemingly knowing smiles. One of our wedding gifts from my mother-in-law was a framed saying: "Equal Opportunity Kitchen." I'm not sure if she believed we could actually live out this ideal. While we have not always maintained a strict three-for-three dinner production, meals for the family continue to be a shared responsibility. One Sunday early in our marriage, we came home from church and discovered a cupboard that was quite bare and funds that were quite meager. We both were too tired to problem-solve and as we headed off to take naps with empty stomachs, we turned to each other quite pitifully and said, "We want a mother." Shared responsibility in the kitchen ultimately created a demand for each of us to grow up and care for each other's (and eventually our children's) basic needs.

When we married, Bruce moved from Boston to New York City to join me, since I was working as a new social worker and his job was in flux. This began a marriage that was slightly unconventional by the standards of many in our family and church. As a newlywed, I happily began hanging some of our things on the walls. Bruce came in and looked at one wedding gift we had received (which in retrospect was quite horrendous) and asked, "Don't I get a say in how our apartment is decorated?" I was not particularly pleased with this interruption into my assumptions. All my friends had decorated without considering their husbands' tastes or thoughts.

This kind of marriage has demanded unexpected conversations, negotiations, and sometimes a pragmatic decision rather than a deeply reflective symbolic resolution. The challenge of these kinds of conversations is that they are ongoing. Living without assumptions about rigid male and female domains demands a willingness to engage in ongoing conversations through life changes and situations with each new change. While we have settled into some patterns according to our strengths (Bruce takes care of the car; I balance the checkbook), there are other tasks that continue to demand weekly conversations. This creates a dynamic shared life in which we have a deep appreciation for the willingness when one of us picks up a negotiated task. There are of course weeks where this also means we are frustrated when our communication has not been as clear as we thought it was.

Early on, we realized the notion of an egalitarian marriage was not shared by all. In college, we sat with another couple and sarcastically talked about our plans to have a marriage where Bruce would always lead and I would always follow. The couple responded with sweetness: "That's how we are planning our lives, too." An awkward conversation followed as we tried to explain our actual, quite different intent.

We added an extra layer of complication when we moved into pastoral ministry. When the calling into pastoral ministry became clear in my life, Bruce and I created the space for me to attend seminary. During this time, Bruce too was able to prayerfully reflect on his call and as a result entered seminary and ministry after I had graduated. This meant that early in our careers I was assigned a position as senior pastor as Bruce entered into full-time studies at seminary. Given the dynamics of our denomination's assumptions that couples would attend the same church together, Bruce first completed his student internship and then joined the staff of the church where I was pastor. Our congregation was supportive of this move, but there were those in our larger community of colleagues and friends who had difficulty accepting my pastoral call, let alone a husband who would serve on the pastoral staff under my leadership.

Bruce and I would often be teased by this switch in roles. There were several models of couples in ministry partnerships, but all the other cases were situations where the men served as senior pastors and the women were on staff. I found that communication via teasing can be a way to express displeasure that doesn't really allow for honest conversations. As the receiver, one is often forced to respond with some spirit of "fun" or be perceived as taking things personally. This can be a difficult conundrum for the often-public settings of these teasing moments. We would be asked questions such as, "Who is the head of your home?" or "Who drove today?" or "Has your boss been nice to you lately?" accompanied by strange smirks. One ministry couple I know stopped going to pastors' and spouses' retreats because they could not bear to fake laugh or to confront these disparaging remarks.

Messages about the cultural "norm" are so pervasive that it's possible not to recognize them. But in the context of my experience I encountered many comments or situations where these assumptions and ideologies prevailed. I heard a visiting professor in a graduate class say that it was a fact that only weak men marry strong women. I have attended many church events for women where they were taught the art of being supportive mates to their husbands and were never given the space to explore when it might be good to ask for support from their husbands. I sat through a seminar where we were told by a speaker that in a marriage there could only be one star and that she and her husband had decided he would be the star. This odd, forced choice seemed to be accepted as necessary. These biases against women fully flourishing in their lives, and against men who encourage women to be strong and able, seem to pervade church culture.

Some of the issues stem from the bad interpretation and teaching on scriptures that refer to marriage. The most notable is the passage found in Ephesians, chapter 5.[1] Verses 21 through 33 are often understood to be prescriptive descriptions of the Christian household. The particular phrase found in verse 22—"Wives, be subject to your husbands as you are to the Lord. For the husband is the head of the wife just as Christ is the head of the church"—has often been used as a mechanism for controlling or subordinating women. It is this passage that served as a root for some of the questions and "teasing" that Bruce and I have faced.

This passage is much richer and more nuanced than a simple read would provide. Good interpretation must begin with verse 21: "Be subject to one another out of reverence for Christ." This verse is the umbrella under which we begin to hear that all Christians are called to submission and service. While the admonitions begin to move into particularities (such as husband, wife, slave, free, child, parent), all are called to offer each other a mutual care and service under this new realm of service to Jesus Christ.

Because the passage shifts between a focus on husband and wife to church and Christ, there is some ambiguity regarding the specific goal of the author. When explicitly looking at the teaching on marriage, it is important to see the extraordinary teaching that the husband was to love the wife as Christ loves the church. This is a love that desires that the church thrive, flourish, and know its full potential. This includes being willing to "give himself up for her" (v. 25). Interestingly, this call to love is often interpreted with parental overtones. Husbands are often encouraged to provide for, care for, and nurture their wives. And yet if the whole of the expression of Christ's love for the church is explored, it is actually a radical statement that frees the church to explore, grow, and be a vessel through which the fullness of Christ is known (v. 23). The church, rather than being protected, is called out to take risks, proclaim the gospel, be a witness, and be willing to suffer for the gospel. Sadly, I rarely hear a sermon on this passage that encourages the love of the husband to be expressed in this way.

The often-assumed paternalistic overtones can be enticing. Marrying at a relatively young age when identity formation issues are at a pivotal

---

1   While I will explore this passage in part, there is far more extensive work provided by many scholars. The website for Christians for Biblical Equality is one resource: cbeinternational.org.

stage regarding the future, one's ability to care for oneself, and vocation, can tempt some to move into a childlike relationship with their husbands. There is some ease in assuming these more traditional roles. The husband conquers; the woman supports. The husband provides; the woman creates nests. And yet these assumptions are unfair to both the woman and the man. The woman is not ultimately called upon to resolve those identity formation issues. Instead of fully engaging questions of vocation, she follows a pattern that, at least initially, has much ease. The man, on the other hand, is forced to meet vocational issues based on the necessity of being at least the primary provider for the family.

While serving as a pastor in churches, I discovered frustrated women who in their forties were asking for the first time, "What would God have me do with my life?" For many, this journey began with a realization that they had no sense of their gifts, strengths, or abilities. I also encountered men who were dealing with great depression in their forties, as they realized the role of primary provider had directed their vocational choices in ways that did not provide anything life-giving or soul-sustaining. They had the additional frustration of not feeling they had the freedom to really ask, "What would God have me do with my life?" For both scenarios this is incredibly sad. The ultimate call of Ephesians 5 is that the husband and wife love and respect one another. The assumed roles layered into the language of submission ultimately deny a couple's ability to truly love and respect each other.

While I do ultimately read this passage as life-giving, there is no way to remove all the patriarchal overtones. Paul cannot be held accountable to modern sensibilities. There is an assumed view of marriage that reflects his context. Nevertheless, there is also a subversive call that belies the notion of household codes, ringing of a new freedom. This is a freedom that calls the husband and wife to be a team who together prays over their shared and unique vocations and how they might make space for these vocations to be fulfilled.

Several years ago, I heard a couple describe their marriage as built on a kenotic foundation. This was a practical application of the kenosis passage found in the second chapter of Philippians:

> Let the same mind be in you that was in Christ Jesus, who though he was in the form of God, did not regard equality with God as something to be exploited but emptied himself, taking the form of a slave, being born in human likeness. And being found in human form, he

humbled himself and became obedient to the point of death—even death on a cross. (v. 5–8)

This passage is not specifically about marriage relationships. Paul is calling the community to a unity through mutual submission that bears the marks of a new community created by Christ. This new community has a nonhierarchical intent. The leadership and service of the Philippian community were to be marked by humility. Paul's point is that Christians are called to make an investment into the lives of others without thought of personal gain. This mutuality of love is to be the mark of the Christian community.

It is not a huge stretch to say that this mutuality of love and sacrifice is the mark of a true Christian marriage. There is great freedom in how this is expressed. I think we make a mistake when we demand that equal flourishing has to look like equal income or equal professional status. It is instead the equal ability to fulfill the vocational call of God. This is to be named and worked out together. Many feminists are rightly concerned about the language of sacrifice and obedience. This can quickly be taken down a road of domination and humiliation. And yet as Christians we cannot throw the notions of humility and sacrifice out because of these distortions. We must live a reflective life that does the work to apply the call to sacrifice in non-gender-specific ways with the goal of all experiencing abundant life in Christ.

This freedom sounds beautiful and winsome, and it is. It is also hard and filled with complex negotiations, conversations, wrestling with each other and God, and a challenging commitment to mutual sacrifice. There have been days when I wished the decisions Bruce and I have had to make were easier and clearer, even if that meant more defined roles and expectations. But those wishes are simply the pragmatic unreflective side of me arising once again. In the overarching view of how we have lived our lives together, I see something beautiful that has been created for both of us to continually discover God's presence and calling in each day. This tone of love and respect permeates our home and our life together. Every opportunity and achievement that has come my way has been fully celebrated by Bruce. There have been significant junctures when we have wrestled with job decisions, where Bruce has sacrificially said, "I think you should do this; this is an amazing opportunity." He believes in my strengths and abilities far more than I believe in myself. At the same time, I have been committed to helping him not only fulfill his professional development but his vocational call, which includes creative writing. We have carved out space for him to do this hard work that may not ever have the mark of recognized success.

After more than twenty-five years, though my husband and I are not so young, and certainly not as naïve, we are even more deeply in love. We have each enjoyed the space created by the other to live out our lives and vocations in response to God's presence in our lives. I give thanks that I was not "protected" from the work that my personal and professional growth has demanded from me. I believe we each stand stronger today as individuals because of our shared life together. I am deeply appreciative of the marriage we have carved out together as we have lived in response to each other and to God.

Negotiating Identity: Retaining a Sense of Self in Marriage and Motherhood

Melissa Burt-Gracik

When my husband and I were engaged, I was confronted with thinking through the life stages marriage would probably bring our way. We were going through premarital counseling and were taking it VERY seriously, wanting to begin this life together well. Two things brought me anxiety in this process: changing my name and the looming idea of bearing children. Both concerned my sense of self.

As a little girl, I had always looked forward to marriage and wondered with anticipation about the golden days ahead. I remember doodling my first name and behind it adding question marks or the last names of the boys I liked at the time. Completely reconstructing my identity and embracing a new life and a new name were things I looked forward to as a young girl. I'm thankful to report that when the time came for me to make the decision about whether or not to take my husband's difficult-to-pronounce Slovak name, many of my perspectives had changed. Letting go of this part of my identity, or any part of my identity for that matter, was no longer a thrilling idea. Instead, it was threatening.

After the name change dilemma came another piece of the future I had always looked forward to as a child: motherhood. My husband Jeff and I had both grown up in pretty conservative homes with traditional gender roles. Neither of us had encountered different perspectives that challenged or provoked exploration of these roles until the time came for us to decide how we were going to live out our male and femaleness in marriage. Jeff was, at first, unwilling to think outside of the framework he had observed as normal growing up. His mother had taken his dad's last name, stayed at home with them when they were little, and as a home economics teacher, had readily taken on the duties of caring for their home. No one in his childhood modeled anything very different from his parents' roles.

This structure of duties and roles in his home seemed to work for his parents and everyone else he knew, and consequently had woven itself into his thinking as the way married adult life should be. I had already started to think outside that framework when we began discussing our life together, and the worldview forming within me was vastly different from his. This was spurred on by my growing awareness of gender inequality in the world, and in particular in the workplace, as I began a career after college. I was left with a deep-seated fear of motherhood in my early twenties. I sensed that with motherhood came a relinquishing of oneself, a letting go of one's dreams and ambitions.

Motherhood as practiced in the gender roles Jeff and I had observed in our childhoods meant stopping my career to take care of my child and home, centering my life around those two things. Only later might I incorporate earning an income back into my life—until I could retire and enjoy children again through grandparenting. Motherhood meant succumbing to cultural teachings that women were better at nurturing than men and were consequently more responsible for it. Mothering meant sacrificing my gifts, talents, and dreams for those of my progeny while my husband continued to pursue his goals, whatever they may be, relatively unencumbered by the obligations of home and children. When this version of motherhood emerged as the version with which Jeff was most comfortable, I quickly learned how uncomfortable I was with making these practices a part of my life.

In early adulthood it became apparent that my observations of gender inequality were not entirely a result of my skewed vision and perspective as a newfound feminist. I learned from current research what I saw right in front of me. Men were earning more than women on average, and always had. In fact, despite the decades-long efforts of the modern feminist movement, the gap between the pay of men and women with college degrees has not changed in fifteen years. If I did choose to work and parent, dire statistics of the workload I would face caught my attention. According to the 2006 survey data from the Bureau of Labor Statistics, one in five men engage in some kind of housework in an average day, while more than half of women do the same. The women I observed around me were very familiar with the reality of the "third shift" they worked when they returned home from paid work. Mountains of laundry and dishes were washed by them rather than the male counterparts sharing their homes.

And it wasn't just the work at home holding married women with children back. As Shira Boss reported in an August 2007 *New York Times* article, marriage with children bolsters a man's career but hinders a woman's.[1] Though recent studies are showing that women and men are closing the gap on hours worked both in and out of the home, women still do twice as much housework and childcare as men in two-parent families.[2]

I was willing to devote myself to parenting, and the workload it came with, but I wasn't willing to parent until I had a spouse who was willing to devote himself to the task, in equal measure with me. In our early talks concerning children and the roles we expected of each other, I felt stifled and potentially pressured into a commitment far outweighing my husband's. This was not okay with me. So, for the time being, we realized we didn't agree, and shelved the issue until it was a little closer to home. We married, I compromised on the name change issue, and for five years I embraced the new name I had so ardently looked forward to in my youth.

By our fifth year of marriage, Jeff and I had grown quite a lot. We'd survived my first master's program, he had suffered through two years of corporate business, and we'd spent three invigorating years in seminary together. Nearing the completion of our program, Jeff let me in on one of the big paradigm shifts of worldview that had occurred within him gradually during our seminary education. He had begun to empathize with my fears of identity loss and suggested that we reconsider our last name, which resulted in us both adding my maiden name. Jeff was beginning to understand how the gender roles we were raised with might contribute to my feelings of fear and anxiety in regard to parenting. He was realizing how gender inequality had created pain in our world and wanted to make strides toward equality in his own life, which meant a few changes in our life together. He was ready to talk about how we could partner in parenting in ways that would be fulfilling for both of us.

Shortly after this revelation, we both agreed it was time to give parenting a go. Enter our daughter, Sophia. After her conception, we assessed where

---

1   Shira Boss, "Wedded to Work, and in Dire Need of a Wife," *The New York Times*, 11 August 2007, accessed 2 March 2011, http://www.nytimes.com/2007/08/11/business/11envy.html?_r=1&scp=14&sq=shira%20boss&st=cse.

2   Robert Pear, "Married and Single Parents Spending More Time With Children, Study Finds," *The New York Times*, 17 October 2006, accessed 2 March 2011, http://www.nytimes.com/2006/10/17/us/17kids.html?scp=6&sq=october%2017,%202006&st=cse.

we were in our vocational paths and it seemed best to both of us for me to continue my career pursuits as Jeff assumed the roles of primary caregiver and household manager.

Motherhood to my daughter Sophia has not been what I feared it might be at the beginning of my adult life. I am quite certain that much of my sense of wellness and wholeness, and the awareness that motherhood has not taken my identity hostage, is due to my spouse's partnership. Being left to manage mothering, work, housekeeping, and all the other components of adult life without his desire to collaborate would have shaped my identity differently. Partnership has allowed motherhood to be a positive contributor to my identity, as opposed to the center of it. Rather than giving up parts of myself, I simply feel like new dimensions have been added. Motherhood has contributed to my identity much like an onion—it's just another layer. The experience of motherhood has wrapped me in a comforting layer of life experience. I've embraced it and made it a part of who I am, but it hasn't taken over. I'm hopeful that each life stage to come will yield the same result: regular old me, just shaped by new life experiences.

New experiences, indeed. My husband's wrestling experience in high school was not something I ever thought I'd incorporate into parenting. But just this week, I remembered Jeff's advice—to go for the hip to leave my opponents unable to complete their planned maneuvers—as I struggled to keep Sophia from kicking and rolling herself into her very soiled and stinky diaper as I, quite graciously, was attempting to give her a new one. I once worried that adding children to our lives would leave me craving deep thought and conversation. It was as if I believed I would be dumbed down by spending so much time with a little person. Memories of the mothers of the kids I babysat in college, eager to be out with adults for a change, probably shaped my thinking.

I am certain that the addition of Sophia to my life has made me smarter, and at the beginning, a little dumber, too. As I recently read in an article by Liz Szabo, mothers' brains must by hyper vigilant. This extra work causes some parts of the brain to be on high alert and others to take it easy. Momnesia was certainly a scary confirmation of my earlier fears. During pregnancy, I asked Jeff to hand me "that thing you pick up hot things with while cooking," because I couldn't for the life of me remember the name for a potholder. All of that physical energy directed toward the creation of our child sapped my brain of the faculties I had assumed would be always present. During this mental fuzziness, I asked one of my good friends, a mother of four, if it would get better. She didn't sound optimistic, but the theorists say there is good news. Mothering is actually supposed to make you more intelligent!

Katherine Ellison writes in *The Mommy Brain: How Motherhood Makes Us Smarter* that motherhood can help women improve in managing stress, multitasking, and dealing with people. Ellison identifies five factors contributing to what she terms the "baby-boosted brain": Perception in smell, hearing, and vision is improved as a mother attunes herself to the demanding needs of her infant. Efficiency is heightened as new mothers develop sharper attention, focus, and prioritizing skills. Resiliency comes with the hormone oxytocin as women become less reactive to stress hormones. Oxytocin is also key in strengthened social interaction, memory, and learning. Motivation is enhanced in mothers who have a powerful drive to be with their babies, nurture them, and provide them safety. Motherhood can enable women to create boundaries, try new tasks, and conquer fear. Lastly, emotional intelligence is enhanced. Empathy increases in a mother as she attempts to understand her infant and what her baby needs. This empathy booster leads to better people-reading skills and a more empathic style of speech.

I'm betting Sophia would argue with that last statistic when I'm trying to create healthy boundaries during meal times. I rarely emote a mite of empathy when she repeatedly wants to throw her food on the floor. But other than a few minor instances, I resonate strongly with Ellison's findings. Mothering has heightened who I am and has improved me. Being Sophia's mom has frequently met my needs for a sense of contribution, giving and receiving love, offering care, partnership with my husband, and so much more.

What Does a Woman Look Like? Reflections on the Multiple, Messy, and Mutating

Bettina Tate Pedersen

"And still I break up through the skin of awareness a thousand times a day, as dolphins burst through seas, and dive again, and rise, and dive."
—Annie Dillard, *An American Childhood*

One of the key questions I seem to be constantly asking myself is, "What does a woman look like?" Perhaps this is none too striking given the fact that I, like all the other women in my modern American culture, am bombarded constantly with images of womanhood. These images are usually of very thin, young, blemish- and wrinkle-free women, and with each passing year, these images look less and less like the woman I see when I look in my own mirror.

There was a time, I must confess, when I felt a secret pleasure that I was young enough not to have to worry about added pounds, or the appearance of wrinkles, or the need for such things as routine mammograms. Those days are behind me now. The question "What does a woman look like?" is, however, still with me, and its answer is far more complicated than the glossy images our consumer culture offers. In the simplest terms, the nature of this woman's life is multiple, messy, and mutating.

One of the most vivid experiences of the multiplicity of my life came to me about six weeks after my older son was born. I was in graduate school at the time, having just completed my doctoral exams twelve days before he was born, on November 30. I have a very vivid memory of returning to my spring term teaching load, standing in my office, and feeling really great to be back "at work," using my brain and remembering that I possessed an intellect. For the six weeks prior, I had been living in the intensity of nursing a newborn. My son had been born a few days before his due date, and his early arrival was only the beginning of his consistent ability to turn my spouse's and my carefully arranged, meticulously planned, and complicated joint schedules on their ears! When we brought him home to our third-floor apartment, he weighed 5 pounds, 13 ounces, and nursed just about every two or three hours round the clock.

Nursing is a learned art, and it takes practice, physical stamina, and the ability to endure incredible fatigue and sometimes pain. It is also relentless and has the effect of literally taking over your life. It felt terrific to be back "at work" that cold January day in Illinois. Getting ready to use my brain to teach a class or two helped me remember that I really was more than just a milk machine for my infant son, and that my identity really was multiple and varied. Nursing was one of the most incredible experiences of my life. I have no regrets about committing to it and carrying it out, but it certainly made me reevaluate the "truth" of all the natural, easy mother-love and nurture I had heard. Standing there in my office, I also realized that in becoming a mother, I had merely added another layer of identity and responsibility onto the ones that were already there.

Several years ago, when my second son was a toddler, I was working, with him in my office, to get ready for the start of a new fall term. Because his childcare did not begin at the same time my week of faculty meetings commenced, I was juggling him and my meeting/course preparation obligations on campus simultaneously. On this particular day, I needed to attend a lunch meeting, so I took my son with me. He played quietly in the corner of the room for most of the meeting. At one point the car noises he was making for his Matchbox cars became too exuberant, so I got up from the meeting, went to the corner, and quieted his play.

Days later, I had an interesting conversation with another professor who had been there. He told me he had seen a totally different person in me as he had observed me dealing with my son. Up to that time, his vision of me as a colleague had been as a hard-driving, totally professional woman. When he watched me interact with my son, he said, he saw a "softened" mother woman, not at all like the assertive image he held of me as a professional woman. I shared this story with my spouse later, and his response was the inverse. My husband has seen me present at a few professional conferences. The confident and professional image he sees of me there always surprises him because he sees me more routinely as a wife and mother. The different images of me that these men see are a little startling, but they effectively illustrate the multiplicity of a woman's life.

§

What does a woman's life look like? Her life is messy. One Saturday morning memory captures this. Saturday mornings for many years now have consisted predominantly of one thing—soccer games—with the rest of life's weekend chores packed in around the day's game schedule. This morning we had hurried as usual to get the car trunk loaded with soccer ball, water bottles, cooler (as the parents on schedule for game refreshments and ice), chairs, sun umbrellas, stroller, diaper bag, jackets, purse, and whatever else we needed. We were running late enough that I had to drive so I could drop off my five-year-old son and my coaching husband nearer the field and with some of our gear so they could be on time.

As I parked, unloaded the rest of our stuff, and settled my five-month-old baby boy into his stroller, I was thinking. "What does a successful professional woman's life look like when she's also a fully committed mother? How does she manage both? What does she juggle and in what ways? How does she get everything in?"

I was pushing the stroller toward the field with diaper bag and purse slung round my shoulders when suddenly a little bell went off inside my head ringing, "*This* is what it looks like! *This* is what it looks like!" It looks hurried, with laundry piles in the way of the door as you're on your way to the garage to load soccer stuff. It looks messy, with soccer gear or office briefcases mixed in with baby stroller and diaper bag. It looks disorganized, with academic papers lying next to homework agendas, flyers from the day's mail, a hopeful recipe for tonight's dinner (maybe), and piles of unopened mail. It looks disheveled, with adult-sized beds made bumpily by little people learning how to do this job right, and living rooms with adult furniture strewn with children's Duplos, Legos, Yu Gi Oh cards, and school backpacks. In short, it looked a whole lot like my actual life and not very much like that other life—my ideal life—that lays out its impossible terrain in my brain.

In that moment it was acutely clear to me that I live at least two lives. One of them is my actual life, in which I work constantly to balance the demands of full-time professional, full-time mother, full-time spouse, and friend or sister. The other life is the fantasy ideal that I imagine in my head. This life is the one in which I have the family Christmas letter written, printed, and folded in August before the school terms begin, so that I can sit down with a leisurely cup of tea on Thanksgiving morning while the turkey cooks and stuff my Christmas cards with gentle thoughts of the friends and family to whom they'll be going in the next day's mail.

This life is the one in which each night after collecting my sons from their bus stop and driving home by 5:30 or 6 p.m., we sit down to a beautifully presented, nutritious, home-cooked meal that we will have eaten and cleaned up just before 7 p.m. so that the evening's routines of homework, English and French reading, violin practice, and baths are all completed and boys tucked into bed by 8:30 p.m. This life is the one in which I manage to go to bed at 10 p.m. every night with my work completed for the next day's classes and meetings, having done some writing or research for my own projects, and with the hallway neatly lined with all our backpacks and briefcases stowed and ready to go for the next morning. This life is the one in which I give a conference paper, or publish an article or book, every year. And this life is the one in which I have time to host bi-weekly dinner parties with our adult friends in our perfectly cleaned and tidy home.

Who am I kidding? What real woman actually achieves this slate of accomplishments? I must confess that I often look at the lives of my friends and the academic mentors I have had, and think that they must be able to pull all this off, and think too that there is just some deep flaw in me that prevents me from doing so.

That Saturday morning's epiphany startled me awake to both the reality and the fantasy of my life. I am a successful professional who finds her work challenging and rewarding; I am a fully committed mother who loves the joys and even some of the demands of parenting sons; I am a contented wife who still finds surprises and struggles enough to keep my two-decade-plus marriage interesting and fulfilling; I am a woman who has good friends who care about the details of my life, and sisters and extended family who love and support me.

All of these things are true about my life even though it is messy, scattered, and imperfect and rarely, if ever, looks like the fantasy pictures that run constantly in my brain. The answer to my question that Saturday morning—and to the question I'm still asking—is that it looks messy. Life can't always look like *Martha Stewart Living*'s latest issue. Perhaps if I spend too much time constructing this ideal life in my head, I'll really just end up squandering bits of my soul in the process, giving up chances to celebrate life in the midst of its messiness or to see that mess erases barrenness and replaces it with life's exuberance. Truthfully, having a career, being a mother, and sustaining a healthy relationship with my spouse simultaneously is much harder and takes far more internal spiritual discipline than I had imagined.

§

What does a woman look like? A woman's life is mutating. "Mutating" is a bit of a distasteful word in my vocabulary. It suggests to me something wrongly formed or unpleasantly shifting—one life form slithering out of one shape and into another—but because of these associations, the word illustrates the messiness of life I've been describing. It suggests the repellent wonder of change and has a truthfulness about it that I like. When I was a new mother, one of my professor friends counselled me wisely about raising children, saying, "Don't get used to anything, because as soon as you do, your children change."

Her words have stayed with me, and I've found myself replaying them in my mind many times in the intervening years. When my sons were doing things that were different or out of character for the way they had been behaving, I found myself becoming irritated and muttering, "What's wrong with you? Why are you doing that?" or something similar. Once they had done the new thing long enough, I finally realized that either yes, indeed, there was something wrong that really needed attention—such as an oncoming illness, school trouble, or an unsettling experience—or that there was nothing "wrong" with them; they had merely moved on to their next phase of development. They no longer wanted or needed those soothers; they had simply moved on from Thomas the Tank Engine and into Yu Gi Oh cards; they really could be left alone at age twelve or even dropped off at Balboa Park for an acting class followed by orchestra rehearsal without me staying there all day to observe. What was really at issue was me. I was the one who needed to adjust, to pay attention to the shifts they were making, to hear and see that they had changed, and to change along with them.

Because children change so rapidly and in such astonishing ways over the course of the few short years you have in raising them, their shifts can sometimes trip you up. This can also be true of the routine process of living and aging—both can catch you off guard in much the same way children's growth does. Suddenly, it seems, you've slammed into the end of another term of school with exams looming in front of you, and the speed of life has surprised you, or you may be graduating from university and the whole world is open to you, which is thrilling and terrifying at the same time. One thing is certain: Our lives are changing, yours and mine. The earth is moving right under our feet, and we must move with it or find ourselves in a heap on the ground.

Sometimes in spite of our best efforts to stay on our feet—to adjust to life's changes, to remain flexible—life lands us in a heap anyway. Our lives mutate and things don't work out as we had envisioned or planned. For me, I never envisioned having a child born with deformed leg bones or waiting for twelve years for the surgery to correct it; I never envisioned losing my mother before any of my children were born, or my father when my older son was just a year and a half old. I never imagined the collapse of my in-laws' twenty-five-year marriage nor the mid-life crisis of my husband's father. I never once thought that the marriages of my college roommates and friends for whom I had been bridesmaid would end in abandonment and divorce.

For everyone, the life events are undoubtedly different, but the effects of the changes are and will be just as powerful and important. Life and the process of aging teach us many things along the way. In the end, what will really matter are our hearts, the persons we have become internally. This is also what our Christian faith teaches us: "As a woman thinks in her heart, so is she." I like the way Joan Chittister describes what matters in the process of aging. In *The Story of Ruth* she writes:

> There are lessons that come with age that come no other way. Age is a mirror of the knowledge of God. Age teaches that time is precious, that companionship is better than wealth, that sitting can be as much a spiritual discipline as running marathons, that thinking is superior to doing, that learning is eternal, that things go to dust, that adult toys wear thin with time, that only what is within us—good music, fine reading, great art, thoughtful conversation, faith, and God—remains. When our mountain climbing days are over, the elderly know, these are the things that will chart the setting of our suns and walk us to our graves. All the doings will wash away; all the being will emerge. (33)

I think we could also say that when our marriages are over, our children are grown, our careers are completed, our accomplishments past, we will still have our internal lives, our internal selves, and what any marriages, children, relationships, careers, or accomplishments have contributed to the creation of our internal selves will be parts of the whole, but not the whole entire. Our lives are moving creations. They mutate, shift, sometimes break, then reform, but they are not static. We shouldn't get used to anything, because life will change. This is also what a woman's life looks like.

§

To say that a woman's life looks multiple, messy, and mutating is to engage in honest reflection that resists the flattening and debilitating effects of some of the essentializing myths about women that surround our lives: that mothering will supplant all other needs for fulfillment that women may have; that caring for infants is natural and therefore should come easily from our maternal instincts; that women need less excitement in their lives than men and are content with quieter pursuits; that women really want, deep down, just to stay in the domestic domain; that real women have all their "Martha Stewart" ducks in a row.

Some women may find fulfillment in an identity composed of only one self, but many women find a multiplicity of selves to be more truthfully descriptive of their real selves, and far more necessary to their healthy living. Some women may actually be able to achieve consummate skill and artistry in balancing professional, maternal/domestic, and relational domains, but many of us struggle in the messy demands of those different worlds and do the best we can. Some women may find a steady continuity to their lives that finds them the very definition of consistent and reliable, always there, always the same, but many of us find ourselves always reaching for an elusive stability that our lives seem to lack.

My reflections are specific to my own white, middle-class, Christian, American, middle-aged situation. They cannot possibly represent the rich diversity of experience and knowledge that is carried by women of different colors, classes, religions, countries, ethnicities, ages, or abilities. Women's lives are truly diverse, and perhaps the greatest harm that essentializing myths do is to make us think (and be) small: to think within tightly controlled categories; to feel our only, or even our greatest, success is in excelling in traditionally feminine things; or to believe that our differences make us inferior or flawed in comparison with men or with other women. We should resist shaming ourselves because we don't fit the categories, or accepting the values of a consumerist society that elevates some womanly skills (like female sexuality and beauty) and devalues others (like mothering or the domestic arts). Too often we as women use language that does not represent our lives or our gender, believe that we are beautiful or valuable only when we are young, and stifle God-given abilities, talents, and gifts because we think they aren't "womanly." When we think small like this, we impoverish not only our own lives, but also the life of the world and the full redemptive movement of God in Christ in the stream of human history. In virtually every example of impoverished thinking I've listed here, we capitulate to values given us by a secular and sexist culture and not to those given us by Jesus's teachings or example. Even when some of these impoverishing myths are taught by the "church," they do not come from God. Even Genesis records the radical sexist division of women desiring husbands, and husbands ruling over them as a curse of sin and not as God's original design for women and men. Resisting these myths isn't just another option we might choose; I believe it is part of the hard and radical call of God on our lives to "be not fashioned according to this world, but be transformed by the renewing of your mind, that you may prove what is the good and acceptable and perfect will of God" (Romans 12:2, ERV).

§

What does a woman look like? In my life, she looks multiple, messy, and mutating. Remembering that my real woman's life looks like this and not like the glitzy images of the advertising or entertainment industries is a good medicine. It encourages me to resist the false values and impossible appeals of a consumerist society. It strengthens me to accept my flawed but genuine humanity. It helps me to see the true beauty in the midst of my imperfect life and to keep an honest humility about my own importance or accomplishment. Annie Dillard describes childhood as a "waking up," a coming to consciousness about yourself, the world around you, and your place in it. I think womanhood is a "waking up" as well. With each added self, the messiness entailed, and the inevitable mutations, I am coming to see more of the truth about my own life, the lives of other women, and hopefully God's redemption as well.

Works Cited

Chittister, Joan D. *The Story of Ruth: Twelve Moments in Every Woman's Life*. Grand Rapids, Michigan; Cambridge, UK: William B. Eerdmans Publishing Company, Saint Paul University, Ottawa: Novalis, 2000.

Dillard, Annie. *An American Childhood*. New York: Harper Perennial, 1987.

Choosing Motherhood: Adoption and the Single Life

Rebecca Flietstra

I never expected to be a single mom. I don't entirely know what I *did* expect to happen in my life—but it certainly wasn't that. During high school and college, when I thought about becoming a parent, it was always in the context of a marriage, never as someone doing it on her own. I doubt I would have even found such a life attractive as a teenager or in my twenties. But I'm a different person than I was twenty years ago—I've had different experiences, additional memories, changing goals. Each past decision has shaped me, allowing me to consider options that once felt alien or impossible or undesirable. Sometimes my first choice hasn't panned out, forcing me to search for a second choice.

"Second choice" fortunately doesn't mean "second best." All of us, at different times, find that our original plans weren't viable. Some of us enter college expecting to pursue a particular major and a related career, but then we unexpectedly discover a passion for a class or a subject that draws us in a different direction. We fall in love for the first time, but most of us end up marrying someone else (or not getting married at all!). Some marriages fail, only to be followed by healthy, new relationships. Just because one option precedes another, it doesn't automatically guarantee the superiority of the first choice.

My choice to become a mother solidified in the fall of 2001. My mom sparked the process during a phone call. She mentioned someone from her church who had adopted as a single woman: "You once thought about adopting, didn't you?" Well, yes. Even in high school I had thought about adopting. I knew that the world's population was skyrocketing, and that there were many young children who needed parents. But, as I mentioned before, I had thought of becoming a mom only after I was already a wife. I had heard, of course, of single-parent adoption, but I never considered it a personal possibility.

Yet the more I thought about it, the more it appeared to be the right choice for me. I started to assess my life. I was in my mid-thirties, and my dating life was fairly nonexistent. I wasn't miserable being single, but I wasn't entirely happy being on my own, either. My world felt a bit small, revolving around work and my personal needs. I had no absolute commitments—no absolute demands on my time. I could spend time with friends when, and if, I felt like it. My time and resources were mine to bestow or to withhold. Becoming a mom would change that—indeed, would change it even more than becoming a wife. The needs of a child are ever present, ever exacting. In choosing to become a parent, I would lose most of my freedom. In exchange, I'd learn how to give of myself, how to sacrifice (at times) my own desires and needs for the sake of someone else's needs and desires.

I also discovered something rather startling about myself: I realized that if I remained single and childless that I would ultimately regret more not becoming a mom than not becoming a wife. I hadn't expected that. I hadn't generally had deeply maternal feelings. I had certainly thought about becoming a mom, but it wasn't the deep desire that I knew a lot of my friends and classmates had. But here I was, realizing that if I could have only one—husband or child—I would choose the child.

I decided to adopt from Guatemala. Although Southern California has many vibrant ethnic communities, I felt that here I would have greater access to the Hispanic communities and events. Thus it would be easier to give my future child a healthy sense of her ethnic heritage if she were Hispanic. I also fairly quickly chose the desired gender of my future child. Unlike pregnancy, adoption typically allows prospective parents to choose. There's an active discussion in the adoption community about the desirability or even appropriateness of making such a choice. For my own part, I had no qualms: I asked for a girl. It just seemed easier as a single woman to raise a daughter rather than a son. I chose the name Anita, a Spanish name that belonged to my grandma. After five months of interviews and paperwork, I was finally ready for a placement. I still vividly remember the day I called the agency to make sure they really did have all my pre-placement paperwork. They did. I inquired about the length of the waiting list. The worker told me there were maybe six or seven families waiting for girls. And then I asked the question that changed everything: "How long is the waiting list for boys?"

"We don't currently have any families waiting for boys. In fact, we have several boys in foster homes waiting for families." Oh.

I still don't know why I asked that last question. It was so irrelevant to everything I was planning on. I was set on raising a girl. I had a name picked out. Whenever I saw a young Hispanic girl, I wondered how much my daughter would look like her. I had bought a couple of dresses. I had never questioned my choice to adopt a daughter—not until the moment I heard the answer to my question.

After I got off the phone with the worker, I called my sister who was, at the time, a mother to two boys. Were boys indeed harder for a mom to understand? How harmful would it be to raise a boy without a father? Having stretched myself this far, how much further could I go? I consulted with friends. I paced. I prayed.

The next day I called the adoption agency and told them I was open to adopting a child of either gender (which, under the circumstances, meant I'd be adopting a boy). On the third day, the adoption agency called me with a referral for a one-month-old boy.

I am so grateful I changed my mind—that I abandoned my initial desire for a girl. In this instance, the second choice has definitely not been second best! It's now difficult for me to reconstruct my previous thinking, the arguments for choosing a girl that had seemed so obviously convincing. Instead, I shudder to realize how close I came to missing out. Jeremiah has been such a joy that the second time around I decided to stick with boys. This time, however, the decision has had some pragmatic support: Having a second boy has allowed for a shared bedroom and the reuse of hand-me-down clothes, among other practicalities. I decided with my second adoption to again adopt a Hispanic child.

Both prior to adopting Jeremiah and in the intervening years, I read a number of books and articles on adoption. I sought out information about international and transracial adoptees. I've been very concerned about a healthy self-identity for Jeremiah, especially since he has been raised by a "white-skinned" mother and was the only "brown-skinned" child within my extended family. By choosing the second time around to restrict myself to a Latino child, I wanted to give Jeremiah a younger brother who could potentially "look like him." I dreamed of two sons who could be mistaken for biological brothers. It would also be easier for me to expose my sons to their culture of origin if they shared that culture.

For my second adoption, however, I chose to adopt through the San Diego foster care system. In 2001, when I first decided to adopt, I never seriously considered domestic adoption. I assumed that most pregnant women who were looking for adoptive parents would prefer a married couple to a single woman. I also completely ignored the foster care system, assuming that they, too, would prefer two-parent families. But I subsequently learned that the foster care system enthusiastically recruits single parents in addition to the more traditional two-parent families. So I began to explore adopting a second child right here in my home town. Although I will never regret going abroad for Jeremiah, the idea of adopting locally held a great appeal. International adoption is expensive, and a local adoption was a more feasible way to expand my family as well as the opportunity to meet the needs of a child in my own community.

The financial aspect of adoption is difficult to discuss—particularly because the general perception of private adoption (whether domestic or international) is of babies being bought and sold. Certainly there have been instances of illegal baby markets. But much of the money I spent on Jeremiah's adoption went to social workers, to paperwork, to background checks, to airlines, and to the nine months of care that Jeremiah received in Guatemala. The costs associated with private adoption are actually quite comparable to the costs associated with delivering a baby. Most American women have nine months of prenatal visits, take prenatal medicine, have an ultrasound (or two), and give birth in a hospital. And that's for an "easy" pregnancy—infertility issues, caesarean sections, and premature deliveries all have their own additional costs. The true cost of pregnancy, however, is not borne by many couples, but is covered by insurance. No such insurance exists for adoption. Thus the cost of obtaining a child is much more obvious when a child is adopted.

So in January 2006 I started the process of foster care adoption. The preparation time once again took about five months. This time, however, the time was spent taking classes rather than filling out paperwork. I still had to be interviewed and fingerprinted, and have the house inspected, but the focus in foster care adoption was much more on the needs of the child. My referral for Jonathan took another sixteen months—not the three days it had taken for Jeremiah. At the same time, one week after I met Jonathan, he moved in; for Jeremiah, I had had to wait eight long months before I was able to bring him home.

I often tell friends that my decision to become a mother through adoption has been the best decision of my adult life. This doesn't mean that everything has been easy, just that it has all been worthwhile. It also doesn't mean that adoption itself is an unmitigated good. Although adoption beautifully brings together a family, it only can occur after the loss of a previous family. My older son's mom was compelled by poverty to let go of her son. My younger son's mom had her newborn child involuntarily removed by the state of California. In an ideal world, no child would be available for adoption because no child would ever lose his or her first parents. No parent would abandon a child. Parents of young children would not die. All parents would be able to provide food and shelter for their children. No children would be removed from their family of origin because a parent was negligent or abusive or mentally incapacitated.

But we don't live in an ideal world. This world is fallen and sinful. At the same time, the world isn't *just* fallen and sinful—it is also being redeemed by God. Redemption always implies that the first act, in whole or in part, failed. Redemption also claims that the second act, the second choice, doesn't simply repair what was damaged, but actually improves the situation. Because of redemption, the second act cannot be considered second best. In Galatians 4, Paul uses adoption imagery to describe the relationship of all Christians to God. It's easy to blithely scan through this text without realizing the power of this image. Adoption meets the needs of a helpless child. Adoption changes a child's identity. Adoption gives a home to an orphan, and transforms strangers into family.

International and transracial adoption can also bring together people with different cultural and ethnic heritages, people who don't initially look like they belong together. Most of my personal challenges from adoption have concerned the "unlikeness" of my sons due to our different ancestries. Especially when Jeremiah was young, many people assumed that we didn't belong together. At the playground, adults would express concern about this young, unsupervised child—not recognizing that his mom was indeed just a few feet away. One time in particular a woman launched into a tirade, telling her friend how "those people" just let their kids run around. "I mean, where is that child's mother?" I calmly informed her I was right there. I love how my sons look and who they are—but there are times when appearance does matter. I don't want us to look alike or be alike, but I do sometimes, somehow, wish that others would automatically assume that we do belong together.

I also wish that my sons will never (or never again) experience racial discrimination. Raising two Hispanic boys has made me even more keenly aware of racism. I now take it very personally when others speak disparagingly of Hispanics or immigrants. My sons have taken my Dutch last name and have participated in my middle-class, white culture—but I, too, have been changed. My identity is no longer just white or European-American. It includes my status as a mother of two Latino boys.

A few years ago, many Hispanic Americans and Latino immigrants took to the streets in our city, demonstrating for civil rights. I decided to bring Jeremiah to one of the marches as it paraded through Balboa Park. Jeremiah was too young to understand the issues, but I wanted him to witness the people and the flags and the music. I wanted him to be in the middle of an event where more people looked like him than looked like me. Similarly, the 2008 presidential election cycle was an exciting time for our family, for reasons ranging far beyond partisanship. Every time I saw Barack Obama on the television or his picture in print, I would picture my boys as adults. Their futures somehow appeared to be less constrained because a man with a similar complexion ran for—and became—the president of the United States.

I like this status, this life that I could never have imagined or predicted. Mothering my boys is a joyful challenge. Like most parents, I sometimes feel stretched to my physical and emotional limits. But being a single mom has changed my life in ways that have strengthened my faith in God and my connections to my community. Not only do I have a rich relationship with my sons, but also with all the people and activities they have brought into my life. My worldview has expanded to cross cultural, racial, and national boundaries. I'm grateful that reality is so much bigger than what I had imagined, and that my final choices were so much better than my initial assumptions.

Shaped by Motherhood: Cultivating Reverence and Irreverence in the Face of Social Roles

Ivy George

O ne of the searing memories of the civil rights movement of the 1960s etched into my mind is the photograph of the Memphis Sanitation Workers strike in 1968. It is a profoundly paradoxical and disturbing cultural document. A black and white photograph of the protesters shows a stream of black men carrying placards. There are a handful of white males sprinkled among the black workers. The white males are dressed in ties, carrying nothing, presumably feeling responsibility and solidarity. The placards say, "I am a Man." The protest is framed by a row of National Guard riflemen with bayonets on one side, and tanks skirting the marchers on the other side.

I have been haunted by the message in this picture. I am not so much unsettled by the police state extant in the Great Society as I am with the emergent truths about the protesters. The primal plea of black men to be counted as fully human through their manhood—at a time when they worked just as hard as white men did, and yet were never equally paid or protected—was finally agreed upon by most U.S. citizens. This underlying principle was in fact the indefatigable raison d'être for the movement. Implicit in the message of these protesters is that being a "man" is tantamount to being wholly "human." It was understood that white men were in possession of this status from birth, and now black men were claiming this full humanity as well.

I cannot help but note the "absences" in the photo, and take pains to imagine what the "presences" would look like. I am thinking about the black women who are absent from the photograph. What kind of a placard would they seek to carry if they were present at the protest? "I am a Woman"? What privileges would accrue from such a claim? Even white women cannot assume full and equal pay, respect, and personhood. What is ultimately evident here is the assumption of white manhood as the apotheosis of humanity. How shaky that scaffolding becomes when we examine our social systems and structures and identify how *all* of us are wanting in self-realization. At issue here is the fundamental question as to whether women are human beings. Nothing less.

Indeed, today many of my students see this photograph as a thing of the past. The veil has been rent. The dream is no longer deferred but has been dramatized. All it takes now, many might believe, is commitment and hard work on the part of the historically marginalized, and they too shall have equal opportunity. After all, it can be argued that these days Barack Obama, Sarah Palin, Hillary Rodham Clinton, Sonia Sotomayor, Elena Kagan, Eric Holder, Clarence Thomas, and innumerable others appear on our dual lenses on race and gender with ease and grace. To such friends of mine I would suggest that there are serious and subtle lapses and slides we engage in when we bring up examples of isolated instances of individuals who have "overcome" structural constraints. But that discussion is for another time.

I mention the civil rights protest photograph to demonstrate how in general the imaginations of men (and women) can be captured by the notion of a "shared humanity," where masculinity is misunderstood as the apotheosis of humanity rather than its subset. In this, there is little recognition of the essential chasms that divide men from women no matter where our time and place in this world. This truth is no more evident than in that most common and universal of women's undertakings: motherhood. I want to make the point that women become essentially *female* when they embark on motherhood through biological or adoptive links. In my reference to mothers as "female," I am referring to the multiple implicit and explicit constraints put on women by societies' perception of their responsibilities to their children.

Writing about motherhood is enormously enjoyable and confining at the same time. I well imagine that I would tell a markedly different story of myself as a mother had I given birth to a child in my early twenties. But that is not how my life turned. I read and wrote a great deal in my twenties. I traveled tens of thousands of miles alone, crossed many cultures, volunteered my skills and services, and met so many people who were outside my familiar realm. I entered into many institutional affiliations, and developed many affinities, and I was introduced to new ideas, new understandings, new possibilities and freedoms. I started to apply these new ideas to the world I knew and had disturbing revelations about myself, and those around me. This process of new understandings continues to be a defining characteristic of my life.

I teach sociology. Sociology opens one's eyes to the complexities of society in ways that are exhilarating, *as long as these complexities don't impinge on one's own life*. When I become the subject of sociology, I am forced to locate myself on the map of the world that I have been teaching and writing about. In my courses on gender, diversity, and social change, I introduce my students to vital statistics about women and their general status nationally and globally. We discuss where women stand in terms of their life chances in the spheres of physical, psychological, and emotional security; education, employment; income; health; religion; marriage and family; media; sports and politics; immigration; and criminal justice. In all these areas, the circumstances of women are often bleak unless they are in close proximity to males in power. It is difficult to avoid the role of male authority in government, the military, economic institutions, religion, the media, and in so many other spheres vital to communal life all over the world. The architects of our public spheres are largely male, with a few nominal women thrown in here and there. This reality is so commonplace that most of us have come to take it for granted, and we have developed adaptive mechanisms to survive in it.

Nevertheless, there are some paradoxes to these structural realities in our time. The first decade into the twenty-first century, the built-in anomalies of this largely male-designed socioeconomic and political establishment of ours has flipped the odds for women and now put them on the front lines in many societies.[1] In industrialized societies, women now are either on par with or have exceeded men in the workforce and in education. Social changes in these societies over the last fifty years—contraception, political progress, and economic crises—have precipitated this push of women to the forefront in labor and education. Increases in female literacy and the rise of microfinance lending for women in developing societies have also resulted in an increased entry and circulation of women in the public square.

---

1   The central tenets of *efficiency*, *profit*, and *competition* in the market economic system require inclusion and advantage of vulnerable populations. Women are attractive as low-skilled, docile, lower-paid and mobile workers in the workforce.

Even so, all these women face the challenge of combining the demands of their domestic lives with the pressures of their public lives in the workforce. There are mirages on the horizon here—more women working in the public sphere does not automatically create social transformation. After all, the present increase of women in the workforce is not a result of increased social justice and equity so much as it is a function of the changes and compulsions initiated by the market. The present recession has hurt traditional male jobs in manufacturing much more than those of females in the service and informal sectors. Women still earn less, work part-time more often, and hold few positions of power and influence. There is a parade of women and girls I know for whom little has changed: the thirteen-year-old maid in my cousin's home who has work only because the family will not or cannot get a male to do the work; the entire South African village of grandmothers of AIDS orphans who are doomed to providing care for a second generation when they are themselves bent double by poverty and health issues; the two women who provide care for my elderly father in India, one of whom was deserted by her husband after marriage at sixteen, and the other of whom goes back to a drunken husband's brawls and beatings night after night to be with her two young sons. And then I think of the lives of many women I know in my circles here in New England who stay home to fan the fires of heart and hearth, and live in captivity. These days I am keenly aware of two very young women with freshly minted doctorates teaching in tenure-track positions under pressure to relocate to where their partners are.

In spite of the daunting global realities for women in social life, my own shocking realization of myself as essentially "female" only came to me when I became a mother. And this realization was a gradual experience. I went into marriage trying to get everything "right." I wanted to learn from my teaching. I wanted to become the subject of my own transformation that I wished for and talked about with regard to women elsewhere. I had made sure that I had an education, that I had some independent life experiences, that I was able to draw in an income. I spent my twenties demystifying all the ideals of romance and resisting the compulsions of hormones. My femaleness was not the centrality of my human identity. I had come of age in my thirties, and it could not have been a better time to embark on marriage and motherhood. I was in for a sobering surprise! In the early years of my marriage, I was relatively free. The marriage partnership was not unlike that of a practical and realistic relationship between two mature adults. It was no problem. We agreed, we disagreed, and we got on with our lives and our various professional responsibilities. The very ground of my being, however, shifted when I became a mother. It was then that I started to see my sense of myself anew. I saw that my husband was not affected by the same pressures I was. Motherhood became a telescopic lens to draw in more distant realities into my immediate purview. I was disturbed. I shall explain.

While it is the case that caregivers who work with children, the elderly, or disabled individuals also attest to the experience of having their lives affected while they are providing care, I believe that motherhood is so universal and all-pervasive that some reflection of its impact on women is warranted. Motherhood the world over has become a key predictor of women's future life chances because it often occurs at a critical developmental stage in women's lives. Across the social and economic spectrum, motherhood has been shown to be a detractor in women's pursuit of social and economic empowerment and mobility. Motherhood is a leveler.

I began to realize that while I had remained a relatively free spirit until I became a mother, motherhood shut me off almost permanently from some life possibilities. All my previous assumptions about the virtues of an independent life for a woman came under challenge by the demands of dependence and interdependence I experienced with our daughter. Further, I realized I was in internal conflict about my sense of self because of the ostensible role of "choice" in my situation. Should I stay home or should I leave the home to work outside? Could I manage both commitments? I should not complain if I felt torn and pressured, because after all, I had made a choice. To make matters worse, women were often my provocateurs in this ambivalence (mostly because they too were affected by these issues). They urged me to go in one direction or the other. I was back and forth in my thinking. At the same time, I delighted in the life of the mind, the transformative power of ideas and the extraordinary privilege of teaching and learning that was mine as an educator. The idea of shelving my gifts was tantamount to dying. I would think about it and find that I had no more choice in being an active contributor to the public good than a woman who is compelled by her economic circumstances to find employment. As women, we seek to exercise our God-given human capabilities to choose, and to choose freely. The very mention of "choice" is a function of the sexist nature of our structures, where no such discussion of "choice" takes place regarding male employment.

Women who become mothers pay a double price in ways that men do not. In the public sphere, I am expected to act as an equal with my male colleagues in terms of my contributions to the institution: my work load, my attendance at meetings, my role in professional organizations, my contributions to research and publications, my contributions to the larger community, and so on. I am given to understand that this is the price of inclusion and equality. The irony is that there is little recognition on the part of these largely male-run institutions that the women and men who service these places are hardly equal! Women's movement (especially as mothers of young children) back and forth from the domestic to the professional is hardly ever seamless. I must underscore that our much-loved daughter was not the *cause* of my constraints; rather, it was the assignment to me of a particular identity as *mother* that limited me.

This condition can be understood only by examining my location in the larger system in which I found myself. As a mother, one is engaged in cultural production and reproduction on multiple fronts. Motherhood is a continuum in work, worry, struggle, resistance, tragedy, joy, and hope. Women effectively become the primary architects of human civilization in their intergenerational efforts and contributions to society. I remind my students regularly that most of them mind their manners and don't pick their noses in public or interrupt conversations because of the massive doses of instruction and positive reinforcement they received in these areas in their early years by their primary caregivers, who have been mostly mothers and women. All the various disciplines of work connected to modern societies were long ago instilled by mothers and later by other agents of socialization, such as schools. Fathers have been frequently secondary players by virtue of the limited time spent with their children, and more importantly due to the ongoing presence of their mothers.

I found that my capacity to mother was overwhelmingly shaped by the way my social, professional, and religious worlds are structured. While the life of an academic can be relatively more conducive to caring for a child, I have been struck by the subtle and not-so-subtle ways in which "motherhood" is a liability for female opportunities in ways that "fatherhood" is not for males. Males dominate academic institutions overwhelmingly. From measures of productivity, to methods of pedagogy and evaluation, to grade submission deadlines and guidelines for institutional leadership and success, the institutional systems are set up to benefit men. Just as women in the wider workforce suffer professionally when they take time out to raise a family or care for dependent family members, women in academia have to negotiate the challenges posed by their domestic commitments. Planning a family, providing childcare and transportation, attending meetings after school hours, participating on committees, appearing at social events with male colleagues who gather regularly to watch a ball game and socialize, coordinating personal vacations with that of the school-going child—many domestic responsibilities interfere with a female professor's optimal engagement with her institution. A stark but commonplace scenario in my institution has to do with those exceptional times when I go to the office either quite early or late in the day. The faculty members in their offices ahead of time or after hours invariably tend to be male. They are relaxing with their morning coffee at their computers, or pursuing their research or administrative duties at the end of the day with no compulsions to run out to pick a child up or to make dinner. There are exceptions, men who do participate in domestic and familial responsibilities. And there are some single or senior women who can also afford to keep outside hours. Nevertheless, these behaviors are largely gender aligned, and they become intensified and more entrenched as one goes up the administrative ladder.

I am struck by the pervasiveness of our culture's assumption that mothering is simply "what women do." Implicit in this thinking is that women take on responsibilities that men do not need to do, that female responsibilities are *natural*, expected, and automatic, while men are not under the same compulsions in the domestic sphere. These female responsibilities exist at multiple levels, from children's physical needs to their emotional, social, and psychological needs. While men are often *helpful*, subsidizing this childcare arrangement with their time and money, the main psychological and moral charge of providing care is on the woman. The burden of "conscience" is on the woman. For suburban, middle-class women, thank you notes for the play dates and birthday gifts, packing the extra set of clothes in the beach bags, purchasing organic meat and milk, making the chicken nuggets to avoid the commercial additives, using cloth diapers for the child's well-being and using the clothesline for the earth's well-being are only a few of their conscientious care responsibilities. As Arlie Russell Hochschild reminds us, women are caught in a "time bind," where tending to home affairs and participation in the labor market become equally necessary but competing demands.

Motherhood, especially in industrialized societies and urban communities, stands as an area of serious contradiction. The historic separation of the home and the workplace and its impact on the provision of childcare as a private matter is a seriously unattended social issue. Because childcare traditionally has been seen as a female responsibility, fathers have been seen as marginally essential for the provision of biological or legal identity to the child. Women are invested in the mothering of their children for many years. Mothering is an all-inclusive process of caring, nurturing, planning, guiding, loving, worrying, and being generally preoccupied with the well-being of children. In the process, many women experience isolation, exhaustion, confusion, inadequacy, alienation, depression, substance abuse, abusive dynamics with their children, and a lack of social and economic support because the underlying social understanding is that these manifestations stem from the woman's personal inadequacies. Corporations, governments, and policymakers have focused their energies on how best they can get women to cope with these challenges individually, making it ultimately the woman's responsibility rather than asking fundamental questions about the systemic assumptions of childcare responsibilities as women's. Further yet is the unwillingness to note that while women are given the responsibility of motherhood, there is little effort to address the fact that these women are denied the power to define the terms and conditions under which they take up these responsibilities.

This conflict and contradiction that women experience will not necessarily be resolved by public policy changes that provide childcare facilities or economic supports for mothers. The dilemma is not only about structural or social changes, but also about women's own sense of identity. Even in previously socialist societies like East Germany with state-funded childcare and equality of opportunity in education, employment, and public life, scholars write of the burden of *bad conscience* and *self-realization* that women had to live with.[2] The bad conscience came with the conflict and contradictions they experienced with their dual commitments to work at and away from home. The issue of self-realization arises when women try to integrate into traditionally male hierarchical institutions and are resistant to giving orders, dominating, and subduing. Women are more interested in, or at a minimum long for, trust, relationship, cooperation, and community.

Why does a woman's brief time spent in pregnancy and childbirth determine her entire life's trajectory in the private and public sphere? Women, whether they have children or not, are treated as mothers (or potential mothers) in the public sphere in many areas: the public regulation

---

2   Elisabeth Adler, "The Image Inside: Women And Profession In A Socialist Country," in *Speaking of Faith* by Diana L.Eck and Devaki Jain, Eds. New Society Publishers, 1987, pp. 114–115.

of contraception, the risks to women's health, the major responsibility of child-rearing, the indirect costs of child-rearing and domestic labor that result in interruptions in employment, the accommodation of work outside the home to the needs of their families, their job choices, location of work, and hours of work.

Motherhood comes to define the essential nature of *female* identity. As Adrienne Rich says, motherhood has dual dimensions:

> One, that the female body is impure, corrupt, the site of discharges, bleedings, dangerous to masculinity, a source of moral and physical contamination. On the other hand, as mother the woman is beneficent, sacred, pure, asexual, nourishing and selfless. . . . [T]hat same body with its bleedings and mysteries—is her single destiny and justification in life.[3]

This is the matrix in which most women find themselves, and it is a no-win situation. If they reject this social ideology of motherhood, they are charged with being unfeminine. If they embrace it, they run the risk of being overly invested in their children, and of social, political, and economic marginalization. The force of these ambiguous cultural expectations takes over women's consciousnesses, leading to great internal ambivalence and conflict.

It is in this context that one is brought to the numbing realization that mothers are at an elemental level reduced to being *female*. Biology becomes destiny and their bodies merely channels for the greater (male) good. Certainly, mothering as a relational dynamic in a mutual relationship of care and nurturance offers up an unparalleled space for creativity and pleasure for women. But when the challenges of mothering are chronicled, one is compelled to ask if women are indeed even *human beings*, given their inferior social treatment and experience. This might then explain their absence at the Memphis Sanitation Workers strike in 1968.

For people of faith, the religious ideology surrounding motherhood further clouds the reality of women's inferior treatment. The language of duty, sacrifice, glory, greater purpose stands as a foil to the serious challenges and contradictions facing women. Christian literature in industrialized societies has referred to women as being so "busy trying to be everything—both professionals and mothers, good housekeepers

---

3   Adrienne Rich, *Of Woman Born: Motherhood as Experience and Institution* (New York: W.W. Norton and Company, 1976), 15.

and intelligent career women—that [their] spiritual vision is clouded by exhaustion and frustration."[4] Implicit in this thinking is the victimization of women for wanting to have integrated lives, and the absolution of men for having one-dimensional lives. Exhaustion and frustration are bound to result in a world that is not user-friendly to women, in a world where men are the normative actors in public life while women are veiled creatures in the private and secondary sphere, unable to use the gifts and potential of both their minds and their bodies to be most fully human. But surely this tragic impasse that women find themselves in cannot be the last word on human possibility!

I think of Mary, the mother of Jesus, and how she might have felt conflicted in her mission to birth and raise Jesus in a world not of her doing. She was aware of the end of this mission even at the very beginning: the immaculate conception, the departure of Jesus from the household at a very tender age, her surrender of Jesus to His salvific mission, and her final loss with His death on the cross. Even so, she cooperated with God and overcame the limits set on her because she knew something about the affirmative aspects of Life here and in eternity.

Daily, I find myself uncovering a great treasure that lies beneath the detritus of women's history. As one who stands deeply rooted in my faith, I stand amazed at the extraordinary privilege of giving my daughter's life a chance. At best, that is what mothers do when they care for their children—they give life a chance. In so doing, they work with God's greatest gift, life itself. Biblical figures like Mary stand as an inspiration for lesser mothers like me. I cannot imagine a greater good than the pursuit of Life for self and for others on this planet. Surely mothers sense this in their intimacy with their children. It is in the midst of this rich experience that I know the transforming grace of God. That God enables this richness to us women through the many oppressive constraints put on us by time and place is a Divine miracle. As a woman, I long for men to partake in this privilege of intimacy and investment. In the meantime, I work toward the examination and transformation of our systems and structures by raising one girl child to understand the importance of cultivating reverence and irreverence as she grows up strong, trying to unmask evil and following the good. I pray she will turn into a Lover, of God, of her life, and of the life of this world. I shall be glad to have had a hand in this, no matter how lonely and peripheral this journey has been!

---

4   Ellyn Sanna, *Motherhood: A Spiritual Journey* (Mahwah, NJ: Paulist Press, 1997), 2.

Between Calling and Commerce: Living in Faithful Vocation

Money. Power. Work. Ambition. Vocation. It takes work to honestly explore and faithfully grapple with these sometimes uncomfortable issues. Both our culture and the church have often given us answers that are too simple—or even silent—when pragmatic questions about making and handling money arise. Is it possible to be a successful, ambitious Christian woman—or is that a contradiction in terms? How do we figure out a career path—especially when most women's lives develop in ways that are more circuitous than linear? The love of money may be the root of all evil, but money is also a necessary commodity in modern society. Perhaps financial savvy and independence could even be a route to generosity and obedience to God. How does making money fit in with discovering our vocations, where and how we are called by God to live in this wide world? As Frederick Buechner reminds us, our callings are not dreary obligations meant to make us miserable—nor are they narrow enough for mere self-fulfillment or personal happiness. How can we draw on our gifts and passions to serve the church and the world by living faithful vocations where our "deep gladness and the world's deep hunger meet"?

The Importance of Ambition for Christian Women: Participating in God's Gracious Work in the World

Linda Beail

Vocation: It comes from the Latin *vocare*, to call, and means the work a person is called to by God. There are all different kinds of voices calling you to all different kinds of work, and the problem is to find out which is the voice of God rather than of Society, say, or the Superego, or Self-Interest. By and large a good rule for finding out is this: The kind of work God usually calls you to is the kind of work (a) that you need most to do and (b) that the world most needs to have done. If you really get a kick out of your work, you've presumably met requirement (a), but if your work is writing cigarette ads, the chances are that you've missed requirement (b). On the other hand, if your work is being a doctor in a leper colony, you have probably met requirement (b), but if most of your time you are bored and depressed by it, the chances are you have bypassed (a), but probably aren't helping your patients much either. Neither the hair shirt nor the soft berth will do. The place God calls you to is the place where your deep gladness and the world's deep hunger meet. —Frederick Buechner [1]

When I was growing up, I heard a lot about the importance of "finding God's will for your life." I spent a fair amount of time wondering and praying about what God wanted me to do with my life, and felt anxious that I wasn't sure what that was. I worried that I would miss the divine signal telling me what to study in college, or what job to pursue, or whom to marry. I desperately wanted to know what God was "calling" me to do.

---

1   Frederick Buechner, *Wishful Thinking: A Theological ABC* (New York: Harper & Row, 1973), 95.

At the same time, I would have rejected the very idea of being "ambitious" as selfish. Ambition was a trait that seemed not very Christian, and not very womanly, either. I never heard people talk about how much they loved and admired their mothers for being so ambitious; when I heard family, friends, or even celebrities and politicians praising their wives and mothers, it was for being so caring, nurturing of others, and self-sacrificing. "Ambition" seemed cold and self-centered in comparison. Yet I wanted to succeed in whatever I did; I was proud of my hard work and accomplishments and wanted to succeed in life, to make a difference in the world.

When I was in high school, I hung out with a whole group of friends who were very involved in all the activities at our church. More than once, older men or women from the church would come up to one or another of my guy friends and ask them if they felt "called" to be a pastor. They would compliment them on their obvious love for God and involvement in the spiritual life of our church, and tell them that they thought they had real gifts for leadership and ministry. While pleased and affirmed by this encouragement, my male friends usually would respond that they did not feel called to full-time ministry (and in fact, most of them are now godly laypeople in a variety of professions). But back in high school, the adults would smile and respond that they felt these young men should be open to a "call," and that they would continue praying for my friends to hear God's voice if he should lead them in that direction.

During those incidents, I was usually standing right beside my guy friends, smiling mutely. Despite the fact that there was no difference between us in terms of our participation in all the many facets of worship and ministry—and that I grew up in a church that had a long tradition of affirming women in positions of pastoral leadership and ordination—no one ever once asked me if *I* were called to the ministry. Once in a while, noticing that I was dating one of these potentially "called" guys, I might be told I would make a good pastor's wife. But it was both obvious and confusing to me that, simply because I was a girl, I didn't fit the image of someone who could be responsible and in charge of shepherding a congregation.

All my life, I'd been told I could be anything I wanted. I'd worked hard in school and excelled in a number of different areas. Yet clearly there were certain things I was not expected to seek out or pursue—and not just in the church, either. As I moved through college, I had an interesting conversation with a male classmate who told me he was envious that I was majoring in

English literature. He'd love to be a literature major, he continued, but he couldn't afford the luxury of such an impractical course of study. He felt pressure to select a major in business or science—something he could turn into a marketable skill—because someday he would have a family to support. Of course, I did not need to worry about choosing a profession, because I would not ever be a serious participant in the world of work.

This reasoning baffled and angered me. Both of my parents were sacrificing a lot to send me to a private Christian university. I was working extremely hard in all my courses and thinking about graduate school. It seemed like an awfully expensive and labor-intensive way to cultivate a hobby in novel reading, as my friend seemed to imply. Many of my classes, as well as my involvement in student ministries, were enlarging my view of the world and challenging me to address complex social problems in redemptive, Christ-filled ways. But what was my "calling" as a Christian, and as a woman? Was it to limit my understanding of my role to certain spheres? Was I to devote myself only to being a wife and a mother? Or was I to take an active role in the larger world? And if so, how?

§

No matter how much women prefer to lean, to be protected and supported, nor how much men desire to have them do so, they must make the voyage of life alone, and for safety in an emergency, they must know something of the laws of navigation. To guide our own craft, we must be captain, pilot, engineer; with chart and compass to stand at the wheel; to watch the winds and waves, and know when to take in the sail, and to read the signs in the firmament over all. It matters not whether the solitary voyager is man or woman; nature, having endowed them equally, leaves them to their own skill and judgment in the hour of danger, and, if not equal to the occasion, alike they perish.

—Elizabeth Cady Stanton, 1892[2]

For women, the question of ambition and vocation is much more complicated than simply the choice to work outside the home or to devote ourselves to the domestic sphere. (Besides, most women these days do not make a clear-cut and permanent choice between those two options, but move in and out of the workforce, sometimes full-time, sometimes part-time, and sometimes at home, at various stages of their lives.) It's really a much deeper question of identity and motivation: Who are we? Why do

---

2   Excerpt from speech delivered before the Committee of the Judiciary of the US Congress, January 18, 1892, from Elizabeth Cady Stanton, *The Solitude of Self* (Paris Press, 2000).

we do what we do? Are we meant to be wholly altruistic and self-sacrificing? If we seek meaningful work, success, or power, must we do it only for the benefit of others—not admitting our own need for affirmation and worth?

Psychologists tell us that ambition is a basic human trait necessary for psychological health and maturity.[3] All of us yearn to master skills and tasks that show our competence and giftedness. All of us need to be recognized for the unique accomplishments and talents we bring to the world. Yet ambition seems difficult for women to own. Psychologist Anna Fels describes asking women who would come to her for counseling, "When you were five years old, what did you want to be when you grew up?" Their answers were quick and sure, filled with big dreams of being a prima ballerina, an astronaut, even president of the United States. But when she asked them about when and how those goals had changed, they grew tentative and silent. Somewhere between girlhood and adolescence, they had tamped down their outsized dreams and become "realistic"—and yet they were not sure when and how that happened, or why they didn't have the confidence to pursue their original goals.

Many of us may not end up being what we dreamed of in preschool. But the question is less about the content of that original dream, and more about the loss of exuberant passion and confidence to pursue our interests. I hear it in my students, who wonder if they should change majors in order to have a less demanding profession, or who are daunted by the prospect of many years of undergraduate and graduate study ahead of them. They worry about how those callings might interfere with relationships, with parents who do not want them to move far from home, or with a potential spouse and children whose needs might cause them to shelve the careers they've trained for. I empathize with the desire to balance vocational goals with intimacy and relationship. I applaud them for thinking ahead, for being savvy enough to worry about how all the pieces of a complex life might fit together. But I worry about the self-limiting, the narrowing down of possibilities and opportunities, that I see in young women more than young men. How difficult it is to acknowledge the importance of one's own ambition while remaining appealingly feminine. If ambition is often viewed in individualistic terms, as "selfish," "competitive," and "uncaring," then it seems the antithesis of warm, giving, supportive womanhood.

For Christians, this becomes even more problematic because the Bible warns us against the temptation of self-centeredness and arrogance. Focusing

---

3   Anna Fels, *Necessary Dreams: Ambition in Women's Changing Lives* (New York: Pantheon Books, 2004).

on my own ambitions and interests seems a failure of both femininity and godliness. Theologians Valerie Saiving and Diane LeClerc are helpful here: They point out that perhaps our very notions of sin are gendered[4]. Masculine theologians and church fathers have exhorted us relentlessly to guard against the sin of pride, and rightly so, as pride and arrogance lead us to rely only on ourselves and not recognize our dependence on a gracious, redeeming God. It distorts our relationship with God to believe that we are the center of the universe. However, as Saiving and LeClerc observe, men, who have historically had more power, opportunity, and authority in the world, may be far more prone to fall into this sin. They would be right to seek some corrective humility and self-sacrifice.

Women, on the other hand, may because of their social experiences be far less likely to become prideful and selfish, but more likely to fall into the sin of idolizing relationships. Putting the desire for (or relationships with) a husband, children, friends, or family first in our lives is also sinful. Those relationships can become idolatrous, taking the place of God as first and foremost in our lives. Our "selflessness" of putting others first, and spending all of our time and energy caring for their needs, is often praised, even in the church. But it too may be a sin, also displacing God from the center of our lives. Instead of placing our "self" at the center, we put others there. Either way, we are distorting that right relationship with our Creator. As Julie Hanlon Rubio explains in *Christian Theology of Marriage and Family*, women are not called just to life in the domestic and private sphere.[5] Women (and men) believers are called by Jesus to a life of discipleship that transcends family ties, to a wider public vocation to serve the body of Christ and the whole community. To follow Christ, we must not merely follow social conventions regarding gender roles; we must be bold to answer the call to however God wants to use our unique gifts, talents, and experiences.

So many bright, talented Christian women have learned to be self-effacing and to discount their abilities and ambitions. Lee Anne Bell describes the phenomenon of "The Gifted Woman as Impostor," showing evidence that women often feel like frauds because they put so much pressure on themselves to meet impossibly high standards.[6] Ironically, it is the *most*

---

4   Valerie Saiving, "The Human Situation: A Feminine View" (1960), reprinted in *Womanspirit Rising*, ed. Carol P. Christ and Judith Plaskow (New York: Harper One, 1992); Diane LeClerc, *Singleness of Heart: Gender, Sin, and Holiness in Historical Perspective* (Scarecrow Press, 2001).

5   Julie Hanlon Rubio, *A Christian Theology of Marriage and Family* (Paulist Press, 2003).

6   Lee Anne Bell, "The Gifted Woman as Impostor," *Advanced Development Jour-*

promising and capable women who set themselves up to fail. They have a hard time seeing competence as "good enough," instead expecting total perfection (and crumbling when they can't reach that impossible standard). Girls and women accustomed to success often have a hard time asking for help when they need it, don't feel entitled to make mistakes, and rebound less quickly from setbacks. They internalize failure, blaming themselves if things don't go well but crediting their successes to luck, charm, or other people. These gifted women are likely to procrastinate or hold back on the brink of achievement, because they feel anxious about the pressures that would come with success. Instead of feeling insecure or sabotaging our own efforts, Bell recommends that women tell each other our stories, ask for help, get mentors (and mentor others), and own their accomplishments. Similarly, psychologist Carol Dweck's work demonstrates that it is often the "bright girls" who experience "learned helplessness" and give up easily in the face of possible failure.[7] Dweck finds that high-achieving young women are likely to equate their performance with innate, fixed qualities of talent and worth. But when encouraged to see their success as attributable to hard work and the ability to learn new skills, as opposed to pre-existing, limited amounts of talent, students quickly begin to persist in the wake of failure. Rather than fearing lack of success at a particular task as proof that they are inherently lacking or "not good enough," those students begin to see the challenge as an opportunity for learning and growth, and express confidence in their abilities to rise to that challenge. As a result, they actually achieve more. Christian women need to give up their fears and false humility—not only for their own sanity, but because we have important things to accomplish as we participate in God's gracious work in the world.

Today, women have more opportunities and choices than ever before in history but feel more conflicted about having their own ambition. A recent study of undergraduate women at Duke University coined the phrase "effortless perfection" to describe the pressure women feel to be brilliant and highly accomplished leaders while still being thin, pretty, and sexually attractive, and to do it all "naturally," without breaking a sweat or showing any signs of stress.[8] One way of dealing with that pressure might be to evade it, by defaulting into more certain and traditional gender roles—and

---

nal, vol. 2 (January 1990).

7   Carol Dweck, *Self-Theories: Their Role in Motivation, Personality and Development* (Psychology Press, 2000).

8   Susan Roth, "The Women's Initiative: The Steering Committee's Report," Duke University, 2003.

for women, to focus on defining ourselves through our relationships more than our vocation and ambition. But studies show that women (and men) need *both* meaningful work and meaningful relationships.

Focusing on marriage or motherhood to the exclusion of wider ambitions or vocational work can actually put women in a vulnerable position, in terms of their physical and psychological health, as well as their economic well-being. On several health measures, marriage seems to benefit husbands while having a more costly effect on wives: Married men fare best in physical and mental health, but married women are much more at risk for depression and illness than married men or single women. While motherhood is something many of us deeply enjoy and want to experience, it can also be difficult, and it leaves women vulnerable in terms of mental health: In 2003, depression was estimated to affect up to 30 percent of mothers of young children.[9]

Many women experience the stress of the "double day," working outside the home but still being responsible for most of the household duties. too. While roles are shifting, and men are increasing the amount of housework and childcare they do, women still do significantly more. For example, men have doubled the amount of housework they do, from 4.4 hours per week in the mid-1960s to 9.5 hours in 2008. Women, however, still do about twice as much (averaging 18 hours per week in 2008).[10] Similarly, fathers participate much more in caring for their children: nearly 8 hours per week, up from only 2.5 in the 1970s–1980s. Yet women still do the bulk of childcare, averaging 14 hours per week in 2008.[11] Working women have better health and report higher satisfaction with life than their homemaker peers. Both working women and their spouses report greater marital happiness than more traditional couples.

The economy has changed, and so have families. In 1960, only 19 percent of married women with preschool children were employed. In 2009, 64 percent were employed. "Working moms" have become the norm, as nearly three-quarters of mothers with kids at home are in the labor force.[12] The U.S. Bureau of Labor Statistics reports that dual-earner couples

---

9   Ellen McGrath, Gwendolyn Puryear Keita, Bonnie R. Strickland, & Nancy Felipe Russo, ed., *Women and Depression: Risk Factors and Treatment Issues* (Washington, D.C.: American Psychological Association, 1990).

10   Suzanne M. Bianchi, "Family Change and Time Allocation in American Families," Alfred P. Sloan Foundation, November 29–30, 2010.

11   Ibid.

12   *Women in America: Indicators of Social and Economic Well-Being*, March 2011, Prepared by U.S. Department of Commerce, Economics and Statistics Administration and

are in the majority, making up 57 percent of all married couples in 2008. Working wives play an essential role in supporting their families, providing almost 30 percent of family income; more than a quarter of wives now earn more than their husbands. And the roles of "stay-at-home-mom" versus "working mom" are not static choices. Most women are moving in and out of the workforce or working part-time. In fact, a majority of mothers (60 percent) say part-time work is their preferred option (with the rest evenly divided between desiring full-time jobs and wanting to stay at home).

Rather than "opting out" of the workforce, many women express feeling "pushed out" by the lack of flexibility in the workplace that would allow them to balance work with family.[13] But the reality is that good part-time work options are exceedingly rare, and it is more difficult than most women imagine to return to the workforce after taking time out to parent. Women who leave the workforce, even for a few years, are at financial risk due to the changing economy, possible divorce or death of a spouse, and the wages, retirement contributions, and Social Security that they forgo. And the gender wage gap persists. Analysis of full-time workers shows that women today make about 80 cents to every dollar earned by male workers—up from 62 percent thirty years ago, but still a significant shortfall.[14] While some of the difference is due to occupational segregation (men abound in science, engineering, and financial fields, while women still tend to be in more service-oriented and lower-paying occupations such as secretarial help, nursing, and teaching), the pay gap holds across all educational levels. Even women who are college graduates or have post-graduate degrees earn about 75 percent of their male counterparts.[15]

Ann Crittenden estimates that the "Mommy Tax" for the average college-educated woman is $1 million lost over the course of her lifetime.[16] All of this can leave a woman in a potentially vulnerable situation if she needs to provide for herself and her children. And women live longer—but more elderly women find themselves in poverty, without the resources they need, after spending a lifetime caring so diligently for others. I'm not devaluing the worth of parenting work here, or insisting that a price tag can be put on giving care to those we love. Rather, I'm sad—and a bit

---

the Executive Office of the President, Office of Management and Budget.

13   Pamela Stone, *Opting Out: Why Women Really Quit Careers and Head Home* (Berkeley: University of California Press, 2007).

14   *Women in America.*

15   Ibid.

16   Ann Crittenden, *The Price of Motherhood: Why the Most Important Job in the World is Still the Least Valued* (New York: Metropolitan Books, 2001).

angry—that so many women do the necessary, important, sacrificial work of mothering and care giving and yet are made invisible and are penalized economically for doing it.

Statistics, patterns, and findings like all of these are not meant as an argument that all women should be in the paid workforce throughout all of their adult lives. Life is complicated, and often comes with unexpected changes. Many of us will negotiate our ways through work and family situations that cause us to change directions and balance things in different ways at different life stages. One can have a meaningful vocation that serves the community or the church without always receiving a paycheck. But we can all make wiser, more informed choices and negotiate our ways through the complexities better if we can honestly confront and discuss the social norms, economic realities, and psychological issues that exist. Many young couples have fairly egalitarian relationships in which they share financial responsibilities and household chores, until their first child is born. It is a particularly interesting and risky time in the relationship: Identities are shifting as both become parents, and it seems natural that the new mother might take more time out of the workforce as she recovers from giving birth or if she is nursing the new baby. Yet this is often when couples default into more traditional roles, as her career becomes permanently secondary and his becomes primary. Couples need to anticipate this, so that they can have explicit discussions and make informed decisions about the kind of roles and relationships that are best for their family, instead of simply drifting into a life they haven't deliberately chosen.[17]

The costs, benefits, and tradeoffs of practicing our vocations are not merely abstract or intellectual issues for me. They touch the core of my daily existence and deepest relationships. A few nights ago, as I was tucking my seven-year-old into bed, she asked me, "Mommy, why do you go to work but some mommies don't? Don't you want to spend time with us?" It was a question I've been anticipating her whole life, yet it still stunned me for a moment. Yes, I reassured her first, of course I want to be with her. (In fact, that is one of the things I love about being a professor; I guard my breaks jealously to be home with my kids full-time for those long, lazy days of summer each year.) I reminded my daughter that she's in school all day, and she agreed that it made sense for me to go off to my classes during that time too. I noted how lucky she is that she gets to spend a few days each week after school with her grandparents, who live nearby, and how much

---

17   Naomi Wolf, *Misconceptions: Truth, Lies, and the Unexpected on the Journey to Motherhood* (New York: Doubleday, 2001).

she delights in having such a close and special relationship with them. She agreed that hanging out at their house was often even more fun than being at home. She enjoys my volunteering in her classroom, and admitted that it was neat when I came and shared with her class about a trip I'd taken with my political science students to Washington, D.C. for the presidential inauguration.

There were other things I could have said: how proud I am of her because she is a responsible, resourceful, kind little girl who pitches in to help, like everyone in our family, because we are all juggling. How I hope she sees how hard her dad and I work to respect each other's time, energy, and vocations, and that she will one day find a partner who values her gifts and dreams that way too. How she's learned that moms and dads both know how to cook and do laundry; that both can wear suits and give speeches; most importantly, that both can pray, teach, worship, and serve. But I didn't say all of those things right then. Instead, I reminded her of another story, a story involving her.

A couple of years earlier, our whole family accompanied me on a trip to an academic conference where I was giving a paper. It was held in a large city, and we were staying in the fancy conference hotel downtown. I reminded her that one night, we all went swimming after dinner in the rooftop pool. Her face lit up as I told the story, for she remembered how magical it was to be swimming at bedtime, the city lights twinkling below us. While we were in the pool, my daughter started playing with another little girl swimming nearby. The other child said their family was staying at the hotel because they were in town to visit her aunt and uncle. "Oh," my daughter said nonchalantly. "Well, we're here for my mommy's conference."

That is what makes the struggle to balance it all worth it to me: that moment, when my daughter voices her assumption that it is perfectly natural for women to be smart, have ideas, and have the expertise and authority to talk about them. To know that in her eyes, it is obvious that our family will be right in the middle of wherever my profession takes me. To my child, it is absolutely normal to be a mom and have a vocation. It isn't effortless. It isn't perfect. But it is both loving the particular people closest to me and using my talents to serve the church and the world as well; it is flourishing as the person God has called me to be, and making space for my daughter to claim her gifts and vocation someday too. I believe God wants nothing less.

Ambition and Vocation: Threads of Our Lives

Maxine Walker

Recently I visited the Jewish Museum in Vienna, Austria with its special exhibit *Beste Aller Frauen*, "Best of All Women." The exhibit shows how Jewish women redefined their roles in the Jewish religion: first woman rabbi, cantors, academicians, social workers, scientists, artists. The large central image of the exhibition is a circular clothesline hung with women's dresses in every style and size, and the line slowly turns to provide a kaleidoscope of patterns and color. The clothes, hardly different from lines of garments hung out to dry by women over the centuries, symbolize the role of Jewish women in religious, economic, and cultural contexts. In the specific biographies of the women who wore these kinds of outfits, the exhibition shows how women stepped over the demarcation line defined by men.

Open your drawers and your closet—what do you see? Don't worry about whether there are brand labels or new clothes! There will be notable times in your life when what you wear will say something special about you: prom night, graduation, weddings, prospective interviews, beach vacations. But in a different way, what do your clothes say about who you are, what you want to be, how your story shows strength and courage?

This clothing image is particularly helpful in thinking about vocation and ambition because it links biblical women, women throughout history, and those of us now. In the story of Tamar in the Old Testament (Genesis 37–38), clothes, in particular a red cord, speak of Tamar's calling and ambition. In the Old Testament narratives, several women experience very difficult circumstances; how will they respond to a very patriarchal society and contribute to the redemption of the children of Israel? For Tamar (as noted in Matthew's genealogy of Jesus), as well as for other women of the Bible, clothes become important. Tamar's widow's garment and scarlet cord tie her thematically to the story of Joseph and God's promise for deliverance. Tamar never had a "plan" for her life, but as a widow in a society of men, she had to find a way to have a child, to secure her future. She had ambition, and her circumstances shaped her vocation. Her destiny, along with that of the Israelites, is served by a woman who acts on her own initiative so that her descendants will inherit the blessing promised by the Almighty.

Many Christian young women shy away from the importance of ambition because they associate ambition with pride that they believe to be unhealthy spiritually and emotionally.

As a professor of literature for thirty-eight years, what has surprised me most in my own vocation is the necessity for ambition, a strong self-confidence. I define ambition as once a woman sees what can be done and has the gifts and graces to do it—do it! But how do you know if you have these gifts and graces? Ask others who know you—both men and women, experts and novices, clergy and professors, a variety of age groups—about "who you are and what talents you have." What is it you want to do? Do you have the training and education to accomplish it? Are you willing to go for it regardless of hurdles or doubts?

Too frequently I have talked to women students who want to earn a Ph.D. or M.D. but settle for something that takes much less than their academic best. Equally troubling, I have talked to women students who have not (or even will not) think about who they are in relationship to their strongest skills and interests. Taking loving care of children is a good thing, but if you are really good at it, why not think about also getting highly involved in local or state government/politics on raising childcare standards, for example? Go beyond your comfort zone. Go beyond the obvious first degree or first step!

I have always believed that if someone else thinks you can do a task, and you are strongly interested, this is frequently a way to your calling. Tamar's story demonstrates that even when she had little power as a Canaanite woman among the Israelites, she heard from others of what was happening in Judah's household, used her own discernment, and went into action. She tricked Judah into giving her a son after her husband died. Her courage and ambition are rewarded in the gospels, earning her a place as one of the few women in Matthew's genealogy of Jesus, the One who too was without earthly power.

My concept of vocation is very similar. You need to do and be what you need to do and be, and it takes *ambition*—that wonderful gift of assurance and confidence. We too can be a part of Christ's redemptive work on earth.

I loved literature as an undergraduate university student, and in my senior year, I had an outstanding Shakespeare professor. The way he taught, the knowledge he had about Shakespeare and the sixteenth century, the challenge of the exams and essays, were so appealing to me. So much so that I wanted to do what he did so very well. And so, married with a small child, and my husband in graduate school, I also began studying for my M.A. in literature. Frankly, I do not ever recall some kind of quest for a "calling"—divine or otherwise. I needed to help support my family, and a Ph.D. in literature qualified me for university teaching, so I set out to earn the advanced degree. Pretty straightforward.

A college in the area needed a literature professor, and I finished my graduate studies, as many of my women colleagues did in their own place and time, as a part of "wearing" the job well. If I had been agonizing over a "calling," I might have missed it! Many evenings, I typed away on my dissertation while my young daughter sat on my lap with her little fingers on the keys too. I think as a grown woman today, she is proud of the academic path I took, with all of its twists and turns.

Now that I'm at the other end of thirty-eight years of teaching in colleges and universities, there is still no sense of "calling," but I do have serenity that I did what I loved best and did well. I thought once about going into medicine, but I'm not as good in science and math as I am in literary studies. Sixteenth-century culture, politics, religion, art, literature—these I can do! I was and am ambitious to do well in these areas and to branch out into interdisciplinary work that links the tough questions between literature and religion.

I do think that women who are academically strong in the natural sciences should be strongly encouraged by those in women's studies to persist in these highly male academic areas. All of my graduate professors were men, and I have always accepted that if I did not do as well as I wanted to accomplish on a paper or project, it wasn't because I was a woman. Simply put, *I* probably had not studied or prepared as carefully as needed. "Men" *per se* do not keep women from pursuing their ambition; often women themselves, even other women, are their biggest stumbling block.

§

The mid-seventeenth-century painter from the School of Rembrandt depicts Judah and Tamar richly dressed. To be sure, the veil disguises who

Judah and Tamar, School of Rembrandt (public domain)

she is, but the set of her mouth and posture suggest an inner assurance. Light falls on Judah's back and highlights Tamar's face. There is no visible sign of "ambition," but that slightly red cord that passes between them will be Tamar's salvation from certain death in the family. At the end of the intriguing narrative, Judah acknowledges her: "Tamar is more righteous than I. . . ."

Women's clothes may seem superficial, but who can forget the dresses of women throughout history—pioneers in the American West, medieval peasants, early colonists, Indian and African princesses, sheepherders and weavers and cooks? Who can forget the clothes women had to give up as they disappeared into the concentration camps; who can forget the chadors and veils in which women closet themselves; who can forget the unheard-of trousers worn by World War II "Rosie the riveters"? Clothes don't make the woman, but they say much about vocation and ambition that connect women over the centuries.

The title of the Vienna exhibition, "Best of All Women," is taken from a Torah curtain that a father gave to celebrate his daughter's marriage and his wife, whom he praised as the "best of all women." We are that indeed, as *our* vocation and *our* ambition bring out the best in ourselves and grace those around us.

Two in a Million: The Gifts of Work and Adoption

Melanie Springer Mock

During the second quarter of my stepson's water polo game on September 25, 2001, I decided I wanted to adopt a child. The desire to adopt came on suddenly, inexplicably, like an unanticipated fever that knocks you cold. I looked at the crowd of doting parents watching their sons play, and somehow determined I longed for a child to adore unconditionally, too. My swimming-centered epiphany caused an immediate physical response: My heart and breath quickened, I began to shake, and I lost complete focus on the game at hand. Such inattention was unfortunate, given I was helping officiate the match.

After the game, I announced my resolve to my husband, Ron, as we were walking to our car: "I think we should adopt." Ron was somewhat shaken by the announcement, for in the first five years of our marriage, I had often proclaimed the beauty of my carefree life. Without children, we enjoyed traveling together, taking last-minute trips to the Oregon coast, and doing whatever we wanted, when we wanted, because we could. From time to time, Ron and I would revisit the idea of having children, and I always said I was content. My husband, with two almost-grown children from his first marriage, had mixed feelings about bringing more kids into the world: He adored his son and daughter, but he didn't feel a strong urge to start another family from scratch. And I had never really wanted to be pregnant, did not have that fierce yearning to birth a child as my friends reported having experienced. While they gushed about the beauty of having a being inside them, or the extraordinary feeling of nursing a newborn, I thought, "Eh. Not for me," this response itself providing confirmation that I best remain married, without children.

But something shifted inside me: A different choice about parenting formed, no doubt, even before my I-want-to-mother declaration in the Newberg Aquatic Center parking lot. Earlier that summer, I had spent significant time with young nieces and a nephew, and saw my sister's joy in raising children. When she hugged her daughters' newly bathed, pajama-ed bodies goodnight, and snuggled with her son on the couch, and laughed at their crazy questions, I felt a pang of longing for a similar mother-and-child intimacy. Shortly after their visit, a friend announced her pending adoption of a special-needs child from India; she showed me pictures of her new son, Babu, unsmiling in Mumbai, and I cried alone after our meeting, sensing an ache I could not name.

When 9/11 happened, and the world seemed to shatter, my heart shifted again. Like many people watching the aftermath of the twin towers plummeting, I felt compelled to reevaluate my own life choices, wondering what God was calling me to in a world that felt utterly broken. My thoughts turned toward whether I was wholly satisfied being child-free, whether I was to play more roles than that of wife and professor. In the aquatic center, a few weeks after 9/11, the tectonic plates guiding my life's journey moved dramatically, a seismic shift that changed the direction my life took.

After the initial announcement, and my husband's nonplussed reaction, we mulled together what it would take to be parents, what resources we would need to adopt, whether parenthood truly was our calling. Almost a year later, after shuffling through reams of adoption agency paperwork, learning more about the complexities of adoption than I thought possible, and traveling to Vietnam twice, we carried home our first son, Benjamin Quan: seven months old, smaller than some newborns, developmentally delayed, but with an infectious laugh and beautiful brown eyes. He was the most extraordinary creature I had ever met. Three years after that, we added Samuel Saurabh to our family: a three-year-old from India who had some special needs, a tiny physique, a politician's charisma, and a captivating smile. Like his brother, Samuel was—is—extraordinary.

And when I held them each for the first time, I knew: This was absolutely right.

The choice to have children radically changed my life. Even getting a Ph.D., moving to the Pacific Northwest, and marrying my husband did not transform me as dramatically as did adopting my two sons. So I am always surprised when some people seem to make a family without much thought, apparently believing childrearing is an obvious and easy requirement for adulthood. This ready assumption, that married people will automatically have children, is problematic, for of course not all are called to be parents. But even more perplexing is the persistent belief that to truly be a Christian woman, to live as God commanded, one must have children. That belief alone binds women and their partners to roles they might not be ready for—might not ever want. And because being a mother is humbling and magical and overwhelming, bringing out both the best—and the worst—in who I am, I am convinced the entire enterprise cannot be entered into lightly, without due consideration for what it means be a parent.

When I made the decision to have children, I did not recognize the million and more other choices resting on the horizon, choices I confront every day, choices that shift and multiply as my children grow, as we all enter different life stages: A few years ago, we were deciding where our children should attend preschool; right now, these decisions range from whether my son should be tested for learning disabilities to whether I should buy both my kids light-up shoes; in a decade, we'll be thinking about where they should attend college. Yet of all the decisions I've made in my seven years of parenthood, the one I thought would be most challenging for me was whether I should work outside the home. Instead, the difficulty did not come from that initial choice, but from the day-by-day, moment-by-moment choices I faced later, long after I concluded God was calling me to be both a college professor and mother of two.

We had no protracted discussions about whether I—or my husband—should stay home full time with our children. Both of us are college professors at the same school and felt our schedules would be flexible enough to allow us to work and raise our sons. Several months before our first adoption, my sister's family and my parents moved to the area and offered to help care for Ben, and with Ron's family also nearby, we quickly decided the juggling act of work and family would not be difficult. Plus, we both adored our jobs, believing strongly we had been called to teach at our university, to minister with students in the classroom. I certainly was convinced God had given me the gift of a teaching job, and it seemed wrong to reject that gift in order to attend solely to my children—especially because my husband also deserved time with his sons, time he would not be given if I took over their care exclusively and Ron took over the role of breadwinner exclusively.

Our plan worked well for us. We moved through our first years of co-parenting delighted by Benjamin's development, by the little person, and personality, opening up in front of us. Although Samuel's entry into our family was a little rockier—he was, after all, a toddler, and would have a much more difficult adjustment from orphanage to home—the formation of our family melded well with the continuation of our careers. Indeed, a few days before traveling to India to adopt Samuel, I submitted my tenure portfolio; several months after our return home, when Samuel seemed finally integrated into our family and was blossoming into a character we hadn't seen before, I was also rewarded tenure. The confluence of these events served as an affirmation to me that my career and my family could coexist, successfully.

But as it turns out, my choice to be a working woman was problematic: not for me, nor for my husband, nor my family, but for some people in my community, whose understanding of the Bible and of church tradition is far different from my own. While my husband and I believe the Bible affirms egalitarian roles for women and men, a good many others would argue that the Bible tells us men are to be the heads of a household, that women are specially made to nurture children, and that only men—and, to a lesser degree, childless women—can successfully operate in the workplace. After I became a working mother, my radar was acutely attuned to discussions about women's roles in society and church, and I heard, everywhere it seemed, arguments for why my own life choices were wrong. At my school, in classes and in chapel, students rehearsed particular Bible verses, securing for themselves—and their potential mates—the hierarchical roles they felt assured God created. A few faculty members at my school echoed this traditional understanding of gender, asserting they too believed scripture dictates a man's headship role, never minding what such assertions conveyed to their female colleagues listening nearby.

In the first years after Benjamin came home, I was especially aware of my students' and colleagues' comments about the biblical mandate for women to stay at home, and I felt burdened by what seemed unfair judgment: about my vocation, about my family, about the choices my family and I were living. A few people made it their business to ask me, repeatedly, whether I was "*still* working?!," incredulous at my response that yes, I was. Some students wondered when I would be quitting to stay home full time, because that's what mothers did. And, of course, no one was asking my husband whether he was still working, or when he was going to quit. That he escaped such interrogation bothered me more, for it was as if being a dual-career family was my choice alone, and the presumed resulting destruction of my children a grave sin for which only I should be judged.

In time, though, I mostly became angry: angry that my choice to work was being scrutinized, and angry that my Christian culture sanctified such scrutiny as "biblical." I was worried, too, about my female students, who were both excited by their vocational calls but also confronted by the predominating cultural ethos reminding them that, once they got married and had children, God had a different plan in mind. In essence, I felt, Christian women were being told they had to choose: either have a career, or have children. Women could not have both—not if they really wanted to follow God's will. The constant thrum of this message aggravated me, especially as I believed that I, and other working mothers around me, have faithfully followed a different path entirely.

I must admit, the day-by-day decision I make to ignore the scrutiny of others has been difficult—more difficult, even, than my decision to be a working mother. Yet over the past seven years of motherhood, the conscious decision I make to reject others' judgment of mothers has become easier. In some part, this is because I have developed a thicker shell. But too, as I have considered—sometimes with righteous indignation—the complicated messages women often receive about their lives as mothers and workers, I feel convicted that we need to reflect, to *be*, another message. And that message is this: God calls women to multiple roles. These roles need not be mutually exclusive. Women should have the freedom to follow the paths God set before them. Sometimes, women have been denied that freedom by being told only one viable choice, that of stay-at-home motherhood, exists. My life, I hope, conveys that message of freedom, as do the lives of those women who model faithful attention to God's calling to parent and to work—to do both.

Right now, I am at home with my boys, trying to write while one son practices soccer against a wall and the other reenacts a recent *Spongebob Squarepants* episode for me, word by excruciating word. I answer emails and grade papers to the background thump of a soccer ball and the somewhat pleasant drone of "and then Patrick says . . . and then Spongebob says. . ." It is my afternoon at home with the boys. Tomorrow, my husband will pick up Benjamin and Samuel from their grade school, while I will stay at the office. We take turns, working, parenting our kids, guiding the vocations of college students and listening to the noise of seven-year-old boys.

We are blessed by this balance. Because my husband and I choose to share parenting responsibilities, we get equal time with our sons—who, in turn, get equal time with us. This does not necessarily happen in cases where one spouse, usually the male, spends most of his time supporting the family, and far less time raising his children. Several years ago, a stay-at-home mom, the wife of a colleague, told me she was taking a Saturday morning for herself, one of the first times she'd done so since her first of three daughters was born. "I'm kind of nervous about it," she admitted. "I don't know how my husband will manage alone with the kids." *But they're his kids too*, I wanted to argue. *Why should a man be unable to manage caring for his kids, for a few hours on a Saturday morning?!* By choosing to share responsibility for childcare, my husband knows our sons as well as I do. He knows their daily routines and rhythms, knows what they eat for lunch and when they need a nap and where they hide their dirty clothes. I trust my husband can "manage" the children just fine without me there. And, in turn, my kids have more access to their father than do many of their peers, who might see their dads on the weekend and several hours each evening.

This has been the greatest benefit of being working parents, affirming for me, again and again, that we have set the right course for our family. There have been costs attendant to that decision, certainly, costs that result from these million and more choices we both make, every day, about how and where we spend our time and energy. While we both attend all our sons' sports games and musical performances, for example, neither of us volunteers in their classes—something a good many mothers (and a smattering of fathers) in our community do. Sometimes, when our schedules are tight, Ron and I hand off the kids in classrooms and offices, so that while we spend ample time with both boys, we have far less time for each other. Once in a while, I grade papers to the tune of *Spongebob*— either the real *Spongebob* on television, or the reenacted version, told to me by a son who really wants my attention. So if our sons benefit from greater access to both parents, they have probably also faced the problem of having parents who are, at times, distracted by their work commitments.

And those work commitments have, no doubt, suffered from our choice to be working parents. Both my husband and I have said no to writing projects, committee responsibilities, conference presentations, and other significant opportunities, knowing that saying yes affects the time we can give to our sons—and the time we can give to each other and to other work commitments. If I agree to teach an extra class one evening a week, my choice to do so concerns not only me, but three other people, and I have to make a decision with them in mind. I know not having a stay-at-home spouse has shaped my husband's career. He works in a department predominantly with colleagues who do not have dependents, or who have wives able to care for children. While they spend some weekends and many holiday breaks at the office doing research, Ron remains at home, caring for his children. While this is a choice he makes—we make—it also means his colleagues are more productive scholars than he is.

Of course, many colleagues are much more productive than I could ever be, too. But because I am a woman working in an evangelical Christian environment, this tradeoff is expected of me. After all, if I cannot be at home full time with my kids, sacrificing career advancement is the least I can do. My husband's sacrifices, on the other hand, are considered heroic, and he receives consistent acknowledgment for giving up his work time to care for his kids.

And so it goes.

The smaller choices though—these are ones I never anticipated when I decided to be a working mother. Choices about whether I can afford the time to have coffee with friends, or lunch with colleagues. Choices about whether I should go to an evening book group, or join a women's Bible study. Each day, I must make decisions that may affect my work life and my home life, and sometimes I am stymied by how difficult these choices can be.

One day several years ago, my sons were with a sitter for the few hours between kindergarten and the time when I could go home. At lunch, I hurried to our campus café to buy a sandwich to eat at my desk, something I did most days between classes. A group of colleagues, clearly enjoying their time together, called me over, invited me to join them. I really wanted to, and on some days I might have. But I calculated the cost of an hour spent eating with friends: the cost of my lunch, of lost time in my office, of the $10 an hour I was paying my sitter to be with my children. I knew the others at the table might sympathize with such calculations, though they could not empathize, lacking a need to do similar calculus. I walked back to my office alone, dejected, feeling a little sorry for myself and the choices other working mothers must make.

Other calculations are not monetary in nature, though they are sometimes just as wrenching—and sometimes just as isolating. For I have found that, although I want friendship with other mothers, my decision to work means I am not often available when mothers gather during the day.

Church programs for mothers are offered primarily during daytime hours, so I cannot be involved with Bible studies for women, or with the Mothers of Preschoolers (MOPS) program our church facilitates each year, or, now that my kids are second graders, with the women's prayer group established by several mothers at my sons' elementary school.

Indeed, sometimes I get discouraged by the many ways our churches offer programs for women who do not work but provide few opportunities to minister to working mothers. This is one more reinforcement of the Christian ethos commanding women into specific gender roles. But then on occasions when I think of attending evening events at our church, I usually must decide if I will leave my kids again, after being away from them all day. And, much as I would cherish this fellowship with others and affirm that working mothers need church programs too, I often make the choice to stay home, knowing my kids need me more.

Such decisions about how I spend my time have often made me feel isolated, both from my colleagues at work, with whom I share a passion for Christian education, and from other mothers in my community, with whom I share a passion for children. I feel that isolation most acutely when I see mothers arranging daytime play dates, knowing my children and I will not be invited, or when mothers gather at the playground, planning weekend barbeques with their families, talking like old friends who have spent ample time becoming acquainted. Although I value my vocation tremendously, I have not doubted my decision to be a working mother so much as at those times: because I know my exclusion from play dates and barbeques and other events often means exclusion as well for my sons.

And fundamentally, it is my sons—my Benjamin, my Samuel—who form the axis around which my world turns. When I hear them playing baseball in the backyard, when I cuddle with one or the other to read, when I smell their sweaty all-boy heads, even when I break up their ridiculous fights: At all times, I know we made the right decision to have children, and I cannot imagine the alternative, the other life we might have had—quiet and uncomplicated, but also emptier. God called these two boys into our lives, and we are blessed.

At the same time, when a student decides she wants to be a writer, or a class opens to a novel we're discussing, or I hear from a recent alum that she's embarked on a teaching career, or even when my husband and I meet with our boys for a quick on-campus lunch: At all times, I know we made the right decision to both keep working, to balance our lives in a way that affirms my husband's role as father and teacher, and my role as mother and teacher. I also cannot imagine an alternative, one that would keep me from the vocation for which God made me.

But while I do not regret my family's choices, I still long for affirmation and support, rather than judgment, from Christians who argue that God demands from women a different life path entirely. And I hope that those still considering whether to be a mother, whether to work, whether to do both, will see freedom, rather than restriction, in making their own life choices. And I still wish for a time when Christian women can pursue whatever they know God is calling them to, without being commanded by others to journey where they do not hear God's voice.

After all, God can give women and men multiple roles, multiple callings, multiple gifts. For sure, God has given my husband and me two distinct gifts: the gift of our children, and the gift of teaching. Neither is ours to squander. So, instead of choosing one gift over the other, we have embraced both, accepting as well the many decisions we've faced as a result. But each of my sons—loving, beautiful, miraculous—is one in a million and more, so worth every choice we've ever had to make.

Riding the Third Wave:
Gender Inequity in the Workplace
LeAnn Wiley Burton

I do not want children—and I am beginning to learn how powerful those five words are. I made this decision before I entered the workplace, even before college, where I learned about "choices." I am learning that many people have an opinion about my choice to not have children. In many cases, those opinions involve judgment against my choice, and I am beginning to realize just how much not having children shapes me as a twenty-something woman in the corporate world.

§

I began working at a national healthcare company a few years ago. As a mid-level employee at a large corporation, I have been surprised at the overwhelming sense of being a "cog in the machine." I work long days (always), long nights (sometimes), and I am consumed with work even when I am not working. My liberal arts college—where people are a part of a community and ideas are explored and validated—did not prepare me for such a harsh and impersonal work environment.

I have always been an achiever. I loved middle school and high school and can't really remember a time when I did not fit in and enjoy school, clubs, extracurricular activities, and church. My father was in the army, which meant we moved every one to three years. This forced me to finely hone my communication and adaptability skills. I was a good student and had lots of friends. I ended up at a liberal arts university and continued to thrive under the mentoring I received from professors and the interest that the staff and faculty took in each student. I was always comfortable and confident. So to find myself in a corporate world where few seem loyal, the demands are high, and some people are ready to throw you under the bus to protect themselves seems surreal.

The strange thing is that my work environment isn't necessarily a man's world. While the company ratio is still 2:1 male to female, my particular department is made up of four men and sixteen women. It has been intriguing to observe how women interact with other women in the office, and how their personal choices affect them in the workplace.

My female manager carved out a place in management for herself at a young age, and I greatly respect her ambition and work ethic. But I am saddened to see that some of the characteristics that have helped her rise in the workplace are often deemed overly assertive and alienating. Men in our office do not seem to struggle with wearing assertiveness and confidence. Even more disheartening to me is that often disapproval comes from other women, making me wonder what chance we ever really have of changing the workplace (or the world) if women are going to be other women's biggest critics. The majority of men in management positions at my work have wives who do not have full-time corporate careers, but no one says they are being exploited as breadwinners. But my recently married manager, who has been the primary breadwinner in her relationship, is judged to be emasculating or simply married to a loser. Will she be judged for having less ambition and dedication now that she's strongly considering having children?

One of our supervisors is a forty-five-year-old woman who is married without children. As one of the few female vice presidents at our company, she is smart—but more than that, she is ambitious and driven. Carol Tavris writes in *The Mismeasure of Woman* that women are judged either as different than men and therefore inferior; judged as different than men and therefore superior; or expected to be the same as men.[1] My VP seems undecided about how she thinks women measure up, and you can see her conflicted feelings in the way she preferences women (she hired so many after all) and yet often seems displeased by "feminine attributes." Of the sixteen women she has hired, just five have children and only five are married. She made the personal decision not to have children, which allows her to be more like the corporate male at work, logging insane hours at the office and putting her career first. Her hiring practices might indicate that she believes women are, in some cases, superior as an employee choice, but that maybe it's a particular sort of woman who is right for the job.

---

1   Carol Tavris, *The Mismeasure of Woman* (New York: Touchstone, 1992).

The underlying message I get is that she expects her employees—both male and female, parents or not—to devote themselves single-mindedly to their careers. A talented coworker of mine, a single mother with two small children, has spent hundreds of dollars on overage daycare fees because meetings are scheduled to begin at five p.m. and do not end until after six p.m. The meetings seem to be scheduled with no thought to the women or men who need to pick up their kids. On the one hand, this manager champions women as capable of doing any job, but on the other, she expects that reproduction and childrearing will not get in the way: discrimination against women who are mothers or would ever expect to be mothers.

Our company believes it is enough to give opportunities to women. After that, it is up to each individual to claw her way to the top, something done by working hard and making choices and sacrifices. This perpetuates the belief that a choice between family or work is the only viable option. Nor is any real mentorship offered. There are just small windows of opportunity in the form of extra projects or bigger responsibilities within the team, and "you better take them when you can, if you plan to get ahead." This structure for advancing your career, of course, specifically stunts those who do have families to care for.

Setting up this model in a department with a critical mass of women is ironic and bewildering. In my company, women at the top aren't changing anyone's mind about the value of women, regardless of whether they are mothers or not. I don't pretend to know what it would be like to try to break down those barriers as a woman in a largely male world, but shouldn't someone start to do it? My managers have carved out little pieces of the pie for themselves, but appear to be comfortable living within the system.

Gloria Steinem wrote in her introduction for the book *To Be Real* that women in this generation of third-wave feminism are not political and do not stand up for each other to fight for women's common interests.[2] When I first read this, I too saw little importance in a political movement for women today. I believed on some level that this previous generation was being hyper-sensitive. After all, I was in college, with a whole world wide open to me. Wasn't feminism over all this sisterhood mumbo jumbo? Hadn't we already had the good fight fought for us? Women work and have families and do what they want, don't they? I am ashamed to say that even when faced with the facts regarding salary inequities, lack of childcare, and

---

2   Gloria Steinem, *To Be Real*, ed. Rebecca Walker (New York: Anchor Books, 1998).

a long list of other missing provisions for women in the workplace, I just didn't believe it until I experienced it firsthand.

Shortly after I was married, the inevitable question began: "When will there be babies?" When I say that I do not want to have children, the reactions are mostly negative. This genuinely surprises me, because I naïvely expected that other corporate career women would understand and even support that decision. I certainly did not expect the complexity of issues surrounding work output pitted against feminine expectations and the overwhelming sense of judgment where no one wins.

I believe that children are a gift. I also believe that raising a child is an enormous responsibility, one that I do not feel equipped to take on. I think that women often feel pressured into having children. It's not only part of our cultural expectation into adulthood, but couples often assume it's an automatic part of marriage. As an adopted child who has grappled with being unplanned and initially unwanted, I have strong feelings about entering into parenthood deliberately, and I believe this is something people need to feel called to do.

Growing up in the church and with particularly conservative friends and family, I felt like *woman* and *mother* were synonymous words. It wasn't until I began seriously thinking and praying about my vocational goals, gaining specific purpose and drive, that I began to feel free to pursue career goals without giving in to unnecessary expectations of motherhood. It is difficult for me that others believe I am less of a woman because I choose not to have children, or that there is something wrong with me as a woman for not wanting them. Vocationally, I am observing that in some cases women may benefit professionally for choosing to not have children. And I also observe women being penalized for choosing to have children. Women are caught in an impossible place, where having children invites a myriad of judgments (the overburdened "working mom" or "just a housewife and mother") and not having children comes with a different yet equally harsh judgment ("selfish"). I really am treated differently when others discover that I don't intend to have children. I was naïve in believing that my decision would not impact anyone but my husband and me. I now see that my decision shapes how people view me, no matter what I choose.

It is bizarre to me that the personal choice of children can be such a strategic yet complicated factor in women getting ahead in the workplace. In college, I figured it was easier not to have children while working, but I didn't ever think of it as leverage. Now, I find that my identity is rooted not simply as a hardworking woman in her twenties, but as a *childless* hardworking woman in her twenties.

I am realizing that my decisions about parenting are shaping me in ways I am just beginning to discover. I once believed that having children defined one as a woman, where the identity of "Mom" superseded everything else. Now I am realizing that choosing to not have children is equally weighty in shaping one's identity. And I am still figuring out what this will mean for me in my career and life.

Twists in the Path

Lindsey Lupo

When I was in grade school, I thought everyone's dad studied at night after work, because my dad did. At the time, he was a school district administrator with a master's degree in counseling and school psychology. He had successfully risen through the ranks of the local school district, but mid-career my dad decided to completely shift gears and go to law school. He was almost forty-years-old, married, with two small children.

A few years earlier, he had found himself at a fork in the road in terms of career advancement. Facing uncertainty, he knew only one thing for sure—both paths in front of him required another advanced degree. And so he enrolled in law school at a local law college. It was a good—but not great—school that offered a part-time schedule with nighttime and weekend classes. Because he was simultaneously working full-time for the school district, it took him four years to obtain the degree. He worked a 40-plus-hour work week, attended classes at night and on the weekends, studied on his nights off, and through it all, rarely missed dinner with our family.

His determination and discipline came from his intense desire to explore his newfound passion for the field of law. In the way he describes it now, he simply loved the classes, and this passion motivated him through even the most exhausting times. Twenty-five years later, my dad has risen to the top ranks of his field and is managing partner ("head honcho," as my family calls him) of a large law firm. On paper, he is an incredibly successful and powerful attorney, but if you ask him, he's a success story because he still absolutely loves what he does for a living.

His story was one that always inspired me, but it became particularly poignant when I hit my early twenties. I found myself sitting in a cubicle in a real estate job that I liked but didn't love. One day on my drive home, a song came on the radio, and it was as though Dave Matthews was singing directly to me: "Twenty-three and so tired of life, such a shame to throw it all away . . . could I have been anything other than this?"

The extent to which I felt deeply uninterested in my work suddenly hit me, and I felt what could only be described as a crushing weight on my chest. I had graduated from college with a B.A. in political science and had loved the field but had never thought that I could make a career out of it, and so made no attempts to further explore that field. I suddenly felt compelled to pursue that passion—I wanted to go to graduate school. But even at age twenty-three I was terrified at the thought of totally changing my career path. I was making it on my own, living by myself in a nice apartment, and I had a job with a solid and stable path in front of me that would offer a comfortable living and a good quality of life. I also recognized, though, that I lacked authentic happiness in my career and was facing a lifetime of even deeper levels of discontent. I thought of my dad's story and decided to take the plunge.

In fact, I dove right into the deep end and applied for Ph.D. programs, despite not even having a master's degree. I didn't really know anyone with a Ph.D., except for perhaps a few of my parents' friends, and they were mostly older men. Perhaps most frightening was that I didn't know any women, let alone young women, with Ph.D.s, save for a couple of college professors with whom I never really engaged. It seemed impossible, scary, and even a little foolish to embark on a journey that was so foreign to me.

I remember standing in my sister's kitchen during the time that I was applying and asking her, "People get Ph.D.s all the time, right? I won't die in the process, right?" Quite honestly, I couldn't quite envision coming out on the other side still intact. The whole idea seemed absolutely absurd, and I couldn't get beyond my need to feel certainty and my inability to feel confidence. My fear and apprehension were palpable, and my sister turned to me, smiled, and said, "Of course they do, and you will too." A year later, I entered my program, still unsure of my abilities and still fearful, but passionate about my area of study. I said a prayer and hoped that passion would help me write good papers.

Fast forward a decade—I've obtained the Ph.D., gotten married, had two children, and landed a dream job at a Christian university. I'm grateful to God every day that I get paid to do what I love. People often look shocked when I tell them that I absolutely love my career. That's not to say that it's not a difficult job—it involves long hours, insane amounts of energy, and an incredible level of discipline. During the school year, I'm often up late working, wondering if I'm achieving balance in even the most remote sense, and worrying about who is suffering because of my long nights and early mornings.

But during those times, I think of my dad, and I remember him on the couch with books and highlighter pen in hand, after a full day of work, with the prospect of a weekend full of classes ahead of him. He set the model for me because during that time, not only did his marriage not fail, it thrived. Not only did his daughters not resent him for his absence, they learned to adore him for his convictions and the way in which he seemed effortlessly to find balance in life. And not only did he find great success in his career, he garnered a deep and profound respect from his peers and colleagues.

§

There is no set recipe for success or happiness. Everyone's path will be different and everyone's outcome unique. We all struggle with big life decisions and have felt the pressure to choose the "perfect fit" career. But the one lesson I've learned is that it's never too late to shift gears vocationally. As a college professor, I often have students in my office conveying to me the intense pressure—both internal and external—they feel to "choose a career" and map out their life plans during college. I have never understood the concept that twenty-year-old students should know exactly what they want to do, what they are truly good at, and what will make them happy. At age twenty, I wanted to be a marriage and family therapist or a physician. I wasn't even a political science major, but a decade and a half later, I'm a political scientist.

I often advise my students to seek balance between being forward-thinking and being flexible. This means being proactive in their career search—seeking internships, researching graduate programs, talking to as many people as possible, pursuing every opportunity, reading all that they can absorb—but allowing room for changes and being open to new paths. One will not be able to figure everything out by the time one graduates. Many people have more than one career in a lifetime, as their personal interests shift and the economy changes. I have found that it's easier to think in ten-year chunks of time—what can I do now to ensure a successful next decade? After that, I allow myself room to grow and give myself permission to shift gears within my career.

Emotional support from family and close friends is critical to a successful career, particularly one that involves shifts and changes. When I recently asked my father about the point at which he decided to go to law school, it didn't surprise me that his response began with five simple words: "Your mom and I talked and . . ." He said it was actually my mom who had pushed him to go for it. She did this knowing that for four years (and more, considering the life of a new law associate) the responsibilities of raising two school-age children would disproportionately fall on her. But she knew that he would do what he could to continue to be present with the family. And he knew that she would help fill in where he was perhaps unable to. They knew this about each other because over their twenty-year marriage they had developed a very strong, mutually supportive relationship. It was, and still is, filled with give-and-take. They are partners, sharing equally in burdens and rejoicing together in blessings.

This kind of equal partnership, this mutually supportive relationship is one I now share with my own husband. When I decided to apply for Ph.D. programs, he was my biggest advocate. Throughout the application process and the GRE exams, I was an emotional wreck. I had finally made the big decision to apply to programs but now had a great amount of fear that I would completely bomb the GRE exam and ruin all chances of getting into a good school. I yelled a lot, I cried a lot, and I pouted a lot. He very calmly would bring me cups of hot tea as I studied, offer a few words of encouragement, kiss my cheek, and walk away. The ritual continued throughout graduate school and into my first years of teaching, when life became even more complicated as we entered our mid-thirties. There was now a house to take care of, a toddler to raise, and even more bills to pay. During my first couple of years teaching, the hours were incredibly long and the work emotionally draining. My husband, without complaint, cooked dinners, got our daughter ready for bed, and went grocery shopping. I did these things as well, but during those first years of my teaching, the household responsibilities fell disproportionately on him, as with my mom years earlier. Now that I have my footing in my career and my job is less time-consuming, I look forward to returning the favor. This is the give-and-take we learned from my parents. "Support" is much more than cups of hot tea—it is emotional encouragement and the physicality involved in literally helping out around the house. And this multifaceted support system is critical in order for each of us to be successful in both our careers and as parents.

Career-life balance is possible. In all those years of my father being in school, while I remember him studying a lot, I don't remember him being absent. I recently asked my sister what she remembers about the time, since she was in her teens. Her most prominent memory is the same as mine— my father sitting on the couch studying. Being older, she had been more cognizant of his choice of study locations and time. He would study in the post-dinner hours in the very open and central living room that acted as a corridor for all the chaos of a household with school-age children. The decision may not have been intentional, but it signaled to us that he remained very present in our lives. My sister also remembers him helping with school projects and recalls his unwavering willingness and desire to read her English papers, making sure she was on track. As we both remember it, his years in law school don't stand out to us as a particularly difficult time in our family. It was only in speaking to one another in our adult years that we realized he was probably intentionally trying to minimize the impact felt by his children.

In fact, I never knew he was as busy as he was. Throughout his time in law school, during the early years at the firm, and still today, he remains a doting and dedicated husband and father. I am certain there are days when he doesn't feel balance. I know I feel terribly out of whack for days— *months*—at a time. But what I learned from my dad is that you can excel in your career while still maintaining a full family life. Some level of balance is possible. I do recognize that there is a gender element here, that men and women face disparate responses at work when it comes to parental duties at home. Men are often rewarded and admired for leaving early for a dance recital, whereas women are perceived as lacking in dedication if they do the same. I recognize this discrepancy, and yet I still look to my father as a model of how career-life balance is possible and how I can be both a good parent and strong professional.

My dad has risen to the top of his firm, competing against those who started at a younger age and who went to more prestigious law schools, and yet he simultaneously excelled in another role, as husband and father. Family and career can go hand in hand. I once asked my father, now the boss, about the life of new law associates who are often told that they literally need to sleep at the office in order to prove themselves. "Are you impressed by them?" I asked. He said he saw them as somewhat inept. "Why can't they get their work done on time?" he asked. "They should go home to their families." Duly noted.

When my dad and I were recently chatting about our individual decisions to go back to school, we laughed at our lack of understanding regarding our choices. When I asked him whether he had always focused on attaining the top leadership position he now holds in the law firm, he chuckled and told me that while in law school, he didn't even know such positions existed. I was similarly confused when I started the Ph.D. program. Early in the process, I happily boasted to my professors about a particular career goal I had until, finally, one very kind professor pulled me aside and told me that such declarations were essentially career suicide. I had to resist the pressure to have the whole plan mapped out with astute clarity and shrewd insight. The road ahead may in fact be a bit foggy, and one may not always know where the new path may lead.

In following my dreams I've also learned that failure is a part of life. Pursuing our passions is an exhilarating experience, but it's wise to be filled with a healthy dose of fear and caution. The reality is that not everyone's dream unfolds as intended. Businesses fail, restaurants close, artists never land a show. But is the prospect of failing a reason not to try? No, because not trying is guaranteed failure. Having a plan B is crucial in following our dreams. For my father, plan B was to quit law school and pursue another advanced degree that would keep him in the school district. For me, plan B was to return to the field of real estate. This meant that right before I quit my job, I did the exact opposite of what one might expect from someone leaving an industry—I worked extra hard and made sure that every door remained open and that no bridge was burned. And, in fact, I was told by my company that I always had a place to which I could return.

One of my best friends recently left her high-paying sales job to do what my dad had done—go to law school. In sales she was earning a six-figure salary, owned her own home in San Francisco, and had just paid off all of her student loans from college. But what she was really passionate about was legal advocacy for women and children. She volunteered when she could but found herself being strongly pulled toward the field of discrimination law. She took the LSAT, quit the job, and began law school. She discovered great happiness in her classes and her studies, but she also found herself in the middle of a divorce from her husband of five years. She was now entirely on her own with a mortgage, new student loans, and no job, and yet she decided to stay in law school. But she needed a plan B. In one very candid conversation, I remember her saying, "I can always wait tables at night." In fact, she had put herself through college working as a waitress. Plan B doesn't need to involve anything very complicated and is probably even better if it relies on some very basic skill. She went on to finish law school, landed a great job, remarried, had two children, and, as it turned out, never had to wait tables. Instead, she taught yoga classes to put herself through law school. Her self-reliance and tenacity have inspired me.

In a similar story, my mother recently told me that she ran into an old acquaintance of mine. We had grown up together, and after college he had gone on to be a rather successful real estate developer. He married, had two kids, and lived a very good life. When she recently saw him, however, he was driving a tow truck. After the real estate crash, he had needed a plan B. My favorite part about the story is that when he saw her, he didn't hide from her in shame. Instead, he stopped, smiled broadly, waved, and unabashedly told her, "I have to make money somehow." As a college-educated woman, I never take for granted that I need to develop basic skills that can help me get through rough, unexpected patches in life. Following dreams and pursuing passions can provide great emotional and financial reward, but it's important to always have a plan B.

I asked my dad if he had any advice for a young, soon-to-be college graduate looking to pursue a passion. "Do it," he replied. To some extent, it really can be that simple. But making career decisions is also a very difficult process full of uncertainty. Making the decision to change careers is even more tenuous. Bumps, bruises, frustration, and despair will all happen— but those happen on the safe path as well. Our faith gives us courage to begin the journey, and sustains us in pursuing those vocations with wisdom and joy.

The Price of Independence: Paying for Life after College

Kelli McCoy

W hen I graduated from college, just shy of twenty-two-years-old, I was excited about truly being on my own for the first time. Independence called to me with promises of fun and freedom: "Do whatever you want! Make your own decisions! Have a fulfilling career! Be the kind of put-together woman who can handle any situation and look good doing it!"

In the midst of graduation and all of my dreams about the future, I didn't fully appreciate that all of those promises come at a cost. A literal, dollars-and-cents cost.

Living on a college campus as an undergraduate prepares a person for a lot of things. I did it for four years, and had some of the very best experiences of my life. I learned how to live amicably in close quarters with other people, and how to participate in a continuous exchange of ideas. I studied, took tests, participated in a variety of extracurricular activities, and traveled around Europe. What college did not prepare me for, however, was grocery shopping.

Like most undergraduates who live on campus, my room and board was all wrapped into one lump sum. I never knew the price-per-roll of that toilet paper in our hall bathrooms, or exactly how much that salad in the cafeteria cost. I didn't think about the electricity bill every time I turned on the heater or left my computer on all night. By the time I was twenty or so, I thought I was pretty independent—no matter how the IRS officially categorized me. After all, I worked a few hours each week in the campus library, and paid for my own gas, car insurance, and clothes. "See?"

I thought. "I'm responsible, capable, and can do this on my own!" I liked that I was young and still single, and relished the idea of launching out into a world full of possibilities.

After graduation, although I was stunned by the price of rent, I moved into a two-bedroom apartment with a couple of roommates. I found this new life to be surprisingly expensive. I quickly discovered that, unlike my years of living on a college campus, every single day of this new life carried with it some expense. I couldn't even get to work without spending money on gas. And that's not to mention the electricity, internet connection, and cell phone that were essential to sustaining what I thought was any sort of reasonable daily existence. So that's how I came to find myself in the grocery store, buying full meals for the first time, totally bewildered by the cost of it all.

Of course, I had purchased plenty of snack foods, pasta, and the requisite Top Ramen in college, but now I had to make *all* of my own meals. I was taken aback by the price of it all. People pay this much for a pound of meat? And which type of meat do you use, exactly, if you want to make a pot roast? I found that everything was more expensive than I had imagined it, and it took a lot of work to do the shopping every week, to drive around town to the stores that had various items on sale, trying to fit everything I wanted into my meager budget. This independence thing, I quickly discovered, is a lot of work.

Earlier in life, I had assumed that financial success would come with my college degree. This success, I thought, would mean better clothes, a nicer car, more vacations, and, first and foremost, no worrying about how to pay the bills. But I had decided to head straight to graduate school after college, which meant that while most of my friends had started full-time jobs, my work—and earnings—would still be on a part-time basis. I knew that my decision would mean that, at least for a few years, I would make considerably less money than most of my friends, but for the most part I was content to pursue the path that brought me the most fulfillment and satisfaction.

I needed to adjust my ideas of what a responsible, independent, adult life would look like in the face of my relatively low income. This would be a life in which I had to make serious decisions about what I could afford to eat, wear, and do. The rent would always have to come first. Independence (and my friends) called out to me, "Go to a concert! Take a vacation!" I now heard a whisper afterwards that said, "If all the bills are paid and you still have money left over." Of course, I still did most of those things, went on trips and out to dinner, to movies and fun days at the beach. It was wonderful and exciting, and I wouldn't have traded it for anything. But I did find that being a responsible, capable woman—who can stand on her own—means having to make careful, sensible decisions, even more than it means enjoying all the delights of a big city with her friends.

The problem is, we almost never see this kind of difficult decision-making on TV. At least, not the sitcoms and dramas that I watched as a young twenty-something. The characters were not generally engaged in creating budgets, figuring out how to pay the rent, debating whether or not they could afford to fix the car that had just broken down, or leaving the air conditioner turned off even in summer to keep down the electricity bill. When single, female characters did star in a show, à la *Sex and the City* or *Friends*, they were beautiful and glamorous, wore designer clothing regardless of their income level, and never seemed to have trouble finding jobs. When a character did acknowledge some cash-flow problem, it didn't seem to stop her from doing, well, anything. In a lot of ways, life on my own after college really was like what I saw on television—it was a lot of fun in an apartment complex and with a group of friends who spent much of their time together. It was full of joy and laughter. But it also brought with it difficult decisions about how to have all of that fun and still be financially solvent.

Of course, it's not like I had learned about life only from the television set. My parents always taught me to be financially responsible—not to rack up credit card debt by spending money I didn't have; to save, to tithe, and to be generous with what I had. It's just that I suddenly found all of that to be much more difficult than it sounded, once I was really and truly on my own. After all, the bright, shiny things that a city has to offer a young woman are so very tempting.

And truthfully, for most of us ends didn't always meet, at which point we relied on a combination of credit cards and the generosity of friends. Being a single woman in pursuit of a career meant that I balanced work, school, and housework on my own, which somehow seems still to be easier than the formidable task of balancing all of those and having a family. I worked as a housecleaner, a nanny, a substitute teacher, and in a variety of academic positions, all so I could keep living in the part of the city I knew and loved best, and so that I could do the things I wanted to do.

I learned that the economic relationship between women and men can be difficult to navigate. I knew—had known for a long time—that I didn't want to have to rely on a man or marriage for my financial security. I relished being independent and self-reliant. I didn't want someone else—especially not a man with whom I was romantically involved—to take care of me and therefore have certain expectations for what my role in our lives would be. So although I still occasionally dated, I did my best to avoid those formal, "traditional" dating scenarios in which a man invites a woman to dinner and then pays for everything. That style of dating seemed to me to be the remnant of an outdated, sexist system and to carry with it certain implied obligations for the women involved. I preferred what I viewed as a more equitable exchange, in which I paid for myself, and he paid for himself. Sometimes I even paid for everything, feeling good about being able to turn the tables on this silly old custom, but I found that very, very few men were comfortable with having a woman pay for them. They understood that the person who was paid for was in the subordinate, dependent position, and they disliked it. It's funny, then, that I should have been expected to like it.

There were a few times when I went ahead, took a deep breath, and went on a "typical" date. On one of these occasions, I was with a man about my age who had a successful career and was quite a bit better off financially than I was. He took me to a restaurant that was much more expensive than I was used to, and spent what, to me, was a small fortune on our dinner. I had not known him well before this, and soon knew that he wasn't the right person for me. But, I thought, when someone spends that much money on you, you owe them a certain amount of your time and attention. And so, our date that evening went on for hours, and I even let him kiss me, and then I never went on another date with him. I later felt rather unhappy about the whole experience, in spite of the lavish dinner and the perfectly nice company.

I eventually understood that what bothered me so deeply was the feeling that I had to give something—at the very least, my time—in exchange for his money. And that was a good lesson to learn. Though as a Christian and a feminist I always knew that there were certain ways in which I would never sell my body or my mind, I came to realize that young women are being asked to sell themselves in little ways all the time. So as I worked at my jobs, planned for my future, and hung out with my friends, I sought the kind of independence that would establish me as my own, individual person. I saw my financial stability as the key to ensuring that only I was in charge of what happened to me. And I never went on that type of date again.

Striving for financial security meant, to me, that I would be able to make my own decisions, live my own life, and not be dependent on a man to take care of me. Meanwhile, and perhaps somewhat paradoxically, I had one of the best communal experiences of my life. The greatest benefit of not being well off in the years after college was that I became part of a deep and enduring community—not an organized church, business, or school, but rather a group of friends who came together and helped each other regardless of the circumstances. There was virtue, I had found, in being able to take care of myself and in not being possessed by anyone or anything. But there was also beauty and love in a community of people who accepted me for who I was, without question, challenge, or ownership. We weren't particularly exceptional; most of us were just recent college grads, and through a web of connections we ended up living in the same apartment complex. Some of us were barely acquaintances at the outset, but our mutual friendships and our shared circumstances brought us together. Most of us struggled to pay all our bills each month; student loans and various other types of debt conspired against us, as did the not-infrequent loss or change of jobs and the sudden, unexpected devastation of family crises. In these struggles, we found great joy and companionship, and so, in many ways, became the Body of Christ to one another.

I watched as people who had little money themselves provided generously for each other's needs time and time again. When someone didn't have enough money left at the end of the month for groceries, a group dinner would appear. Those who were better off at any given moment helped to take care of those who were particularly struggling, and then, sometimes, the roles would reverse. It was one of the most purely selfless communities in which I have ever had the privilege to participate. I have never known another group of people, unrelated by blood, who shared so freely. This, then, is one of the greatest lessons of my life: that no matter my income level, it is possible to give, and that giving is transformative for the people who give as well as receive. I think our lack of economic prosperity actually made us more generous, more open to the sense that these precious moments were fleeting and that we all ought to cherish them together while we could.

"Treasure every moment." That was one of the last things my grandmother ever said to me, and she was right. Because I felt like I didn't have a lot of money, it was all too easy to spend my time looking around me and wishing that I had the same things other people did. I too often judged my life and level of success by what others possessed. For the most part, I figured I had a pretty awesome existence . . . until I saw that someone else my age had a new car, or hundreds of television channels in contrast to my paltry handful of local stations. Though I certainly cannot say I never feel that way anymore, I recognize that sort of longing is a waste of time. It is also fundamentally in opposition to how I want to define myself, as both a feminist and a Christian. I know that material goods—including the expensive shoes and clothing I see paraded in front of me every time I leave the house or turn on the television—not only do not make women better, but also serve as a way of objectifying us and imprisoning us in a web of fleeting, temporal delights. Although I have more "stuff" now than I did when I was twenty-three, it has made me neither more nor less happy—for me, the deepest joy has come from cherishing every moment spent with friends and family.

I really never intended to get married, and I was thoroughly enjoying life with my friends and my work, when the totally unexpected happened, and I fell in love. This amazing, unanticipated person entered my life, and I underwent another financial transition. Leaving college had meant, for me, a move from economic dependence to independence. Being in a serious relationship, and ultimately marriage, in which finances were equally shared meant another transition, to interdependence—not to a relationship in which I would lose my independence, per se, but to one in which my decisions would inevitably affect another person, and vice versa. I imagine that I have more to learn in this new stage of my journey.

During my first few years out of college, my thinking about money revolved mostly around my immediate needs—what it could do for me in terms of groceries, rent, and entertainment. Now, in the next stage of my life, more of my focus has been on the long-term: what money can mean in terms of a stable, secure life for me and my family. Every new stage in life brings both joy and struggle, but I wouldn't trade those years when I was first out of college for anything. Financial independence gave me a way to carve out my own identity and pursue my dreams. Though I discovered that there was a literal cost to independence, measured in hours of work and the sacrifice of some material goods, I also learned that my life had deep joy and meaning when it was shared generously with others.

A Husband is Not a Financial Plan

Becky Havens

Paradoxes: My Identity

I am a mid-life economics professor who has not had to spend much of my life worrying about money. I am a wife who does not believe a husband is a financial plan, but whose husband is an expert in finance who supported me in paying off graduate school loans, getting started with my career, and purchasing a home for our family. I am a mother who believes adult children should be financially independent, but who myself gained advantage from my parents' support, and who now, as a parent, intentionally does everything I can to use my financial resources to give my adult children access to college and graduate school, and to launch them into professional careers.

I am an economist who cares more about relationships and understanding people's needs in my professional work than I do about money. In fact, I care about money and how economics works precisely in order to care for the needs of people and make people's lives better. I am also a professor and former academic administrator who has studied gender issues and lived out management practices to make a way for flexible work arrangements. Research reveals that while women are economically disadvantaged and have less access to power and position, they have some of the best qualities to offer organizations. And while leaders can alter systems to make workplaces function better for women—and men—to care for their families, and create more productivity in the process, public policy and many organizations are stuck in old, outdated practices that aren't working for families.

How do my values, my experiences, my journey, and my research lead me to these seemingly paradoxical positions and understandings?

Perspectives: My Journey

I was raised by two working parents in a middle-class Christian home. My parents loved me and believed in me. They told me I was smart, that I could be anything I wanted to be, and they encouraged me to dream big professional dreams. My upbringing shaped me to believe that becoming educated and seeking a well-paying professional career, one that fulfilled my dreams and calling, was in keeping with God's will for me. I wanted to pursue a helping profession, and I wanted to become financially independent enough to give back to my parents some day.

My parents also shaped me to believe hard work and education were important. I worked from the age of sixteen as a secretary, graduated high school early, and worked full-time at a fabric store between high school and college. My parents supported me through college with tuition, and I paid for my own room and board to live on campus, because I valued the relationships and community engagement of a small liberal arts college. With savings, I paid for an educational trip to Europe at age nineteen. But without my parents' support for college tuition, using my financial resources for educational enrichment would not have been possible. The balance between my own efforts and outside support is a recurring theme throughout my life. It is also a concept that permeates my life's work and calling.

During college, as a pre-med student, I soon discovered I had a weak stomach, and so I changed to mathematics. I realized that God has given each of us gifts, and that mine involves analysis and problem-solving as well as using those gifts to help people. I discovered economics and philosophy in my junior year, and I realized that the field of economics connects mathematics and social issues. It was then I felt called by God to care about the disadvantaged members of society, and to use my intellect to study poverty and inequality. I made the decision to pursue a graduate degree in economics.

I lived with my parents during graduate school and worked as a teaching assistant, research assistant, typist, and adjunct professor, so I could pay my own tuition expenses and minimize debt. I studied income distribution, labor, and the economics of education. It was a tough program, and while I believe my own determination helped me to continue during extremely challenging times, the grace of God helped me believe in the ultimate purpose of my graduate work and finish the program. I met my husband during graduate school as I was moving into the dissertation phase. My husband entered our marriage with financial means, and he supported me at the end of my Ph.D. to enable me to work on my research full-time.

We started our family when the end of my graduate program was in sight. Our daughter was born four months before I defended my dissertation, and my husband cared for our daughter nearly full-time during those months, which was a critical factor in my successful completion of the Ph.D. It also gave him sensitivity to the role of infant caregiver and drew us into the partnership of parenting as a practical means of survival. Later, I took on the role of caregiver while he finished his graduate studies.

Our early career years after we both completed graduate school were definitely give-and-take. We each alternated part-time and full-time work, depending on our opportunities, and we both partnered in the care of the children and the home. There is no one right way to organize family-work balance. I believe each young family must negotiate those arrangements for itself. Still, organizations can create structures to assist young parents in family-work balance. When I began to study women's workforce issues, I realized our society can also use public policy to assist young families in work and life balance.

My first position after graduate school became my long-term career. My alma mater, Point Loma Nazarene University (PLNU), invited me to join the full-time faculty upon completion of my Ph.D. But my daughter was only seven months old, and the offer included six new course preparations during the first academic year. I didn't believe that was humanly possible for me with an infant, though I did love teaching and wanted to use my degree and put my education to work immediately, and I loved Point Loma. So I turned down the full-time offer and accepted a part-time teaching position with PLNU instead. The part-time contract gave me no future promise of employment and no job security. I soon learned that academic hiring is structured so one must be full-time to climb the rungs of the promotion and tenure ladder, and gain access to job security. I began to wonder if the hiring system had to be structured this way, or if there was an alternative system that would be more sensitive to young families and flexible in the work arrangements necessary for them to balance work and family. At the risk of sounding self-serving, the reality was that I was a female economist with a Ph.D. from a top-ranked graduate school, an alumna of this very college where I sought to join the faculty, and a third-generation member of the school's sponsoring denomination. Was I not an ideally suited young faculty member with significant potential to bring great value to the university and advance its mission? Was I not worthy of fighting to hire and retain?

The answer was to come in my future years of employment at PLNU, now numbering twenty-four. I was hired full-time in my fourth year and quickly given increasingly responsible leadership assignments. I became department chair and later academic dean. I moved up the rungs of the promotion and tenure ladder and served on numerous committees, often in leadership capacities.

My son was born between my first and second year of part-time employment, and my husband and I entered into the hectic domain of navigating work and childcare as a two-income family. There were years I worked part-time and my husband worked both a full-time and a part-time job. There were later years when my career began to take off, and my son needed more attention, so my husband provided full-time care for our children and support for me in household management. My husband's willingness to work part-time or provide full-time home care for our family enabled my career to advance, much like traditional wives of post-war Caucasian culture historically supported the successful full-time work of their husbands.

I am not self-made. Yes, I worked hard. But the support of my parents and my husband enabled me to accomplish the things I have accomplished. My early career experiences also began to make me question the structures of academic hiring practices. My intuition is that when we allow more flexible work arrangements, it is more productive for our organizations and increases the access to opportunities for women. My work in gender studies finds evidence to support this.

Later, my work as an academic administrator helped me test and implement those insights. My study and experiences both lead me to believe that women bring a unique perspective into workplace management practices, and allowing more flexibility in workplace arrangements helps not only the families, but also the organization by retaining excellent faculty. Through my firsthand experience, I observed that simple adjustments to our systems can provide huge benefits to the productivity of our workforce.

As our children grew up and went off to college, my family work arrangements became more flexible, and my husband and I could both resume a more intensive career life. But financially the needs of our children changed, and so supporting them through college and on into graduate school presented new financial challenges and pressures. I don't think I expected the financial pressures to increase as we went into our mid-life careers, but they have. What I've learned during this era of life is that there is no single correct way to handle financial stress, but that several things are critical: ownership and partnership, communication between partners, sharing common values, and planning for the future. I am also fortunate to have a husband with an MBA in finance who is creative about working out financial arrangements, but even so, I believe it is important for me also to "own" the financial responsibility of our household, communicate with him, talk about our financial values, plan together, and for me not to relinquish the responsibility entirely to him. Not everyone is fortunate enough to have a partner, and life circumstances can change quickly and without warning. That, along with the general fragility of women's financial situations, leads me to believe it is even more important for women to own our own financial futures.

During my years as a college professor, my colleagues helped me discover gender studies, a natural fit for my calling to care about the disadvantaged. I realized that as a group, women have less economic power relative to men. I feel called as a Christian to work toward a better understanding of the economic challenges faced by women, and to advocate for changes that can make a difference for them. Improving the quality of life for women also improves the well-being of their children, and increasing the economic status of women and children improves society overall. The study of women's economic empowerment fits my root calling to care about the less fortunate members of society, and to use my intellect to study economic issues that can make lives better.

A few key economic realities facing women have emerged from my studies. I believe these are important for women to keep in mind as we progress in our education and careers. I believe awareness and proactivity can help us better plan our futures and improve the well-being of our families. And I believe that becoming responsible financially for what we have been entrusted by God—both in talents and material resources—is part of our stewardship as Christians.

Principles: Economic Trends

Women are at risk for economic insecurity in America. This is well-documented by economists for many reasons. There is a gender wage gap of 23 cents, meaning that women make 77 cents for every dollar men make, which is only partially explained by differences in education and experience (Boushey, 58). Motherhood is fraught with economic disaster, because mothers face blatant discrimination in the labor force, as opposed to men who are rewarded for being fathers (Boushey, 61). Mothers typically bear the financial burden for children should the family unit dissolve (Tilly, 26), and family units are breaking up at much higher rates than ever before. Economists have discovered that in many cases it is economic insecurity that contributes to family breakup. The significant increase in female-headed families is a huge risk factor in poverty, with women and children making up a high percentage of the poor (US Bureau of the Census, Snyder 600, Weitzman 217).

The economic insecurity faced by women only makes it even more important for women to plan our financial futures by tracking our situation—recording our spending, knowing what is happening, and planning prudent action steps to live within our means. Being financially responsible is one way we can care for ourselves and our families, and honor our Christian responsibility to be good stewards of our resources. Financial responsibility can be learned. In my case, some of the knowledge I have gained and the practices I have employed throughout my life were intentional, and some were accidental. During college I got a credit card in my own name and paid off the balance at the end of each month. I can't say I knew at the time that this practice would be good for my future creditworthiness, but it was. So later when I needed a graduate school loan, or when my husband and I applied for a home mortgage, it ended up being good preparation. Having a credit card in your own name and paying off the balance monthly is one way to establish a good credit history. And as a general rule, acquiring credit card debt that cannot be paid off monthly significantly increases future economic insecurity because the interest rate (cost of borrowing the money) is ridiculously high on credit cards.

Despite the current and real economic disadvantages women experience, families are becoming increasingly dependent on women's earnings (Thurow 214; Warren 23), and only the families with working wives have experienced real (inflation adjusted) income growth (Boushey 2010, 35–36). The lead story of the first *Economist* of this decade was about women constituting more than half the workforce, described as "arguably the biggest social change of our time" ("We did it!" 7). In married couple families, working wives now contribute 42.2 percent of family earnings, nearly 40 percent of mothers are primary breadwinners, and another 24 percent are co-breadwinners (Boushey 36). Because of structural economic changes, including the fact that women dominate jobs in the fastest-growing industries and have lower unemployment rates than men, these trends are expected to continue ("Female power" 51).

In addition, despite the increasing financial contribution to the family and new economic power, women still suffer disrespectful attitudes and obstacles to leadership in their organizations. Women who work full-time in the home raising children, caring for elderly family members, and taking care of the home are considered to be "not working" by the U.S. Census. Women who work providing caring labor are called "dependents" and "liabilities" and are "supported by" their husbands (Crittenden 60-61). We have a very narrow definition of what "work" is. Women who work in the labor force hit a "glass ceiling" while men have a "glass elevator," invisible barriers or opportunities to rise, respectively (Haslam 530). The model of corporate America is male-centric, requiring individuals in senior leadership to work 24/7, not have any interruptions in their career paths, and be completely mobile (Desvaux, *Women Matter* 6–8). This does not mesh with family life or responsibilities. And workplaces still tend to be quite inflexible in work arrangements, and do not meet the needs of today's families (Boushey 10). Yet the economic reality is that women bring needed qualities to senior leadership positions during times of economic crisis, and corporations with a critical mass of women on their leadership teams perform better financially (Desvaux, *Women Matter* 12–14). Furthermore, experts observe female leadership behaviors to match those needed for the businesses of the future (Desvaux, *Women Matter* 13–14).

So, what do these trends mean for Christian women? I believe we must become aware of these social and economic realities, and take action in our own spheres of influence. We should press for social change to better accommodate work-family balance, revise outdated social policies, create flexible workplace arrangements, and acknowledge women's contributions to senior leadership talent. We should intentionally work toward increasing the diversity of leadership in American organizations.

I particularly believe we should better align our values with our actions. If we as Americans believe in the importance of family and shaping the next generation, then we need to take action to value caring work, and make that work possible within the existing economic realities facing families. If we as Christians feel compelled to care for our families and be good stewards of our talents, we must honor our own individual calls by God to both parent our children and find meaningful work in the marketplace.

I greatly value my family, but I also feel a strong call by God to follow the passions of my heart and make a contribution in the workplace. My husband and I found ways to partner together so that we share the responsibility of family and work. I believe there is no one right way to figure this out, but that each family must work out their own way to balance family and work responsibilities. I believe it is important to put Christ first in my life, and then to align my values and my actions.

Reflections: What I Believe

Personal finance is just that: It's *personal*. And it can be difficult to talk about, confusing, and hard to know when and how to become completely independent financially as we transition from adolescence to adulthood, and these same feelings can follow us into adulthood. It's often easier to just avoid it altogether, relinquish the responsibility to others—our parents or our spouse—and hope everything will turn out okay. I know I have myself been guilty of these tendencies at different points of my life. But it's never too late, or too early, to begin thinking about our finances and planning our financial future. Even if we are fortunate enough to have supportive parents and/or a supportive spouse, taking charge of our own financial future will give us a sense of proactivity and positive control, especially given that circumstances can change quickly, and it will allow us to become good stewards of our material resources.

A leading economist once said, "Women are men with less money." ("Womenomics" 2010, 48). This is only true in the worst possible sense, because our society only treats women like men when it comes to acting like they have equal access to earning power following divorce. But we know from the evidence this is only wishful thinking. We do not treat women like men in giving them access to Social Security for their countless hours of unpaid work to care for children and elderly family members. We know women work longer hours than men, and make less money for it, even with equal qualifications, and that despite the gender pay gap, women still bring home a significant portion of the family earnings. We know that without women, family earnings would not be keeping up with inflation. We know that a significant percent of women are primary breadwinners. We know that women bring excellent leadership skills to corporate America but are significantly under-represented in boardrooms. And yet, if we embrace more women in senior leadership, our organizations will perform better, and be better prepared for the future. We also know that workplace arrangements are inflexible and hiring practices discriminatory to mothers. We know that there are not good part-time professional positions available for parents who would like to continue working part-time after they have children, and even though families need two incomes to survive, our public policies have not caught up with that reality. We know that children suffer the most from the refusal to change public policy. Most importantly, we know that if we want to change workplace arrangements and public policy, we can.

My life journey—what God called me to care about, my studies, and my experiences—has taken me to a place of concern. What I know, and what I have come to believe, is that not only can we change America, we must. We must set up systems that allow greater access to disadvantaged groups. We must give children improved access to educational opportunity and a way out of poverty. We must change public policy for immigrant women doing domestic work, to allow them access to living wages and a better quality of life for their children. We must give both men and women improved public policies that allow them to navigate the balance between work and family responsibilities. These changes will be good for individual people and families, and right for society. Not only will individual people have a better quality of life, but our organizations will be more productive, our society will be placing a higher value on caring for our families, and we will be better caring for the next generation and as a result, improving our own future. As women gain access to greater economic power, we must use our leverage to change the world for children, disadvantaged racial groups, and global women who live in oppressed environments. And ultimately we must use our new economic power to make society a better place.

I believe that all resources belong to God, and that becoming self-sufficient as a contributing member of society financially, and caring for my family in partnership with the members of it, is my responsible stewardship as a Christian. I believe that God did not promise any of us material rewards, but God did promise us something far more important—salvation and eternal life. I believe that relationships are far more important than things and that whatever financial resources I have should be shared. I believe in financial interdependence and that I am not self-made. I believe in give-and-take, and that to whom much is given, much is expected. As my parents and husband supported me, I would like to use my financial resources to support my family and enable my children to access educational opportunity or professional careers, become financially self-sufficient, and utilize their God-given talents in the process.

I believe that structural forces, or the way our systems are set up, determine at least to some degree the outcomes of the financial rewards in society, and that those systems advantage some and disadvantage others. I believe that we can change these systems if we take the time to analyze their outcomes and think through the effects in keeping with our societal values, and that if we do, our organizations will become more productive and our families better able to function with two working parents. I have been called to study and care about the underserved, particularly the economic realities facing women and families. I believe in the ability of smart men and women to collaborate and change systems and policies that will make people's lives better and create space for all of us to flourish.

Most importantly, each of us has to live our own lives, live our own dreams, and follow God's call on our lives. I encourage women to be responsible, be aware when society's expectations try to squelch God's call, and allow the transforming work of Christ to fully use our talents and financial means in wise, God-honoring, and empowering ways so that we can be change-agents in the world.

Works Cited and Consulted

Boushey, Heather, and Ann O'Leary, eds. 2010. *The Shriver Report: A Woman's Nation Changes Everything*. A study by Maria Shriver and the Center for American Progress.

Buvinic, Mayra. 1997. "Women in Poverty: A New Global Underclass." *Foreign Policy* Fall 1997: 38–53.

Crittenden, Ann. 2001. *The Price of Motherhood: Why the Most Important Job in the World is Still the Least Valued*. New York: Henry Holt & Co..

Faludi, Susan. 1994. "Don't Be Happy—Worry." *Race and Gender in the American Economy*. Edited by Susan F. Feiner, 413–27. New Jersey: Prentice-Hall.

"Female power." 2010. *The Economist*, January 2. 49–51.

Desvaux, Georges, Sandrine Devillard-Hoellinger, and Pascal Baumgarten. 2007. *Women Matter: Gender Diversity, a Corporate Performance Driver*. McKinsey & Company.

Desvaux, Georges, and Sandrine Devillard. 2008. *Women Matter 2: Female Leadership, a Competitive Edge for the Future*. McKinsey & Company.

Desvaux, Georges, Sandrine Devillard and Sandra Sancier-Sultan. 2010. *Women Matter 3: Women Leaders, a Competitive Edge in and after the Crisis*. McKinsey & Company.

Haslam, S. Alexander, and Michelle K. Ryan. 2008. "The road to the glass cliff: Differences in the perceived suitability of men and women for leadership positions to succeeding and failing organizations." *The Leadership Quarterly* 19:530–46.

Havens, Rebecca A. 2003. "Are American Women Down and Out in a Global Economy?" Paper prepared for Midwest Economics Association, March 2003.

Helgesen, Sally. 1990. *The Female Advantage: Women's Ways of Leadership*. New York: Doubleday Currency.

Maher, Kristen Hill. 2010. "The Gendered Migrations of Sex Workers, Domestic Workers, and Correspondence Brides: Limits of the Trafficking Paradigm." Lecture given for the Margaret Stevenson Center for Women's Studies, Point Loma Nazarene University. March 30.

Masterson, Kathryn. 2009. "Harsh Economy Drives New Brand of Communication from the Top." *The Chronicle of Higher Education*, November 29.

O'Toole, James and Warren Bennis. 2009. "What's Needed Next: A Culture of Candor." *Harvard Business Review* 87.6 (June): 54–61.

Rosener, Judy B. 1990. "Ways Women Lead: The command-and-control leadership style associated with men is not the only way to succeed." *Harvard Business Review* 68.6 (Nov-Dec): 119–25.

Snyder, Anastasia R., Diane K. McLaughlin, and Jill Findeis. 2006. "Household Composition and Poverty among Female-Headed Households with Children: Differences by Race and Residence." *Rural Sociology* 71.4: 597–624.

Stern, Stefan. 2009. "How to Be a Good Boss in Bad Times." *Management Today* (September): 38–42.

Sutton, Robert I. 2009. "How to Be a Good Boss in a Bad Economy." *Harvard Business Review* 87.6 (June): 42–50.

Thurow, Lester. 1994. "The New American Family." In *Race and Gender in the American Economy*, edited by Susan F. Feiner, 213–15. New Jersey: Prentice-Hall.

Tilly, Chris and Randy Albelda. 1994. "It's Not Working: Why Many Single Mothers Can't Work Their Way Out of Poverty." In *Real World Macro*, edited by Marc Breslow, et al. 12th ed. Somerville, Massachusetts: Dollars and Sense. November/December: 26–28.

U.S. Census Bureau. 2011. "Poverty." Last revised January 5. http://www.census.gov/hhes/www/poverty/poverty.html.

Warren, Elizabeth, and Amelia Warren Tyagi. 2003. *The Two-Income Trap*. New York: Basic Books.

"We did it! The rich world's quiet revolution: women are gradually taking over the workplace." 2010. *The Economist*, January 2.

Weitzman, Lenore J. and Jad H. Abraham. 1994. "At Issue: Do Men Experience a Huge Rise in Their Standards of Living After Divorce?" *Race and Gender in the American Economy*, edited by Susan F. Feiner, 216–18. New Jersey: Prentice-Hall.

"Womenomics: Feminist management theorists are flirting with some dangerous arguments." 2010. *The Economist*, January 2.

Recommended Reading on Personal Finance

Bach, David. *Smart Women Finish Rich*, Broadway Books, 1999.

Hamilton, Adam. *Enough: Discovering Joy through Simplicity and Generosity*, Abingdon Press, 2009.

Kiyosaki, Robert. *Rich Dad, Poor Dad*, Warner Books, 1998.

Orman, Suze. *Women and Money*, Speigel and Grau, 2010.

Ramsey, Dave. *Financial Peace Revisited*, Viking, 2003.

Ramsey, Dave. *The Financial Peace Planner*, Penguin Books, 1998.

Ramsey, Dave. *Total Money Makeover*, Thomas Nelson, 2009.

Stanley, Thomas and William Danko. *The Millionaire Next Door*, Taylor Trade, 2010.

Loving God with our Hearts, Minds, Souls ... and Money

Melissa Tucker

Several years ago I was asked to describe, "What is money to you?" I answered with these five qualities, which still sum up my position today: power, temptation, a distraction from the best that life has to offer, a need, and useful. As my list might imply, I have a contradictory relationship with money.

I think money can both ruin and free people. It is the elusive dream for which many sacrifice time with their loved ones. At the same time, it allows loved ones to have vacations, long lives, and fun together. As I go through my phases of sometimes loving and often hating money, I still have to figure out what to *do* with it. At thirty-three, I actually have some money to work with, so I have moved from theorizing to real choices and a bank account. It's fun to think about how to spend money, but another and much more daunting thing to actually manage it.

In college, when I was desperate for guidance on how to live as a hopeful Christian, stay part of the church, and commit to my budding new ideas, I spent late nights working all this out with friends. My conversations with friends who were studying religion and sociology opened my eyes to new issues: social justice, redistribution of wealth, the U.S. impact on the world economy, corporate sin, the gospel's approach to money, and how I was still responsible for the way my financial choices might harmfully impact someone on the other side of the world. Whew. I left college nervous to earn a paycheck, unsure how I was going to convert those dollars into my ideals. Would I be able to live up to the high standards I was setting for myself as a Christian? In some ways, it was a lot easier when I was working as a hotel front-desk clerk, sharing a room in a small apartment, skimping on movies to buy organic veggies and pay my car insurance instead. I didn't have money to work with, so I wasn't confronted much with how to use it. All I had room for were the essentials.

And then I got a teaching job.

I could finally tithe and save, so I was committed to figuring that out. I had been so formed by those late-night chats during college that I already had a strong sense of stewardship. *Money needs to be something I hold loosely. Because I belong to God, my money belongs to God, therefore it is ultimately not my own. I cannot love money, but I need to spend and save it responsibly and carefully. Most of us here in the U.S. use more of it than we really need to for fulfilled living. Others in the world need some of the resources that I have such easy access to.* These were, and still are, the bedrocks of my financial philosophy.

In college, I learned of John Wesley's profoundly simple directive to "Make all you can, save all you can, give all you can." I had certainly inherited the "make all you can" messages from general U.S. society and culture, but I was being challenged constantly to bring these concepts together and maximize the money I'd someday make to truly save and give it away. Another college revelation was how much Jesus talks about money. Friends and I actually counted up and compared his statements and lessons about money against all his other sentiments. His words became my compass for navigating my way through thoughts and decisions about money. Obviously, money is a big deal. Jesus gets that, and he wants us to recognize its complexities. It has personal and public impact. It both is in our power to control and has the power to control us. There is enough of it, but not everyone has access to it.

I am captivated by Jesus' words in Matthew: "For where your treasure is, there your heart will be also. . . . No one can serve two masters, for either he will hate the one and love the other, or he will be devoted to the one and despise the other. You cannot serve God and money" (Matthew 6:21, 24). I am both challenged and comforted by Jesus' command to "Take care, and be on your guard against all covetousness, for one's life does not consist in the abundance of his possessions" (Luke 12:15), and epistle reminders that "the love of money is a root of all kinds of evil" (1 Timothy 6:10) and to "Keep your life free from love of money, and be content with what you have, for he has said, 'I will never leave you nor forsake you'" (Hebrews 13:5). I'm committed to practice generosity and help those in need as I'm guided by the following scriptures: "If a brother or sister is poorly clothed and lacking in daily food, and one of you says to them, 'Go in peace, be warmed and filled,' without giving them the things needed for the body, what good is that?" (James 2:15–16); "In everything I did, I showed you that by this kind of hard work we must help the weak, remembering the words the Lord Jesus himself said: 'It is more blessed to give than to receive'" (Acts 20:35).

As these scriptures and my faith community continue to shape me, I am more empowered to make wise and compassionate decisions with my money. This is the heart of stewardship: empowerment to make wise and compassionate decisions with money. Stewardship is about caring for yourself and others around you—done through thoughtful analysis of what we own and save, and faithful obedience in giving and spending.

It's dangerously easy—even with protective, careful constraints on how to use the money we have—to let money slip in and out of our hands rather thoughtlessly. This is precisely why constraints are necessary. Without thoughtful consideration of financial priorities and a good amount of soul-searching surrounding the ethics behind those priorities, negative habits slowly creep in. First I rely on credit cards for just this *one* purchase . . . then forget to shift money into savings before spending the whole paycheck . . . then promise myself I'll double my lagging tithes next month. Actions like these morph into patterns that can ultimately make me feel owned by my money, instead of the reverse.

The task of stewardship is to manage the way we interact with money. This involves more than just the particulars of spending and saving money, but also my orientation toward money. The way I view money will determine so much about the way I use it. It's been an essential process in my adult life to return to questions like the one I posed at the beginning: *What is money to me? How much should I keep for myself? What are good and bad ways to spend money? How do I feel about debt? How much do I want to prepare for my future now? How does my faith guide my financial choices?* These questions drive me to look deeper, to ask more of myself about the greater purposes of life and my guiding values.

Each of us will come up with our own set of answers that provide a compass for financial decisions. For some, a desire for future security will affect current investments. Others might apportion more than 10 percent for charity and actively research causes and organizations to donate to. Some will see their money as the vehicle to build a lifestyle that advances their careers. The answers to these questions draw upon our understandings of our faith, calling, obligations, and the state of the world around us. Our money flows out from us in unlimited possibilities, and it is quite a weighty and important exercise to find the best channels for its movement. The moral judgments we assign to monetary categories such as debt, saving, spending, investing, charity, and earning become the foundation from which we know how to move about in the world in extremely practical ways.

After identifying financial goals and priorities, the next obvious matter was how to organize money to actually match my theories. For years I extolled the idea of "living below your means," before I actually whittled down my credit card debt that collected ridiculous interest because of my lazy unwillingness to make some sacrifices for a few months to pay it off.

Throughout my twenties, I felt that my careful spending and thriftiness meant I didn't need to budget. There was always money left over every month, so I must have been doing well enough, right? While I had managed not to get myself in grave financial trouble, I also wasn't funneling that leftover money into anything worthwhile. My checking account grew a little more each month and became a zero-interest savings of sorts. Meanwhile, I was paying the minimum on my student loans and was nowhere closer to my goal of saving up for dreams like adoption, returning to school, or prolonged travel. Realizing this, I called together a group of friends whose financial lives I respected, and we started meeting once a month to discuss our finances and share strategies. After the initial meeting, when I confessed that I hardly budgeted (and they all collectively gasped), they each opened up their tidy Excel spreadsheets, Quickbooks files, and mint.com accounts to show me their budget categories and amounts assigned to each.

This eye-opening evening motivated me to review my fixed and variable expenses. Fixed things were the constants that never changed month-in, month-out. Variables were the kinds of things I could count on spending money on, even though the monthly total would vary. I then broke my monthly take-home income across categories, assigning amounts to each until I could cover all and shift a reasonable amount into savings. It took about three months of tracking my actual spending to see if I was even close. I found I allotted far more for gas than I actually used and severely underestimated how much I spent on gifts. I discovered that though my dining-out category used far more money than my married friends', my lifestyle as a single person had adjusted to accommodate my social needs. Consequently, I consistently undershot my grocery category and used about a fourth of what I initially designated. Tracking each purchase was annoying, honestly. It was time-consuming and required near-daily maintenance. The practice, however, has revolutionized my spending and saving, and the reward has been increased peace surrounding this huge area of adult responsibility.

Tightening up my budget gave me the knowledge and the freedom to begin to imagine a debt-free life. I could see the overall landscape of where each dollar was going, which enabled me to pare down enough to allocate nearly half my monthly income for a year to my creditors. I had carried a small balance with me on my credit card for years, so I set out to pay this down first. From there, I moved to the balance on my car, and recently just paid off my last student loan. This required multiple sacrifices, but I could make them once I knew exactly where I could cut. I turned down entertainment opportunities, brewed coffee at home, moved into a room with much cheaper rent, and set a gift limit. Not only did that year provide me financial freedom from obligatory payments with mounting interest, but I also proved to myself I can live on far less than even I thought possible. Faced with the awareness that I have lived on less, I'm challenged to re-route that hefty monthly amount into new, creative avenues. I am able to give more away and have begun investing my money in profit-yielding ventures that still honor my ethical convictions.

Part of the Christian commitment is to live life together. We are excellent at that when it comes to weddings and funerals, sharing emotional and physical burdens, and opening our homes for hospitality. Concerning bank accounts and salaries, however, just like everybody else, we keep to ourselves. Money is viewed as a private matter, and protecting information from each other is even seen as virtuous. I have tried to expand my notion of stewardship to include careful examining of the movement of my money *with* those I trust and care about. One benefit (and challenge!) of marriage is that partners are forced to deal with each other's attitudes and choices about money. Perspectives naturally have to change as one makes space for the financial priorities of the other. As a single woman, I have found that extending this privileged view to faithful friends gives me new eyes to see my own predicaments and possibilities. We can keep each other accountable to our individual commitments and communal values in relation to money.

Like anything else, what is best for me may not be best for my neighbor. Ultimately, we must seek God's guidance in how we view and use money, tread with humility in these, and recognize that just as we belong to God, so do our bank accounts.

Wholeness and Holiness: Living an Embodied Life

Our thoughts, our memories, our experiences, stress, setbacks, triumphs, our joys and sorrows—as humans, we carry all of these things in our bodies. The most powerful gift we can offer the world is to truly embody our hopes, our dreams, our convictions, right relationships, a healthy sexuality, and bold spirituality. That we not only have bodies but are bodies is essential in developing and maintaining healthful habits for navigating the transitions and challenges of our lives. Our physical practices—what we eat, how we move, how we delight our senses—help shape how we think, love, worship, and act in the world. Life-giving routines and relationships move us forward into fully flourishing. The interconnectedness of our physical, mental, emotional, and spiritual health demonstrates how the pursuit of wholeness is also the pursuit of holiness. How can we best ground ourselves as full members of the body of Christ, as women created in the image of God, so that we can know the freedom that comes from faithfully reflecting on and adequately embodying our deepest beliefs and convictions?

Wonderfully Made or Wonderfully Made Up?

Kristina LaCelle-Peterson

When I was in high school, I had a friend who spent an hour every morning on her hair unless, of course, it didn't turn out and she had to wash it and start all over again to get that perfect look. I thought she was excessively preoccupied with her hair (and she certainly didn't care about sleep as much as I did), but my own efforts to be attractive then were probably a lot more harmful. I used to skip breakfast and run to the bus with a fruit bar in my hand, which my mother assumed I ate on the bus. But I would save it for lunch and often eat nothing else until dinner. For months on end, I ate essentially one meal a day, which often left me dizzy and drained, but I still believed that I needed to lose weight.

Why did I think that? I am sure I was trying to avoid the scorn of the guys in my life who clearly preferred skinny young women, but I also feared the judgment of my girlfriends. I didn't want them to think I was fat, either. We all bought into the idea that thin was better, more beautiful, and really, really important. This meant, of course, that I was never happy with my body. But there were a couple of things that began to change how I thought about beauty and thinness.

Things that got me thinking

I became impatient with how women were portrayed on television and in movies. One time in particular, I was watching a movie on TV with a bunch of my male cousins, and even though I had never minded action films before, this time I was embarrassed and irritated. The men did the thinking. They showed courage, and they were at the center of the drama. They wore shirts, long pants, and even socks and shoes. The one woman

173

in the film, on the other hand, wore a mini-bikini and high heels, and she usually appeared leaning on a man's arm or throwing flirty glances. It made me angry: Why is she so helpless and so ridiculously underdressed for the setting? Can it really be true that her part in this movie is just to show off her perfectly skinny body? Is that what a woman's role is in a larger sense, just to look thin and sexy and to be some guy's lover while men handle the rest of life?

These were troubling questions for me, because I wanted to do something meaningful with my life but at the same time found it hard to struggle against the idea that I needed to be thin and beautiful in order to be valued. This was a message I received from high school culture, but it was also perpetrated by the media, and even though I didn't watch four hours of television a day like the average American, I was still affected by the images of perfect women I saw in shows and commercials. Later I learned that I wasn't the only one, that millions of American women have a horrible body image because they compare themselves to what they see on TV and don't measure up.

Of course, we can't possibly measure up because the ideals aren't even real; we are constantly bombarded with images of air-brushed, surgically altered, or even digitally created images of women, not real women. And then the whole advertising industry came at my adolescent insecurities with messages of "You're not thin enough, your hair isn't shiny enough, your lashes aren't full enough, your breath isn't fresh enough, but if you buy this product you will be sexy, beautiful, happy." I began to realize that the industry is all about making us feel that we are lacking so that we will buy more products, which not only does make us buy things, but also has the side effect of making us more dissatisfied with ourselves.

A book, *The Obsession: Reflections on the Tyranny of Slenderness*, also helped me rethink my conception of my body. Kim Chernin asks a couple of basic questions that pushed my thinking in a whole new direction: Why do so many women hate their bodies, and particularly those aspects of their bodies that allow them to carry and bear children? Why wouldn't we celebrate broad hips and solid thighs as signs of the wonderful capability of bearing new life into the world? Why is it a given that women should always try to take up less space in this world? The dieting industry has largely targeted women with the message of reduce, reduce, reduce. The cosmetic surgery interventions to alter body size are also predominantly performed on women. And women's clothing is often advertised with signs such as "Look ten pounds thinner." Women in this culture are told in a million different ways that they should be smaller than they are. Is it that we are taught to look young and dependent for our entire adult lives, instead of taking ourselves seriously as partners in the human project?

These questions helped me take a step back and think about my own strivings to make my body a certain size and shape. I began to see my body as a place to express myself, rather than simply a medium for slavishly following cultural messages.

What my church said about bodies

Did my church have anything helpful to say? Well, no, not really. I mean, I learned about the verse in Psalm 139 that says I am "fearfully and wonderfully made," and it did inspire some feelings of gratitude about my body. Other than that, though, the church seemed just to repeat what the culture said. One older Christian woman told me I should always take care to look nice in order to honor God. But that seemed like very strange advice to me. Did God really care if I wore stylish clothes or makeup? Unlikely. Even then, it seemed to me that the Bible had more to say against vanity than it did about the importance of achieving beauty ideals.

More recently, one of my friends told me about her daughter's Wednesday night Bible instructor, who was teaching fifth grade girls how to put on makeup. The main lesson for the evening was, God doesn't want you to be ugly. This sounds more like *Teen* magazine than the Bible. The Bible never instructs us to try to match our society's beauty standards. It teaches that we are already beautiful in God's eyes. After all, God made us and pronounced us very good. Or in the words of my friend to her daughter's Bible teacher: "God doesn't want them to find ways to be beautiful; God already MADE them beautiful."

Some churches put too high a value on physical attractiveness, just as the culture does. But at the other end of the spectrum are Christian groups that devalue appearance. In fact, they seem afraid of bodies. They generally want their women to wear long sleeves, long skirts, and their hair pulled into a bun. This is not because they deem the body so beautiful that it doesn't need adornment, but because they think the body isn't worth adorning. Or, probably more to the point, they view women's beauty as a distraction to men's spirituality.

We had a little bit of that attitude in my church as well. In youth group, I received a lot of messages about girls being careful about what they wore because they would cause the guys to stumble. Sure, modesty is important, and so is dressing appropriately for the setting. But this all didn't seem fair, because the boys were never given any sort of lecture about their attire, as if the girls couldn't be distracted by boys' bodies. Why didn't anyone take our sexual desires into consideration? In addition, we were always told that girls had to be the gatekeepers in a dating relationship, the ones who didn't let the physical expressions of affection go "too far." It all added up to a picture of teenage boys (and men) as helpless before their sex drives, which good girls had to control by dressing modestly and by being the responsible ones in romance. At the time I bought this message to some extent, but now I think it is a terrifically insulting picture of men. They are not, after all, animals with uncontrollable desires. They are human beings with choice. To say that men just can't help themselves is ridiculous. And this creates an unhealthy picture of women, because it makes them responsible for men's sexuality and ignores the fact that they have sexual desires as well. Even the ancient writer of the *Song of Songs* could recognize and celebrate female sexual desire.

The church gave me two opposite messages: God wants you to be beautiful, so make sure you try to be. And your attractiveness is dangerous to men, so be careful not to cause them temptation.

A few thoughts from the Bible

Does the Bible actually teach this? No. While reading the Bible with these churchly instructions in mind, I noticed a few interesting things. The Bible is not silent about appearances; we hear of beautiful women, such as Sarah, Rebekah, and Rachel, and handsome men, such as Saul and David. But at the same time, the Bible stories do not leave the impression that these individuals' appearances are their most important features or the reasons for their places in the stories. Even Esther, who is put in a king's harem because of her beauty, is in the end commended for her courage, her decision to risk her life for the sake of her people. In the New Testament, women's physical characteristics are not described at all. Neither are men's, for that matter, except for Zacchaeus being vertically challenged. Nowhere are women (or men) instructed to look beautiful for God.

I thought the Bible would have a lot to say about the danger of women's sexual attractiveness, since the church sure did. But there is shockingly little. In the Old Testament, Joseph is seduced by his master's wife (Genesis 39), and in the early chapters of Proverbs a mother and father instruct their young son to avoid the wiles of the loose woman, but there is nothing like that in the New Testament at all. And here's what really strikes me: When we look at Jesus' interactions with women, we don't see any of this. We never see Jesus treating women as if they were too dangerous to interact with. Even when a prostitute shows up at a dinner party in Luke 7, Jesus doesn't pull away from her touch, afraid of being seduced. He recognizes her sexuality, but he doesn't see it as the only important thing about her. He knows her sexual history, but he doesn't allow that to define who she is. He doesn't reduce her to her sexuality, and he treats her as a full person.

I always wished Christians would follow Jesus on this one. It frustrates me to be treated as "just a woman," especially in situations where my gender has nothing to do with anything. When I was in seminary in my mid-twenties, I loved my theology courses because of all the new ideas I was exposed to. What I wanted most was to talk to people about what I was learning, but more than once when I sat down at the lunch table where my classmates were having an intense theological conversation, someone would turn to me and make a comment like, "My, don't you look nice today." If I tried to throw in my own theological musings, they would wait for me to finish but continue the conversation between them as if I hadn't spoken. Many of my fellow seminarians simply could not have a discussion about ideas with a woman. One guy even said that to me outright: "I have never had a theological conversation with a woman before." Two thousand years ago Jesus had theological conversations with women, and you think it is a novelty?! Think about the woman at the well (John 4), Mary learning at his feet (Luke 10), Martha and then Mary after their brother died (John 11), women as the first recipients of the news of Jesus' resurrection, and even women as leaders in the early church.

I am a whole person with a mind, a spirit, a body, created by God. I am not "just a woman" who measures up or doesn't measure up to someone's particular ideas of femininity. My classmate's comment was simply a Christianized version of society's habit of valuing women primarily by their sexiness quotient. Either way, women are reduced to something much smaller than human personhood when they are valued only for sexual attractiveness and/or gender role compliance. And the problem for women when we internalize this value system, when we judge ourselves on our looks or on our ability to meet femininity standards, is that we devalue all the other wonderful things about ourselves. What about that artistic flair, the quick wit, the poet's soul, the merciful heart?

There is further the serious problem of violence against women in our society. Once people are valued solely on the basis of their bodies, they have been dehumanized, reduced to the status of object. Once people have been dehumanized, any type of violence seems justifiable. This is the root of the vast and growing problem of sex slavery in the world and in this country. The humanity of children and women is forgotten. The particular aspects of their personhood, even their preferences for tomato soup or soft pink slippers, are completely ignored—all that matters are the ways in which they can fulfill the needs and desires of others.

As Christians, we take our cues from Jesus, who remembered the humanity of the women before him. People didn't have to be beautiful, rich, powerful, disease-free, one particular race, or even male to be treated well by Jesus, because all those categories turn out to be meaningless. I have been learning, when I assess myself in front of the mirror, to remember that beauty and thinness are not the ultimate categories. Rather, I am a full and complex human being made in the image of God. (Saying that every morning a number of times might be a good discipline to start the day!)

And if beauty and thinness are not primary determiners, then overemphasis on our looks and bodies can lead to a focus on ourselves that is not particularly healthy, or even Christian. Should our lives really be about us all the time? Should we really spend enormous amounts of time, energy, and money trying to live up to the beauty ideals in our culture that are unattainable anyway? We know that God does not expect that of us, or even want that for us. God gave us bodies, and created us as embodied beings, so that we might enjoy life in them.

Enjoying our bodies

That very phrase, "enjoying our bodies," would have sounded hedonistic and not terribly Christian to me earlier in my life. I think this attitude came from a misunderstanding of the language of "flesh" in the Bible. When I was young, I had the impression that flesh was bad and spirit was good. After all, there were "sins of the flesh," and there is a war between flesh and spirit described in Romans 7. When I finally sat down to look at the text on my own, I was shocked to discover that the war is not between my flesh and my spirit, but between the flesh and the Spirit. It is not the physical part of me at war with the spiritual part, "the spirit is willing but the flesh is weak" applied to all of life. Rather it is my flesh—my old sinful nature— at war with the things of God, the Spirit. The writers of Scripture never encourage us to hate our bodies or to think of being at war with our bodies. Instead they remind us that our fallen, broken nature struggles against the Spirit of God who wants to reorient us—body, mind, spirit—to the things of God. The Bible calls us to reject our sinful desires, but it never calls us to despise our bodies. We are supposed to care for them and use them well as members of the body of Christ and temples of the Holy Spirit.

The other reason I couldn't really embrace the thought of "enjoying my body" was that I thought Christianity was all about spiritual things. Growing up in the church, I had a hyper-spiritualized idea about faith. But embodiment is central to the Christian story. God created us with bodies and declared us very good. Then Jesus as the Son of God became human flesh. This is a huge compliment to us all, because it suggests that God, rather than being afraid of or disgusted by bodies, actually joined us in embodied existence. Jesus had to grow up like a normal kid and do mundane things like eat and rest after a long walk. He was executed in an excruciatingly painful way and then he was raised—his body was raised, the tomb was empty—and now he has promised to raise our bodies as well. His body was taken up into heaven, where we will eventually join him in our own new bodies. In the meantime, we are instructed to engage in the Lord's Supper or Eucharist, a celebration of Jesus' body using physical symbols. This is not a body-denying story. It is a body-affirming story.

In addition to overcoming the thought that bodies were somehow bad, or at least unimportant, I had to embrace much more consciously the idea that bodies, and particularly my female body, is good in God's eyes. After God created the human race, Genesis says, "God saw that it was very good." I had to recognize that everything about me could please God, which was not easy. Somehow it was obvious that God would treasure our hearts, which are capable of love, and our minds, which are capable of creativity and rational thought. It was strange to think about God valuing our bodies and, specifically, *my* body. These amazing bodies, capable of expressing love and creativity as well as enjoying the stunning world around us, *are* delightful to God.

In fact, I began to see that it is as a body that I know God. I suddenly saw how many of the Psalms use our experiences of nature (through our physical senses) as reminders to worship God. I found myself drawn to the prayers of ancient Celtic Christians, who allowed all the aspects of nature to draw them to God: the wind blowing against their faces, the sun warming their shoulders, the greening of the fields in spring, the thunder of the waves at the ocean's shore. I realized that it is as a body that I come to worship God.

When I finally believed deeply that God created me with this amazing body (and as I studied human anatomy in a college bio class, the incredibly complicated systems of our bodies helped me see just how amazing this body is), I could relax. I could simply enjoy my embodied experiences, even those that don't necessarily lead to worship: skiing in the Alps, singing harmony with a friend in an empty cathedral, kissing the soft head of a baby, throwing a Frisbee, smelling a rose just after it opens. I no longer feel guilty for these simple pleasures, nor do I spiritualize them in order to make them acceptable to God. All of them already are gifts from God.

In this context I can engage in exercise as a means of enjoying physical strength and skill, or at the very least, as a means of keeping my heart healthy and muscles strong. I want to be a good steward of the body God has given me, regardless of whether I have abs of steel that anyone can notice. (Full disclosure: It still would be nice to have people notice how fit and trim I am, but it just doesn't matter the way it used to.) For me, exercise has always been intrinsically enjoyable, though more so now that I don't expect it to sculpt my body into something it could never be.

I believe sexuality is also one of the ways I have been learning to enjoy my body, but never the only way, not even the dominant one. It is one more wonderful aspect of being human. When we have a healthy sense of our bodies as part of the complex of the whole person we are, we will not value ourselves (or others) on this one aspect of life alone, but rather we will see our sexuality or our sexual attractiveness as a component of our identity. In the same way, sexual expression will be part of the whole range of our interactions with people. Since God created us as integrated beings, sex belongs in the context of one whole person expressing love to another whole person, which is why it is best in marriage, where people have pledged themselves to one another. When we come at sexuality as whole people, rather than thinking of it as something we do with our bodies, we are much less likely to engage in self-gratifying (read selfish), damaging sex.

Conclusion

There are no real instructions in the Bible about how we should present our physical selves in any particular way to please God. I don't think God cares whether or not women wear makeup, gain five pounds, or dye their hair. Piercing your nose or getting a third tattoo may even be a healthy thing, a way to say, I am enjoying this body. (Of course, this might be done out of insecurity or to spite parents, but this is more about motives than whether the action itself is good or bad.) Maybe, just maybe, God is delighted when we take delight in our bodies—after all, they are gifts from God.

I am grateful for all the ways in which I can embrace the idea that "I am fearfully and wonderfully made" with more and more of my whole self.

I am thankful for the beautiful diversity of looks and body types that God created in the human race, and I long for the day when all of us love our bodies even if they don't fit a narrowly prescribed cultural ideal. I hope for that time when, without devaluing our physical selves, we learn to embrace all the gifts we have been given as complex human beings and use them well as we join in Christ's work in the world.

Gratuitous Sex within the Reign of God: A Gift that Grounds and Transcends

Heather Ross

About a year and a half after my son, my second child, was born, I really began to have true doubts about my mental health. It's not like until that time everything had been smooth sailing in the old noggin.' But in the midst of caring for his older sister, then three-years-old—who was constantly sick owing to her love of the preschool ritual of placing disgusting, cold-virus-slathered toys into her mouth—and teaching full-time on no sleep, I was not entirely at my mental best. I had, just the year before, begun to teach philosophy at a liberal-arts university—not the kind of employment one can just coast through. We had moved across the country for my job and knew almost no one. I had a couple of kids, and not just kids, but toddlers, for goodness' sake. A full night's rest was still a year away. My husband and I would pass one another at night like two members of the Flying Dutchman in the Bermuda Triangle—a strange combination of ghost and zombie.

By this time, my son had finally moved into his crib, out of our bed. This was ostensibly an improved situation for my husband and me. Finally, just the two of us, right? Wrong. This forced autonomy did not bring joy into the heart of my communitarian child. He would wake frequently, and upon becoming cognizant of his solitude, would cry out, loudly, for company. My husband and I would dream of a mythical night-nanny who would care for our wakeful little ones while we spent time in bed as we should—sleeping the recommended seven to eight hours every night and having a little romance. Of course, no such nanny exists—or if he or she did, we couldn't afford one—and neither did that fairytaled sleep/romance combination.

All of this bleary-eyed wakefulness resulted in an overall dulling of our spirits and thus our sex lives. The sharpness that comes with enough sleep seemed like a dream—unavailable to us. The years of losing time and sleep to other, more demanding forces left little for my husband and me to share. The very idea that once in bed, the time could be spent doing anything other than crashing unconsciously into oblivious, all-too-brief sleep seemed downright irresponsible.

There was a cruel irony to our infrequent intimacy. At a time when we truly needed the sustaining connectedness with one another that comes with that time spent in physical intimacy, it occurred less and less. The philosopher Georges Bataille gave us one of the best analogies of all time when he wrote, "the sexual act is in time what the tiger is in space." The potency of Bataille's beautiful analogy is both heavy and light. Heavy because of his comparison of sex to a fearsome predator, at home in space. Light because time, where Bataille claims the sexual act resides, is without mass. It is always escaping from memory to anticipation and back again. With the dearth of sex in our marriage then, sex became this fearsome lack. It was something in our past—reduced to memory and only hoped for in the sense that real hope is only for what can't be anticipated. Time does not wait, and yet it is always lying in wait.

As I think back to the difficulty of that time with small children and a new job in a new city, strangely, I can't help but feel an immense and profound gratitude for that difficulty. Having been without the expectation of regular physical intimacy with my husband for quite a long time in my marriage, I have had the benefit of both a new understanding of what sex means and also of being able to live out that difference in my life. I now appreciate, at all levels, that sex is not a foregone conclusion. It is, by its nature, ephemeral and fleeting, and hence a reflection of the most fundamental aspects of our humanity. We are, as human beings—at our best and worst—finite, time-bound creatures. The more we know this and live our lives reflecting that, the more truthful we are about who we are and, more significantly, who we are not. We, my husband and I, can never again pretend that sex is a given. Or perhaps, we see that sex is only given. It is only ever a gift—gratuitous.

To be without regular sexual intimacy is not the same as being without water, food, or sleep. It's not the kind of thing that will kill you. Seriously, you won't die without it. So, I ask, what is it about sex that when it is not happening, for whatever reason, I miss it? Of course there is the obvious aspect of pleasure, and I would be dishonest to leave it out. I mean, I'm an old-fashioned kind of girl and all, but to suggest that sex isn't about enjoyment would be lying. But it is not quite enough to say that I miss the pleasure per se. Whatever the pleasure that goes along with sex turns out to be is an incredibly complex pleasure that can't be separated from the vast web of experiences, desires, fears, memories, and hopes that make up the content of our lives. Desire itself, for anything, doesn't come from nowhere. It is always situated in the context of a life, which, in turn, is situated in time.

To say that sex is an important part of my life, worthy of being missed, and, further, to say that sexuality is an important issue for human beings to address overall, is, for me, to have already placed the question under the purview of what it means to be a Christian. In order for an act, any act at all, to be a good act, it must have its meaning in whatever it means to be a good Christian. What does it mean to say something is Christian? It's not anywhere near enough to say that, by default, because I am a Christian, whatever I do is Christian, like Christian ice-skating or Christian karaoke. Nope. For something to be Christian it must depend, for its meaning, fundamentally and necessarily on the truth that Jesus of Nazareth is God.

What, then, am I talking about if I'm talking about Christian sex? Is that any different than something like Christian bowling? Sadly, the very coexistence of these two words, Christian and sex, can evoke for me images of drudgery, obligation, and prudishness. To attach "Christian" to the idea of sexuality might seem to take the joy and vitality right out of the act. And to connect "sexuality" to the word "Christian" runs the risk of trivializing whatever it means to be truly Christian by reducing it to self-help or worse, self-worship. I really want to avoid equating the word Christian with generic ideas of self-satisfaction or happiness. I believe Christian life and action is much more demanding of me than those things. There is a particular potency to the claim that something is a Christian act, and a unique danger that comes with the overuse and trivialization of the word. So the question becomes, what does Christian sexuality have to offer by way of making me live my life in a more Christian way?

To go around asking questions about Christian sex is a dicey affair. It can be dangerous on almost all fronts. For many, the weighty expectations that come with the very notion of sex governed by the logic of good Christian practice are enough to seal otherwise open mouths shut. And often those who do choose to speak say unhelpful things. There are more than a few of these unhelpful specters haunting discussions around Christian sexuality, ranging from worry about the tempting length of someone's skirt all the way to justifications for hate crimes against perceived sexual deviants. The church may give young women positive reasons to avoid promiscuity, but it may also send unintended messages fetishizing virginity. The church is right to critique pornography and sexual objectification of women, reducing them to the sum of their body parts. But an overemphasis on the importance of virginity can be the flip side of the same coin, reducing a woman's value to her body and sexuality in a different way. To be sure, sexuality can be used in sinful and harmful ways. But sexual immorality is one of many possible sins, not the sole criterion of a woman's spiritual worth. An all-or-nothing approach to any level of sexual activity may instill fear, guilt, or repression about healthy desire and pleasure. Moving from forbidden taboo to celebrated good in the space of one short wedding ceremony may be a difficult psychological or physiological transition for some women; inhibitions that once seemed to protect purity may remain barriers to intimacy in marriage. Yet Christians often speak as if those changes will occur immediately and easily, leaving those with different experiences to grapple in silence or shame. It is long since time that Christians actively speak out and think differently than we have previously regarding our existence as human beings, our relationships with those we encounter throughout our lives, and our bodies, the meanings of which have too often been filtered through dominant culture. I have heard intimations all my life that sex itself is a form of depravity. Too often this is propagated by folks in the church. Instead, I'd like to have heard more of the suggestion that sex, like many human actions, is neither a natural edification nor an inherent defilement of Christian purity. Sexuality is a gift that can be used well, or misused horribly.

Sex is as good a place as any to start that process of reimagining life, not by calling us backward to what has been previously, but forward to what could be if we work at it prayerfully. I am wary of any hint that a return to the good old days of yesteryear, when things were supposedly simpler and more pure, is the way to go. I do not buy the fantasy of the so-called ideal family life of my grandparents' generation. Nostalgia for an overly idealized past will rarely aid in any ethical quandary, and least of all in regard to the question of sexuality. In fact, I would like to argue that sex is primarily about the future. It is always about what could be, but is not yet, because desire is about what could be, but is not yet. There is always an aspect of each human life that can and will escape the dominion of both the past and the present. What I have been and what I am keeps on moving as long as I continue to exist. Sex is an event that, at its best, says yes to the openness of that future. Sex does not nail anything down. It does not hold anything in place. It takes whatever boundaries and limits we have had and exceeds them.

In our discussion here on Christian sexuality, it is important to remember that, at its heart, we are dealing with issues of embodiment. This means that while sex is often about strength, it is also about vulnerability. Bodies are always vulnerable to material conditions like the possibility of not having enough to eat, not having access to medical care, environmental hazards, physical violence, warfare, etc. as well as conditions of ideological violence in the form of institutionalized and legal structures. When two people have sex, it's not like what it means to have a car or have the cucumber soup. These images of ownership and consumption, while pervasive in the sexual imagination of many cultures, do not do the act justice. Sex is more like having a party or a wake or having church. So corrupt consumptive desire of another human being, while common, is, in fact, misguided desire. I'm not simply speaking in terms of morality here, either. If one human being wishes to consume another human being in the sexual act or in anything, that wish will inevitably fail to be fulfilled. To want to consume another human being and to actually consume another are two different things. This statement is tethered to the hope that there is always an aspect of each human life that can and will escape the dominion of not only other people, but our own pasts as well. The violence of consumption is the very violence I am called out of as a follower of Jesus. I am called into the repetition of gratitude for what I have been given and, more importantly, what I am able to give away. We are called, as Christians, to offer up vulnerability and power to one another in love, just as these things were offered up by Jesus himself as the ultimate enactment of the reign of God.

Sexual consumptivity as a kind of violence affects women with a particular force. All too often, in so many cultural circumstances all around the world, what it means to be a woman is so pathologized that it can be difficult to imagine what redemption of the idea of "woman" would look like. For me, in my cultural context, the idea that there is an essential part of my being, my identity as a woman, for example, that is timeless and universal and makes me biologically disposed to play with Barbies or enjoy doing laundry like other females is a common assumption. This, however, does not clarify the issue for me. It does not make my life make more sense or help me become a better wife or mother. Whatever is meant by my set identity as a woman is, for me, a temptation not to have to deal with a difficult issue. The assumption that I already know what it means to be a woman, in advance of being one, too often allows a false sense of security regarding the fundamentals of my life. When the declaration that "I am a woman" becomes a prop rather than doxology, the words take away so much more than they give.

The particularity of my womanhood runs as deep as the particularity of my existence. There is not one part of myself that is left untouched by the fact that I am a woman, just as there is no part of me that is not human, or the daughter of my mother or beloved by God. There is no aspect of my womanhood that is left untouched by who I am. I am certainly not claiming that it doesn't matter that I have the biology that I do or that I have the letter F on my driver's license. These things matter quite a lot. It also matters quite a lot that I think of myself as a woman and that I identify myself in that way fairly often. And surely my own sexuality cannot be divorced from the truth that I am a woman, and yet it does not prescribe, before the fact, what that means. More often than not, the content or meaning of the word woman eludes me. When I am honest about the question of what it means for me to be a woman, I am more troubled than quieted. The answer to that question not only escapes me continually, but the very prospect of an answer is a temptation to put to rest what should never be.

So, then, what is Christian sexuality? This will always remain a question for me as long as I give it the serious consideration it deserves. I can tell you, though, that I am grateful for it in my life, for what it reminds me about the constant slipping away of time, my own finitude, about how little I know about who I am and how much more there is to know about who my husband is and will be. I am grateful for the lives of my children and the abundance of their futures that could not have been without the felicitous acts of love that preceded them. In my life, sex is gratuitous. It is not necessary, it does not have to be, and yet it is—from time to time. I would say that sex is our, my husband and my, own impossible desire to overcome the difference between us—to overcome our individualization. It is our prayer to reject the fate that determines that "we all die alone" while, at the same time, affirming that very thing. It is the quest to slow the onslaught of time while inhabiting the moment of the event itself in time. Sex happens, and there is no discernable beginning of that happening. It stretches out and back through the worlds that gave us life—finally coming to rest at the edge of the world's first moment. That moment, as the singular act of first creation, is that moment of grace that found its way into the event itself—impossibly distant and yet so. Sex happens, and then it is done. My husband and I joke that we should quit wasting our time doing anything else. But truthfully, the event never really ends. It propels our lives forward into the openness of our future together—more together than we were before and less than we will be later.

Sheep among Wolves

Jenell Williams Paris

Behold, I send you out as sheep in the midst of wolves; so be shrewd as serpents and innocent as doves. Matthew 10:16 (NASV)

"What do you think I should do?" Sarah asked me. She explained that she and her husband, Mike, both lovely, thriving, recent Christian college graduates, had attended a church event with another couple, Kevin and Michelle.[1] At the event, Kevin took Sarah aside and said he sensed a connection between them. He asked if he could call her sometime to see where things might lead. He promised not to tell Michelle and asked Sarah to keep the secret from Mike. She told Mike within the hour.

Sarah said she and her husband were united in alarm and disgust, but also in uncertainty about how to respond. Kevin and Mike are pastors in the same small town, she explained. Mike knows Kevin has a reputation for this kind of behavior, but complaints against him have never stuck. Kevin's father has clout in the local religious community and has protected Kevin thus far. If Sarah politely declines Kevin's offer and pretends to keep it secret, Kevin will likely repeat his offense with someone else. But if she tells, would any good come of it? A formal charge could easily slide right off Kevin, and the backlash could harm Mike's ministry and their family's livelihood.

Sarah also began to wonder why this ever happened. She said to me, "I never sensed a connection with this man. I hardly ever made eye contact with him! But did I somehow send a signal? Did I ask for this?" And, with no vanity whatsoever, she wondered, "Is it my fault because I'm beautiful?"

---

1   Throughout the essay, names and identifying details have been changed to protect privacy.

"Now Sarah, you earned an A in my anthropology class," I gently teased, trying to ease the weight of her questions. "Surely you remember the discussion about the anthropology of sexual violence, how our culture legitimizes sexual misdoings with the belief that women's irresistible sexuality diminishes male responsibility."

"Oh, right," she said with a slight smile. "Everything relates to anthropology."

"And besides," I said, "a wolf on the hunt is hoping to satisfy his hunger, not gaze on the beauty of the prey. This wasn't your fault; you just happened to be there."

§

Sarah's story brought to mind a time when I, too, just happened to be there. When I was a teenager, a fifty-year-old married pastor said he sensed a connection between us. Unlike Sarah, I took the bait. For several years, into my early twenties, he and I studied God's Word together, prayed, and discussed our spiritual lives. I considered him one of my most important mentors. We almost always met behind closed doors. We gazed into each other's eyes, and he confided his struggles with aging, marriage, and ministry. I believed what he said—that I was exceptional, and that I "got" him in a way no one else did. Once I started to ask him, "This thing between us—do you think it's wrong?"

"Shh," he interrupted. "Let's not talk about it, or it might go away."

It was never physical, not even a little bit, so our intimacy didn't seem to really break any rules. Growing up as a conservative Christian, I had learned that sexual purity meant sexual intercourse was restricted to marriage. And toward that end, any stimulating physical touch (including dancing) should be avoided. Indulging in sexual chemistry with a married pastor intuitively seemed wrong, but it didn't exactly break the rule. I had also learned that by virtue of his age, gender, and profession, he had biblical authority in our relationship. Who was I to question a male pastor?

Eventually I moved away and moved on. Years later, I learned the full story. Turns out I was one among many "special" young women who cycled through this man's life. When one singular young woman grew up or wised up, he found another. Complaints were raised against him, but, like Kevin, he had connections with influential men who protected him. I heard complainants (women all, as far as I know) labeled angry and manipulative, their stories minimized or dismissed altogether.

That is, until she appeared. Like many biblical heroines, her name isn't part of the public record. When this young woman saw she was being used, she didn't get weepy—she got a lawyer. Though the pastor offered her concessions and tried to diminish her reputation in the community, she stuck to her story. He was fired.

When I heard about the whistleblower, I felt ashamed. Why hadn't I spoken out as she did? If I had, it could have protected other women, including her. I hadn't because I couldn't. A tranquilizing mix of shame ("It's my fault for attracting him") and loyalty ("He'd be upset if I told") kept me silent, unable to admit even to myself that I had been used.

When the intimacies of the whistleblower's relationship with the pastor were aired publicly, I felt an irresistible urge to revisit mine. One evening, with dinner dishes unwashed and three children left to be bathed by their father, I found myself rifling through boxes in the basement storage closet. I read old notes and letters I'd exchanged with my pastor—the originals of his, and first and second drafts of mine. I shamed myself, thinking, *You're a middle-aged fool. Fool for reading these. Fool for saving them. Fool for ever having written them.* My writings were painstakingly set forth, daisy chains of emotional melodrama tied to sophomoric wisdom tied to U2 lyrics. His were composed with careful innuendo and double entendre. What was true of our writing—his crafted, mine naïve—was true of us as individuals at that time.

I remembered my conversation with Sarah. It had taken me seconds to speak this truth to Sarah, but nearly twenty years to say it to myself: *It's okay. You weren't the fool. It wasn't your fault.*

§

So tame, these stories. No sex at all; not even a kiss or a fondle. Our stories may be tame, but they echo the moans, wails, and gasps that provide the soundtrack for full-blown sexual scandals. Each story I've heard about in my circles is uniquely atrocious, but also so common it could have happened anywhere. A boy commits suicide, and his family later discovers he was being raped by their pastor. A man is abandoned and devastated after his wife pursues an affair with a member of their church. A youth pastor leaves the church in disgrace when his pornography addiction is revealed. Numerous children complain about sexual advances made against them by a church leader, and it takes years for authority figures to take them seriously.

Other stories are known nationally. Jim Bakker paid Jessica Hahn to downgrade her rape charge against him. Jimmy Swaggart paid women for sex. Ted Haggard lied to his family and church to pursue sex and drugs. These examples are all from Protestant churches, but the Catholic Church has also been scandalized for harboring priests and nuns who sexually abuse children.

There are plenty of juicy bits in the Bible, too. Abraham disguised his wife as his sister and gave her to a king for sexual use. Just because he wanted to, King David had sex with Bathsheba, the wife of another man. David's son Amnon raped his half-sister Tamar. The Levite threw his wife (or concubine) out to be sexually abused and murdered by a group of strangers.

Maybe leaders like Bakker, Swaggart, or Haggard, or Abraham or David, or Kevin or my pastor, believe they are doing Jesus' work, but find it to be anything but a light burden with an easy yoke. Instead of rest for their souls, they find an anxious need in their bodies for a little something on the side. Maybe they think they deserve it. My pastor may have thought a teensy compromise of marital fidelity was a price worth paying; special young women energized him to persevere in ministry. Abraham feared the king would kill him; by risking his wife's life and his marriage's fidelity, he saved his own life so he could proceed with the promise God had given him. Maybe building God's kingdom can become like building any other. Construction projects incur collateral damage—heaps of broken bricks, piles of scrap metal, and dust in the air. In what all too often passes for God's kingdom, that damage takes the form of mistreated people. Children are vulnerable, simply by virtue of their age. Women are vulnerable, not only because they are often physically weaker than men, but because in many Christian settings, deference and subordination are seen as God-ordained feminine traits. Although such beliefs distort the true value of women created in the image of God, they make women especially vulnerable to sexual harassment or abuse that is perpetrated by religious leaders. Boys and men are sometimes vulnerable, too; some perpetrators, even, are repeating abusive practices that were forced on them at an earlier point.

§

I once believed sexual purity was about being innocent as a dove, the virtuous woman wings away from sexual sin. I still believe that is right and good, but I also believe that Jesus knew there's more to being a godly woman than just preening lily-white feathers. I'm still learning the shrewdness of the serpent: to keep my beady eyes open for predators, to spit and hiss when endangered, and when danger gets too close, to sink in my teeth. This could mean telling the truth to a loved one, as Sarah did with Mike, or pursuing justice through the courts, as the whistleblower did against my former pastor. It could mean standing up for vulnerable people, despite the personal cost. For me, it means telling my story and sharing its wisdom with young women such as Sarah, helping them become bolder and stronger than I once was. When even the shepherd turns out to be a wolf in disguise, it's time for the sheep to wise up.

Nurturing Body and Soul
Janell Lundgren

"[The] bias against the natural body [encourages] women to turn their attentions to a constant monitoring of body, thereby robbing them of deeper and finer relationships with their given form. Angst about the body robs a woman in some large share of her creative life and her attention to other things."

—Clarissa Pinkola Estés, *Women Who Run with the Wolves*[1]

Holistic Living: Embracing the Whole

Whether we love and take care of them or not, our bodies are what we have to carry us through our lives. We are spiritual beings having a physical experience. In many ways, we exist outside of and beyond our bodies. And yet our bodies are an inextricable part of our experience of being alive. We have so much to learn from our bodies, so much to express, encounter, and experience through them. Our bodies are the way we interface with reality, the way our spirits are manifest in the world. If we desire to live lives full of vitality, then creating healthy habits and a holistic way of living is how we take care of our precious bodies so that we live life at its most abundant, as Christ promised in John 10:10.

I first became interested in nutrition and healthy living when I discovered that we can actually prevent illness as we grow older through the choices we make today. We live in a country where healthcare is viewed as a variety of reactive measures to be taken after someone has already become ill. And it is likely that those reactive measures will have to do more with operations or medication than with changes in lifestyle and food choices, although this is slowly changing. Most American doctors do not receive

---

1   From *Women Who Run with the Wolves,* copyright © 1992, 1995, by Clarissa Pinkola Estés, Ph.D. Used by permission of Ballantine, a division of Random House, Inc.

more than, at best, a single course concerning food and its power to heal the body during all their years of medical school. [2]

This heavy reliance on reactive treatment through expensive medicines and surgical procedures is not the case in many other countries around the world. In parts of Europe, it is a widely respected and commonly observed practice for employees to take up to several weeks' vacation at a mineral hot springs for personal wellness and prevention of stress-related diseases and conditions. In Asia not so long ago, doctors received payment for their services only as long as their patients remained healthy. The community expected them to *prevent* disease and illness rather than simply treat it after the fact. Imagine what a difference this kind of mindset could make. Imagine what a different life we all would live if we practiced preventive healthcare throughout our lifetimes in the daily choices we make around food and lifestyle. I began to imagine living to the ripe old age of 100 without losing my mind, my breasts, or my mobility.

Preventive healthcare has become one key for me in living a vibrant and vivacious life. Practicing preventive healthcare means I have to listen to my body's messages. It means learning to slow down and rest *before* I get sick, and making small daily choices that support my greatest health and highest happiness.

The term "holistic" has acquired a number of connotations and interpretations, but at its core, it means to take the "whole" into consideration: the whole person, the whole situation, the whole system. Rather than treating our bodies or our lives like a set of unrelated parts, we learn to look at the whole picture and begin to understand how things are connected. We understand that what we ate for lunch today has its own part to play in affecting what kind of mood we'll be in this afternoon, and whether we come down with a cold this evening. But so does that argument we might have had with our boyfriend or the moments we took this morning to still our minds and pray.

Holistic health is about paying attention to all areas of our lives, including work, relationships, spirituality, creativity, and physical activity. Nourishment is a two-way street. The foods we eat play a major role in our ability to be fully engaged in our lives. When we're eating well, our bodies grow strong and vibrant, and we can bring ourselves fully to the things we are most passionate about. However, we're more apt to make healthier food choices when we love the life we're living and we aren't using food

---

2   Clifford Lo, "Integrating Nutrition as a Theme throughout the Medical School Curriculum," *American Journal of Clinical Nutrition* 72.3 (2000): 882s–89s.

to numb out at a stressful job or avoid an unhappy relationship. To live truly inspired, healthy and fulfilling lives, our food and life choices must symbiotically work together to nourish us.

My Story: A Sordid Tale of Self-Love

Despite the constricting messages of stereotypical beauty so prevalent in our culture, several years ago I began to notice an exquisite contradiction. The women in my own life seemed to be beautiful, not despite their so-called "imperfections," but because of them. This epiphany slowly permeated my views of myself, and I came to believe that I am no exception—my beauty comes no less from my pear-shaped frame, gapped front teeth, and the mole on my lip than from my more stereotypically beautiful traits. But I did not start out in this enlightened, self-embracing way.

My relationship with my body image and food began long before this on a day when, at age twelve, I stayed home to baby-sit for the first time by myself. I had never been alone and in charge before, and I was terrified. I sat on the couch in the living room and listened for every unusual sound, any hint that someone was about to break into the house and kidnap us all. But soon I began to see the upside of being on my own: I could do things without my parents finding out. As my first foray into this newfound freedom, I decided to scour the kitchen cupboards for candy, cookies, and any sweet thing I could get my hands on. Sweets, in particular, were a coveted food in my house, and very closely monitored. I began to smuggle and hide them at every opportunity. I ate them in secret after dark or as a source of comfort on especially difficult days. I stuffed myself until my stomach hurt. And so began my compulsive behavior around food.

As I got older, my obsession with food only grew stronger, and when I entered college it developed into a wild and untamable monster. College was a time of stress, intensity, and change for me. I made a lot of good friends. I loved my classes. I fell in love with travel and the man I planned to marry. But I also faced a maelstrom of earth-shattering transitions. My faith underwent a painful questioning process that ultimately transformed it forever. As a university student on the West Coast, I compared my body to the Southern California standard—the super-thin, yet curvy, tanned, athletic beach babe—and never measured up. I felt overwhelmed with my responsibilities as a student and as a privileged American woman in a world filled with poverty, racism, sexism, and environmental destruction. I felt a strong sense of calling and obligation to spend my life serving God by working toward healing, social justice, and sustainability on a global scale, but I had no idea where to start. I went through long periods of depression, unable to pray or socialize or even get out of bed on some days.

From the outside, I seemed like a normal, if somewhat intense, student. But on the inside I wasn't dealing with all the pressure very well. I watched with one eye shut as my growing food addiction erupted into a full-blown eating disorder. I started bingeing in a whirlwind, out-of-control way. Whenever I felt despairing and anxious about school, relationships, or my current image in the mirror, I would eat everything I could get my hands on. I could not stop even when I was thoroughly bloated and sick. Food became a twisted sort of comfort to me. It was my outlet as well as my reward. It gave me a private way to express my internal chaos while flying under the public radar.

I didn't know at the time that I had an eating disorder. I knew about anorexia and bulimia, but I wasn't purging or starving myself, so I didn't fit into those categories. Years later I would learn the name for my behavior— compulsive eating disorder. But at the time I didn't have any language for it, and I didn't know where to turn to get help.

What I did know was that I had *disordered eating*. Beyond the narrow clinical definitions of eating disorders, there is a lot of disordered eating in our culture. Many women, and a growing number of men, develop unhealthy, imbalanced relationships with food as a result of our image-obsessed culture or the stresses of life but can't find the ways to move forward and free themselves. Caught in this vicious cycle, I began to seek ways to deal with my addiction. I brought piles of books home from the library. I joined a support group for women who struggled with food. I watched a video presentation about the manipulation of women and their body image through the media and advertising industries. Some of these things helped in their own limited ways, but life barreled on and my disordered eating continued to wax and wane.

The turning point came the spring I graduated from college alongside the man I was planning to marry that summer. Through an excruciating discernment process, we decided to break up, and I was catapulted into a year of intense solitude and grieving. I suddenly found myself standing amid the rubble of my carefully planned future and realized I had hit rock bottom. I also discovered that I had become a bit overzealous and arrogant in my assumption that I could perpetually give of myself to help and heal others when I couldn't even take care of myself.

Unable to manage much of anything else, I began a long process of learning self-care as I started to take my own healing seriously. I began to listen to my body and its natural cycles of hunger and satiety. I started to take seriously the idea that my body is a temple where God's Spirit dwells (1 Corinthians 3:16), and slowly, many parts of me died and were reborn as my relationships to my body, my self, and others were transformed. As more and more aspects of my life came into balance, my disordered eating gradually subsided. I didn't need to use food anymore to fill the aching voids in my life because I was learning to fill them with their proper inhabitants. Loving relationships filled the well of loneliness. Anger was released through kick-boxing and long walks on wintry nights. Depression was channeled into creative projects and candlelit baths. And my longing to make a difference in the world eventually found its expression in a newly emerging career path.

I decided to attend a holistic nutrition school, where I was immersed in a community of love, wellness, and a shared passion for fabulous food. I reconnected with my body and began to trust my intuition again. I experimented and played with my food. I came to love the skin I'm in— this beautiful body that faithfully carries me through each day. I decided to be my own best friend instead of my own worst enemy and developed a stubborn loyalty to myself along with a fierce protection of my most vulnerable places. Over time, I developed the skills to help others to draw on the innate wisdom they also possess that will carry them into a life of health and joy. Now I make a living by guiding and supporting people to rediscover balance, energy, and vitality in their lives by healing their relationships to food and creating the fulfilling lives they dream of.

I have also learned that the foods we choose to put on our tables have significant personal, spiritual, cultural, political, and economic implications. As Frances Moore Lappé writes in *Hope's Edge*, "Food is about more than fueling our bodies. Embedded in family life and in cultural and religious ritual, food has always been our most direct, intimate tie to a nurturing earth as well as a primary means of bonding with each other. Food has helped us know *where* we are and *who* we are."[3] At the center of Christian community practices, the Eucharist remains the primary ritual for reminding us of who we are and of how we are to live. Through the elements of bread and wine, the body and blood of Christ, and the simple act of eating and drinking at the Lord's table, we are made mindful not only of God's faithful provision of daily bread, but are strengthened to become the body of Christ in the world. Through the simple act of eating, we are

---

3   Frances Moore Lappé and Anna Lappé, *Hope's Edge: The Next Diet for a Small Planet* (New York: Tarcher, 2003).

also given an opportunity to live out many of our core beliefs and values. Eating with awareness means consciously choosing our food based on its nutritional value, how it was grown, and its impact on the world. Because it is a choice we make several times a day, eating with awareness is one of the simplest and most powerful tools we have to keep our bodies, our local and global communities, and our earth alive and thriving.

Eating well and with awareness is certainly an important factor in health, but it is only one aspect. As Dorothy Day has said, "Food for the body is not enough. There must be food for the soul." Happiness, that is, the joy and thrill of loving our particular lives, is by far a better determinant of health than which foods we eat or the number of calories we consume and burn. And happiness stems from how fulfilled we feel by the other aspects of our lives. These other aspects are as varied and unique as each individual. They have the potential to feed our souls and bring us a sense of joy and fulfillment.

Three aspects I am learning to embrace for wholeness include rest, lifelong learning, and balance. Rest is more than sleep. It means having downtime and spaciousness in your life. Richard Swenson has written a few books about what he calls "margin overload."[4] Too often we overload our lives such that we no longer have room to breathe or think or transition smoothly from one thing to another. We have to learn to set boundaries and say "No," to protect space for replenishing our own energetic reserves, because when we don't, we eventually find ourselves running on empty. I have learned that creating spaciousness and downtime in my life allows me to be fully present when I am with others. Lifelong learning is an overall approach to life and a healthy way to keep things fresh and interesting. Just because I finished school, degree in hand, didn't mean that the learning chapter was over and the rest of the book would be about action. A friend of mine created a game she likes to play in groups of new acquaintances or strangers. In conversations with others, she practices setting aside her own knowledge and opinions and pretends she knows nothing about the subject at hand. By simply listening and asking questions, she learns things she would have missed out on if she'd been busy spouting off her own views or assuming she already had a handle on the topic. In my own life, developing a habit of curiosity has served me well, and I am continually discovering an abundance of creative ways to let learning continually seep into my life.

---

4   Richard A. Swenson, *Margin/The Overload Syndrome: Learning to Live Within Your Limits* (Colorado Springs: Navpress Publishing Group, 2002).

At times, the many things for us to consider in nurturing our own journeys can seem overwhelming. One of the most important things I can do is try to maintain a sense of balance. Life is always in flux. Rather than trying to do all things, all the time, all at once, I remember the wisdom of Ecclesiastes 3:1, which says, "There is a time for everything, and a season for every activity under the heavens." As a friend said to me recently, "I can do everything I want to do, just not at the same time." At any point in our lives something will take precedence over something else. When you're a brand-new mom, you might not have time to get a solid eight hours of sleep, much less take that art tour in Europe. When you're falling in love, you probably won't be focused on overhauling your finances or spending a lot of time alone. Balance is about regularly assessing your internal state of equilibrium and continually making small reasonable adjustments to bring yourself back to center.

I've learned that it's important to be patient and gentle with myself as I attempt balance in my life. Setting realistic expectations and goals is crucial. The things that are important always seem to resurface, and I've discovered that there will be opportunities to prioritize them later. A dynamic tension will always exist between doing and being, giving and receiving, stillness and activity, relationships and solitude.

It has been more than ten years since my college graduation and the breakup that served as a wake-up call to step fully into my own skin. I can truthfully say that my growth and healing have been hard-won and undeniably worthwhile—though, to be honest, I have felt pretty selfish at times. I set out with so much passion for how I would change the world, and I've spent much of the last ten years focused on changing myself. But what I'm finding is that I have grown from that idealistic though floundering young woman into a wiser woman who knows how to care for herself so that I have something consistent and self-replenishing to offer the world. I know I am not alone in my experience. Most women in our culture struggle with loving themselves and their bodies unconditionally. Riffle through almost any women's magazine and you will find the message that you are not enough just as you are. Insidiously, the messages seep through: Your breasts are too small, your hips are too big, your skin is flawed, or your hair is too frizzy. Through interviews with thousands of women all over the world, author and playwright Eve Ensler discovered that almost every woman she met passionately hated one part of her body and was desperately trying to fix it. In China, women break their legs and add bone in order to become taller. In Iran, women break their noses to get rid of the ridge and create a ski-jump effect. In Japan, women surgically add creases to their eyelids. In America, women pump their faces full of Botox and their breasts full of silicone.[5]

Why are we doing these things to ourselves? Who decided what we're "supposed" to look like, and what do they get out of it? Somehow we have been convinced to wage war against our own bodies, as if they are our enemies. *If I just force myself to work out an hour a day . . . If I could just stop craving sugar . . . If only I had better genes . . . If only I had enough willpower . . . I could win this battle with my body.* But our bodies are not the enemy. They are very wise guides. They know things we cannot learn anywhere else. And so it is our responsibility to begin to protect and listen to these bodies that have been so "fearfully and wonderfully made" (Psalm 139:14). We must learn to love the unique beauty of all women, just as they are, because in that journey of embracing flesh and blood, of loving ourselves as beautiful, worthy creations, we find a map for moving forward into love for the rest of creation as well.

Women's bodies are complex, vital compositions. They cannot be reduced to a set of mass-produced, interchangeable, and seductively marketed parts. Women are powerful; we are capable of holding immense suffering in our bellies and our strong, proficient hands. And, by God's grace, we are capable of transmuting that suffering into joy.

---

5   Eve Ensler, *The Good Body* (New York: Villard, 2004).

Moving Beyond Balance to Fullness in Christ

Jennifer Lang

When I finally reached my college graduation, I was excited and anxious about the life ahead of me. Where would I go? Where would I live? What work would I do? Whom would I meet? Whom would I marry? The time ahead of me seemed to be abundant. I looked forward to being able simply to breathe, read a book just for fun, relax, and catch up on sleep (I probably lost about a month's worth of sleep to many all-nighters in college).

The strange thing is that life just seemed to pick up speed. Life flies by faster and becomes busier the older I become, and our culture encourages this frenetic pace. We are constantly available anytime, anywhere thanks to the bounty of electronic gadgets that keep us connected. Staying balanced is a genuine struggle. I am a woman, a therapist, a wife, a daughter, a stepmother, a sister, an aunt, a church member, a friend, an artist, a volunteer. So many roles and demands, so little time!

At first, I struggled to juggle all of these multiple roles and dimensions of my life. I'm continually discovering as my life unfolds that my real goal is not "balance," a static, perfect arrangement of time, energy, and relationships. Instead, I have come to realize how dynamic life is, and that these roles and responsibilities ebb and flow over time. I am learning to be attentive to how my emotional, physical, spiritual, and social health are connected. Pursuing health and wholeness rather than an image of perfection has helped me to honor my emotions instead of repressing them, to create relationships with healthy boundaries, and to change my attitude toward my body. Relinquishing the ideal of perfection has required me to identify and name unhealthy patterns of thought and behavior in order to move toward healthier ways of living.

Often women take care of everyone else before meeting their own needs. I had to unlearn this and see myself as a priority. This isn't selfish—it is good and necessary. On an airplane, the flight attendant provides instructions about the oxygen masks: "If you are traveling with a small child, please secure your own mask first and then your child's mask." I used to be curious about this. Why wouldn't you secure your child's first? But if we don't attend to our own basic needs, we won't be any good to anyone else in our lives. I have found that pouring myself out to others can happen only when I am being filled.

Growing up in the church, I learned to feel guilty if I wasn't constantly meeting every need that I encountered. Talk about a fast path to burnout. I now realize that part of taking care of myself is knowing who I am, my unique personality and spiritual gifts. I enjoy and feel comfortable operating within the realm of my talents and gifts. God creates a passion in each of our lives—teaching, art, business, counseling, medicine. I once thought that if I enjoyed something, then it couldn't possibly be God's will! I was convinced that it had to feel difficult and uncomfortable. I now realize how absurd that was. Why wouldn't God take pleasure in and receive glory from how He created me? I think of Olympic runner Eric Liddell in the classic film *Chariots of Fire* saying, "When I run, I feel God's pleasure." For each of us, learning who we are and God's specific purpose for our lives is a process.

The moment a leaf is pulled off of a plant, it dies. It may take a while to show signs of withering, but the leaf *is* dead, because it is no longer connected to the plant. Jesus said, "I am the vine, you are the branches. Those who abide in me and I in them bear much fruit, because apart from me you can do nothing" (John 15:5). I may be able to coast for awhile, but eventually I will show signs of withering. Staying connected to the vine and daily inviting the Holy Spirit to dwell within me more fully is essential. I am constantly reminded to stop stepping ahead of God and trying to do things on my own strength. Whenever I do, I fall short.

When I began working as a counselor, I over-stressed myself with reading and planning. I felt I had to be prepared for anything and everything, to be able to answer all of life's questions. There is nothing wrong with being a good steward and doing my work with excellence, but I was more concerned about pride in not wanting to look incompetent than I was in allowing God to work through me. Quoting Philippians 4:13—"I can do all things through him who strengthens me" —calms my anxieties, kills my pride, and reminds me who is really in charge. Staying connected to God is vital to being used by God.

Our minds are amazing, and we need to take care of our brains. Neuroscience has exploded in recent years, showing that brain health affects our physical, emotional, mental, and behavioral well-being. Knowledge of the different areas and functions of our brain enables us to identify strengths and problematic areas. Exercise, nutrition, relaxation, healthy release of emotion, and positive thinking all increase good brain health. An average amount of stress doesn't hurt us; often it pushes us toward excellence and helps us to respond appropriately to situations. But studies have shown that an enormous amount of stress releases too much cortisol in our bodies and increases the release of epinephrine into the bloodstream. This has the potential to cause heart problems, exhaustion, lowered immunity, and other health problems.

Our emotions are God-given protective and life-enhancing tools for understanding ourselves and what we need. When we feel our emotions appropriately, we can learn from them and take appropriate action. Sometimes we are taught to ignore our emotions, or to amplify them. When this happens, we aren't learning what we need from them. When I attended college, my parents went through a divorce. I put on my strong "I'm okay" mask, and I really thought I was. I spiritualized my pain and denied its existence. It wasn't until I attended a divorce support group for students that I realized how angry, sad, and depressed I really was.

The signs were all there. I slept all the time, took many showers to escape, and was more prone to illness. My grades plummeted. I knew very little about normal grief symptoms. I obviously didn't pay attention to my body or connect it to my grief. I had lots of support from my friends, especially my roommate. She loved me, listened to me, supported me, nurtured me, and laughed with me. She was a gift from God as well, and we remain very close friends to this day. The chaplain's assistant at my college became a mentor to me: a wise, older woman who loved me and walked with me during that tumultuous time. I cannot imagine how I would have felt or functioned without having these amazing friendships.

During the time of my parents' divorce, I recall one of my siblings saying, "If anyone can get Mom and Dad to stay together, it's Jen." Well, I must have taken that to heart. I have carried this sense of responsibility with me for a long time. I played the role of supporter, negotiator, interpreter, and relationship mediator in my family. If two people in my family had conflict, it would increase my fears and anxiety. So I would intervene to help "fix it." I felt responsible for fixing all relationships. (No wonder I became a therapist!) In addition to the incredible loss, I also felt like a failure when my parents did divorce. This sense of responsibility carried over into my work as a therapist. I tried to fix people and their lives based on my sense of responsibility and my own efforts.

After years of embracing this role in my personal and professional life, it was taking a toll on me. This negative thought that I was using to organize my life did not change until I processed my parents' divorce through therapy. Processing my grief and sense of responsibility has helped me to heal, adapt, and clarify boundaries. Sometimes I still step into relationship issues between family members even when I really should not. I recognize it now and don't become as anxious to fix the conflict. It has been much easier to allow others to resolve their own problems. I also have clearer boundaries with my clients about their responsibility to do the hard work of therapy. I have learned how important it is to recognize points of unresolved grief and trauma, and to work through them with trusted friends or caring, skilled professionals.

I also wish that I had spent less time being so self-critical and self-absorbed. Looking at photos of myself from twenty years ago, I realize that I was fit and healthy. But I remember my dissatisfaction with my body then, thinking my thighs were too big or my arms were too short. I regret spending so much time negatively obsessing over my body. I wish I had learned about needing a healthy balance between caring for my body and giving it too much importance. The Bible refers to our bodies as temples: "Or do you not know that your body is a temple of the Holy Spirit within you, which you have from God, and that you are not your own?" (I Corinthians 6:19). All that I am and have comes from God, including my body. We are inundated with images of bodies in this culture, and we are promised that the perfect body and flawless skin are attainable. If I pick up a magazine at the hair salon, I'm comparing and wishing I looked like Jennifer Aniston or some other beautiful actress. I have those "nothing fits and I hate my hair" days. I chastise myself for eating that occasional bowl of ice cream.

It becomes easier to have a healthier attitude toward my body when I remember that my body is not an object, but a part of my wholeness. Our bodies are designed to help us to be in relationship to ourselves and others, to enjoy eating, sleeping, dancing, bicycling, painting, and so many other activities. Being good and nurturing toward my body positively affects all of the other parts of myself. Avoiding certain magazines has also been helpful for me, as well as wearing clothes that are comfortable and flattering, and allowing grace for an occasional bowl of ice cream. I try to remember that what I contribute to my inward and outward body affects my mood, my thoughts, my spirit, and how I relate to others. Good nutrition and exercise are connected to our physical, emotional, mental, spiritual, and social well-being.

Life has twisted and turned in ways I didn't expect, and I'm glad that I didn't spend my twenties simply waiting for the perfect mate, perfect job, or perfect place to live. I read, painted, rented my first apartment, was a "mother" to two cats, took a trip to Paris with my college friends, worked, participated in missions work in Belize, reconnected with my mom, and played volleyball. I learned that I could pay my bills with my own paychecks, even if at times I had only coins left to pay for gas. Experiencing life as a single person allowed me to learn, grow, and build self-confidence.

I was thirty-three when I got married, and I found that there are positive things about marrying later. I felt that I knew myself better, and I had changed a lot within one decade! I was able to finish my graduate degree before marriage. I visited family frequently and spent time with friends. Don't get me wrong; I looked forward to finding "the right guy" and getting married. I did meet him, and he was the first man I had met who felt like home to my heart. He is not perfect, but neither am I. Marriage is very fulfilling, but it is hard work. I think that I had a preconceived notion that marriage is easy when there is an abundance of love. Even with the emotion of love present, the commitment to continually act in love is more challenging. My emotions, thoughts, behaviors, and choices affect my spouse. I have also found it challenging to balance my individuality with our unity as a couple. I don't think anyone feels completely prepared and ready for marriage. In hindsight, I understand the importance of being reasonably ready for that important step. It is a huge decision that has long-term impact.

There is really nothing as vital as attachment and nurturing. Without them, babies don't thrive. We absolutely need them and will go to great lengths to have them. From relationships, we learn that we are not alone and learn that we are lovable. Loving looks and affection actually increase oxytocin, "the hormone of love," in our systems. So does laughter (even faking a good laugh increases oxytocin!). Research at the University of California San Francisco reveals that oxytocin is involved in attachment and bonding. It mediates emotional experiences in close relationships.

I've learned that even in the midst of a great romance, it is essential not to neglect friendships. It is unfair and unrealistic to expect my spouse to meet *all* of my emotional needs. Other women provide support, understanding, laughter, and companionship. For generations, women of many cultures have gathered together to share in each others' lives. Recently, I spent the weekend as a small group leader at a retreat for women who have experienced the death of a child. During this weekend, the women cried, laughed, created, played, hugged, and supported each other. Friday night they arrived with trepidation, and by Sunday they had experienced an amazing and healing connection from being together. Having a community of women to share life with can be a rich and supportive experience.

I have given up on trying to achieve balance in my life. Instead, I have learned to pursue *fullness* in my physical self, mental self, emotional self, spiritual self, and social self. All of these selves make up the whole person, created in God's image, that I am meant to be.

Transitions and Change: Finding the Still Point

Lois Wagner

"Pretty soon, now will be a long time ago!"
—Annika, five years old

After sixty-six years and many changes and transitions, one would think that I would have much wisdom about how to deal with the changes of life with grace and some degree of comfort. I have a friend who says "Embrace change!" and she seems to really live that motto. Her eyes light up and energy gets going when something new presents itself. I often wonder if she ever experiences middle-of-the-night questions and ambivalence as I do with every change.

Times of Transition—We Seek Them and Yet We Resist Them

I have to admit that I don't do change well. I seek change and desire the new, but I also like to hold on to the familiar, the known. I sometimes experience a great deal of angst whenever I am faced with change—even that which I have sought and desired. This seems ironic because, as a nurse and teacher, I have spent my life assisting people through the changes involved in birth, illness, and death. Though I have learned a great deal through these experiences and often draw upon these lessons as I go through my own transitions, I am aware that I still have much to learn.

Resisting change for most of us begins in our earliest stages. I think of toddlers and the various ways they resist changing from one activity to another—often with crying and temper tantrums. My daughter says of her three-year-old, "She doesn't want to leave whatever it is she is doing even if she didn't want to do it initially."

208

Another image of transitions is of a woman in labor and giving birth. When the contractions become the strongest, sometimes women will experience a period of disorientation, often hollering, "What am I doing? I want out of here. I can't do this." But of course she can and does go through this period. In fact, the birth of her baby provides an amnesia that allows her to even consider doing it again.

So what helps when we are going through times of transition and change? One of the most helpful and simple pieces of advice comes from Al-Anon, the organization for friends and families of persons with alcoholism. The acronym HALT is used to remind people of how to take care of themselves during difficult times: don't let yourself get too Hungry, Angry, Lonely, or Tired. This is taking care of the basics first—good food, emotional care, relationships, and sleep. And the basics are so important because they help us make healthy and sound decisions to all the questions we face during times of transition.

For me, some kind of regular exercise and getting out in nature is important for both my body and soul. It is easy during times of change and transition to get so busy with activities that I don't take care of the basics. A helpful question to ask during any time of stress or transition is, "What do *I* need at this moment, and how do I take care of that?"

One of the most unexpected lessons I've learned is that transitions can and often do lead to grief. Many of us do not recognize our grief over losses, especially when those losses are a result of choices we've made. We can get so busy preparing for times of transition that we don't allow ourselves to grieve the losses resulting from a new change. But grieving these losses as we move toward something different and unknown is extremely important.

Also, when we are in new situations we often make harsh judgments about ourselves, others, or the situation itself. It is helpful to recognize this tendency and to hold our judgments very lightly, knowing that we are seeing through the eyes of our own discomfort and that as we become more comfortable, these judgments may change. During these times I have found it helpful to remember the four most important things to say: *Thank you. I love you. Forgive me. I forgive you.*

As I face retirement from teaching at a university, as well as a big move across the country, I wonder how similar my responses to this transition resemble those of students who are about to graduate. I find myself vacillating between being more emotional than usual to almost being numb. I find myself thinking about all the people I wish I had spent more time with, the classes I wish I had taken, the places I intended to go, but didn't. I feel very grateful for the time that I have had and feel a deep ache as I prepare to leave even though I am clear that this is what I am choosing to do.

When I was in my forties, I was trying to learn to rock climb. Once, as I found myself on the side of the mountain with my feet on small ledges and my hands barely holding on, I felt absolutely stuck. I could not see where to put my hands next. I could see only one spot where I could put my foot. The young guide from below hollered to me, "Just make the move that you can. The others will become clear when you do that." And sure enough, that is what happened. When I finally reached the top, I collapsed in sobs as I realized that this mountain climb was a sharp metaphor for the uncertainty I was experiencing in my life at the time. Often all we can do is to make the next move that we can see.

Resting in the In-Between

It is also important to think about the spiritual journey during times of change and transition. The practice of pausing, reflecting, and meditating is a great tool that helps prepare us inwardly for the inevitable changes before us. Practiced by many members of Benedictine communities, *Statio* is the practice of stopping outside the chapel for a few moments before entering the service. The intention is to be more fully awake to the present moment and the next steps, and therefore to be present to God in that moment as he is always to us.

Frederic and Mary Ann Brussat further explain the practice of Statio:

> Using this Christian practice, we can reframe the many transition times and places we experience during the day. Instead of regarding them as wasted periods, unavoidable delays, or inconveniences, we can see them as divine invitations to stop, to re-center ourselves, and to become more aware of God's presence in the world around us. . . . Just consciously choose to stop, close your eyes, and relax your body. Take a deep breath and as you exhale, let go of any anxieties. Shrug your shoulders or shake out your hands. Rest in the moment and know that this special moment will never come again. Savor it and give thanks to God.[1]

---

1   Brussat, Frederic and Mary Ann. "Transition Times and Spaces: The Practice of Statio," accessed 2 March 2011, http://www.spiritualityandpractice.com/practices/features.php?id=16837.

If your life is anything like mine has been, there will be wonderful moments and difficult moments, wonderful years and difficult years, and sometimes ones that are wonderful and difficult all at the same time. As you continue to face life challenges, you will find strengths in yourself and from the most unexpected directions, persons, and places. I have found hope and solace in remembering that there are many ways to live this life. I'm reminded to keep perspective in my own granddaughter's simple but profound statement: "Pretty soon, now will be a long time ago!"

My prayer for each of us is that, as we go through the many transitions throughout life, we will take really good care of ourselves—physically, emotionally, mentally, and spiritually—and find the Christ whom T.S. Eliot called "the still point in the turning world."

Learning to Embrace the Mystery of Faith

Cassie Lewis

The possibility that there could be any merit at all to "blind faith" is tough to swallow for a woman like me. My mind insists that faith should be well-informed and thoroughly tested before delving into its wily, unpredictable ways. Yet, beyond my own doing, I have been increasingly drawn down a path that is requiring of me that very thing: following the path set before me, blindly, darkly, laying aside my usual intellectual handrails. It has been a surprising journey.

It is good, sometimes, to stand back and take stock of whom one has become, to trace the winding path of what leads one from a certain beginning to a very different place today. From the admittedly limited vantage point of my thirty-three years of life, I can name three major seasons of my spiritual journey thus far. There was the earnest faith of my childhood and adolescence, where the world made sense and right and wrong were a simple matter of black and white. This season was followed by the predictable collapse and transformation of that faith into its overly intellectualized young adult form, at the exclusion of any openness to matters spiritual. Finally, there came a metamorphosis of that young adult faith into its current spirit-driven state after my being tossed into the crucible of devastating personal crisis.

§

I grew up in the suburbs in a good-hearted pastor's home, with our large, conservative, evangelical church at the center of my family life. The churches we were part of were like a beautiful extended family that loved me and raised me, laying the foundation for the person I am today. It was a beginning that taught me the heart of religion, centered on selfless love of others and the fruit of the Spirit. We were ever aware of the potential for missing the point and taking pride in one's achievements, learning the difference between doing good and becoming holy. My parents raised me with a grasp on the best that evangelical faith has to offer, an upbringing filled with conviction and passion, a discipline of personal prayer, commitment to a body of believers, and compassion for the world outside of the church.

Eventually, I bounded off to a Christian college with an eager, passionate spirit oriented toward serving and loving God—the God around whom I had organized my entire life and understanding of the world. I used my time there to prepare for a life of serving God among the urban poor, a life to which I had felt an explicit call while on a high school mission trip to Skid Row in Los Angeles. But I was also irresistibly inclined toward intellectual endeavors and found myself fascinated by discussions and debates about the deeper layers of life, the mysterious and the provocative. I was introduced to Christian authors who made a compelling case for the possibility that God might have used evolution as a means to create life on earth. My new mentors challenged me to see that having compassion for the poor meant not only doing charitable acts but also engaging political structures to enact real justice—which might entail taking political stances farther to the left than many Evangelical churches seem comfortable with. My ministry with men who were dying of AIDS launched me into all kinds of questions about finding Jesus in unexpected places, about being present to the "untouchables" of our day, and about setting aside judgment and offering hospitality in its stead.

All of these new encounters catapulted me toward the possibility that there may not be an objective, clear-cut way of interpreting God, the world, and our roles within it, given Christians' vastly diverse responses to the world's realities, in spite of their using the same Bible to base their convictions upon. In my very first semester, at age eighteen, my faith came crashing down in a stormy swirl of frightening new ideas that threatened everything I had ever known or presumed to be true.

The experience was shattering, as I discovered that my faith might now include uncertainty and questions. I was afraid to reveal my doubts to anyone and was thus completely alone in my inner turmoil. I came to realize that much of my scriptural interpretation had been made in ignorance of the historical and literary context in which the texts had been written. I began to see that Truth is far from linear. Mystery abounds.

Thus began the slow and confusing process of piecing together a worldview that might make space for my new understandings of the universe. I wondered how God could possibly be at work in the world, yet seem to daily ignore the world's suffering. If God were truly just, and Jesus' resurrection had really conquered the dark side, how could such evil continue to exist? Why would God help my middle-class self in some insignificant moment of distress (like granting me a longed-for parking space) while ignoring the cries of a mother whose child was starving in some far-off land? I had no answer to these disturbing questions, and I hungered to reconcile my faith that God is somehow present and just in spite of the persistence of suffering and evil in the world. Thus the pendulum swung for me all the way from an easy, unexamined faith, to a faith reduced to only what I could rationalize.

As I considered the essentials of what had constituted Christian faith for me up to that point, I confess I felt rather numb. I was not inspired by what I saw as the church's focus on people accepting Jesus in their heart, as if faith in Him was a simple ticket for entry into heaven. I was also uninspired by a moralistic focus on individual piety. I wanted to follow Jesus not for the hope of receiving a heavenly reward, but because to follow Him is to participate in something beautiful and good here in *this* life as well. For faith to have any meaning at all, I had to see that it was relevant to the real-life, here-and-now concerns of Creation. I wanted to see churches engage in love of neighbor to the point of self-sacrifice, or to embody the profound stories in the Bible where the very God of the Universe modeled humility and was moved to compassion by the plight of suffering people. I wanted to hear the church call its people to take radical stands against the great social ills of today, such as consumerism and environmental desecration. The church could be involved with creating an alternative lifestyle of simplicity, generosity, and hospitality to the poor. I longed for the Church to call us once again to embody the radical, society-transforming cries of the prophets and of Jesus. These were the themes that ignited a flame in my soul and compelled me to give my life to following Jesus.

As I processed my growing faith, I was terrified that I might no longer be considered an "orthodox" Christian. As my focus shifted away from a theology of personal salvation to one more centered on the redemption of social structures that wreak havoc on the disadvantaged of the world, I carried within me a deep fear that if I opened my mouth to share truthfully about my new perspectives on God, others would exclude me from the Christian camp. But I wanted desperately to be included! I loved who I understood God to be, was enamored by the person of Jesus, and felt deeply committed to the life of service I felt called to.

After graduation, still in the midst of trepidation about my place in the Christian church, I spent a year in Washington, D.C. in a vibrant church community where I discovered a theology and spirituality that actually resonated with my own. The very thoughts that I was keeping silent in my heart were actually celebrated and considered the norm in the context of this quirky, passionate church. It began to dawn on me how wide and deep and broad is God's house, and that there perhaps could be room for diverse expressions of Christian faith. In this community, we spoke of "the Way" of Jesus as being more important than "right belief," holding with humility the myriad, unanswerable mysteries of God but still walking forward and living our lives as they believed Jesus would have us live. We prayed using ancient monastic practices such as centering prayer, Lectio Divina, or the Stations of the Cross. We wrestled with the Bible's teachings in a way that acknowledged human authorship and the authors' sometimes poor translation of what God may have intended or what the authors thought they heard. We viewed other religious traditions graciously, making space for their contributions to our own faith.

I found a place that nurtured and affirmed my long journey of taking apart my initial childhood rendition of the world and its Creator, and urged me along to rebuild my theology into something that would take into account all of my surroundings, my intellect, and my experience. That group gave me, once again, a sense of belonging within the Church.

My faith continued to be driven primarily by my intellect after my year in Washington, D.C. I delighted in my newfound freedom to explore and wrestle with the mysteries of life and God. I sought to unearth new expressions of the depth and beauty of Christianity and was deeply moved by what I was discovering. For all of the precious depictions of God's compassionate heart I encountered, however, it would unfortunately be a while before spiritual practices and prayer could once again fit inside this framework. I felt much more comfortable expressing my "prayer-life" in actions of service to neighbors in need or within deep, communal, loving relationships, at the exclusion of private renditions of prayer where stillness and silence were allowed to do their work in my heart. This action-oriented prayer felt safe to me, protecting me from having to face any personal encounters with the Divine. Furthermore, at that time, I was doubtful God was even interested in a personal encounter with me.

Such a perspective served me well enough for several years, but like many, when my first true personal crisis struck, I found myself jolted completely. I was not accustomed to sorrow or soul-wrenching grief. When my husband of five years suddenly chose to end our marriage, I was hurtled into depths of emotion that I never knew existed. So much was yanked out from under me in that moment—my prospect of becoming a mother in the near future, my sense of stability and direction in life, my source of emotional support, my identity and status as a married woman . . . my whole world unraveled before my eyes, leaving me with the wind knocked out of me, literally struggling to breathe.

Life's challenges would normally find me analyzing my situation and mapping out strategies to forge my way ahead. But this was the first challenge of my entire life where the fog felt so thick that I could not make out the way ahead. I had a startling sense that this problem was far bigger than what I could steer myself through—a rather foreign feeling in my overly self-sufficient history. I felt this unmistakable prodding, deep in my gut, telling me that in order to survive this event, I had to *let go.* Instead of wielding my inner strength in an effort to hack away at the obstacles in my path, I was challenged to release my grip on my journey and simply listen deep within. I heard a resonant call to regularly sit in silence, with my candles, a cup of tea, maybe a journal, sometimes my guitar or piano, and listen for my deepest needs to emerge, and then heed the nudge to address them. This is how I would learn to pay attention to the subtle cues that would guide me on the path to healing. This flew in the face of the intellect-based theology I had been crafting since college: securely navigating life with my head while ignoring that other essential aspect of our humanity—heeding the heart and God's prodding within it.

The following year I declared for myself a "Sabbath Year," one of the wisest things I've ever done. I still went to work every day, but I removed myself from all other responsibilities and involvements. Beyond employment, my only obligation that year was to practice this deep listening that had been asked of me. It really was all I could do, since I was not capable of strategizing or thinking my way out of the grief that had paralyzed my heart. When my heart demanded that I plant wildflowers in my garden, I did so. When I was in need of friendship, I sought out time with friends. When I needed solitude, I obliged myself, even if it meant canceling previously made social plans. When my soul hungered to be lost in the expression of music in the middle of the night, I poured myself into the keys of my piano with Beethoven's "Moonlight Sonata" or in the mournful songs I was learning on the guitar, letting the music carry my heart's cries in ways words could not. My only task was to learn to hear God's voice and to simply heed the gentle wisdom contained within it.

That simple practice of allowing myself to be led from a place deep within me rather than depending exclusively on heady ideas is what enabled the desperately needed healing from the pain of my divorce. But now that I am beyond that period of tumult and grief, I see that the lesson was not for that season alone. Instead, it has come to define and transform the next phase in my spiritual journey. The experience of that crisis and the year of restful healing that followed reoriented my entire identity and spiritual life. It was like that classic metaphor of the hot crucible into which raw materials are placed and then are transformed under the extreme heat and pressure, turning them into something profoundly more valuable than before their exposure to the seemingly fatal and unbearable heat.

My approach to faith no longer requires that the mysterious world of the Spirit fit into the tidy boxes of my finite mind. I have consented to live within the innumerable paradoxes that litter my earthly reality. I can now make space in my worldview for the miraculous. While I certainly can't explain every miracle story I hear, I can at least remain open to the possibility of God intervening in reality. For example, I once felt deeply conflicted when pondering the stories told by my rambunctious Grandpa Roy. I adored him, but what was I to do with his crazy stories of praying for the half-constructed new church building where he was pastor, to be protected from the coming torrential rains? After an all-night prayer vigil, the tale ends with a rain-soaked earth surrounding the construction site where the not-yet-roofed building has been spared, completely dry. Grandpa Roy also told the story of my mother's birth, when during my grandmother's labor the doctor came to my grandfather and declared that he must choose between his wife and his soon-to-be-born baby girl, because they would not be able to save them both in the critical labor scenario. My grandfather refused to accept these options and told the doctor he would simply have to save the lives of both. He proceeded to gather together the elders of the church for yet another passionate prayer vigil, yielding yet another miraculous ending.

Rather than listen with skepticism, this new perspective of openness allows me to hold such stories gently, to give them space to live in my consciousness, even when they don't fit our culture's exclusive dependence on the earthly senses for our source of truth. It is not that I no longer permit my mind to voice its protests to these scenarios, but it no longer gets to shut out the possibility that God might have the capacity to act outside of the natural and ethical laws perceptible to our finite minds.

Prayer is another facet of the spiritual life that I engage in differently now after emerging from the wreckage of my heartache. Recently, a homeless man wandered into the courtyard of my church during coffee hour, asking for any leftover food. I knew that a woman had earlier delivered a large basket of figs from her tree to distribute to people at church, so I offered the remaining fruits to the tired, ragged man. As I later recalled the exchange, I found myself uttering prayers for his well-being. Perhaps one of the gifts of prayer lies in its capacity to promote compassion in our hearts, teaching us to care about the right things, giving us the opportunity to practice responding rightly to someone in need.

I no longer feel a need to be held back by my theological quandaries of whether or not prayer really makes a difference in our earthly reality, and the apparent injustice of it all if prayer *does* make a difference (Why should God oblige the demands of some of us and not of others? What about the people whose homes flooded during the rainstorm my grandfather was spared from? Or all the mothers who have lost their lives or their infants in childbirth?). I choose to submit to the reality that the universe is beyond my ability to understand. Rather than be mired by my mind's questions, I intend to live within the tension of honoring and engaging those questions while also bowing, when the moment is right, to the supremacy of the Mystery. The willingness to be led by the stirrings in my heart rather than be led strictly by the confines of my mind continues to play out in my evolving faith. While my theology presently lies in a heap of mismatched pieces at my feet, I still have a deep desire for my life to reflect the profound *Way* presented by Jesus, regardless of whether I am able to find meaning in the classic theological doctrines that my mind struggles to ascribe to. In other words, my beliefs may be a work in progress, but that need not hold me back from attempting to live out the true essence of Christ's call in my daily life.

Now when I sit in church, my senses are engaged and awakened in the fragrance of the incense, the unbearably beautiful sounds of the choir and pipe organ, the light filtering in through the colorful stained glass, the sponginess of the bread on my tongue, the tingly warmth of communion wine in my throat. Even in the midst of my most searing doubt, the experience of the liturgy draws me in, calling me to bow to the mystery that is God, to continue walking forward in faith, in spite of the darkness. Worship becomes not an exercise in knowing things intellectually, but a repetition that week after week allows me to come to know God's spirit in my bones, beckoning me to a deep knowing beyond the surface of intellectual perception.

This new lesson is not a call to abandon my intellect but rather to honor both the heart and mind, giving each their proper place. I still give my head permission to wrestle with questions of faith, theology, and right practice. When I encounter words or thoughts that I still struggle to affirm, my hope is that the utterances of the faithful saints surrounding me can carry me and my doubts on their believing shoulders. And when it is time to partake in the Eucharist, I keep coming to the altar. The best I can do is to repeatedly show up at the table, extending my hands in humility to receive the gifts of bread and wine. I open myself to the possibility that God might make God's self known to me, or perhaps even to enable me to ingest, on a weekly basis, more and more of who Jesus is and to let that person become incorporated into the very fiber of my being. It makes no sense at all; it's not even remotely possible. And yet, I know better now than to let such impossibilities limit my awareness of God's mysterious love and presence in my life.

In Search of Spiritual Mothers

Carol Blessing

There is a woman hidden in the pages of Judges who defies categorization, disrupts boundaries within which patriarchal interpreters try to enclose women, combines life roles, and does all this successfully. Her name is Deborah, and the account in Judges 4 and 5 lists her as judge, prophet, military leader, wife, mother, woman. The fact that she is included in scripture both encourages me and rebuts those who view the Judeo-Christian traditions as utterly misogynistic.

Despite extensive Bible study at the conservative churches I attended from infancy, I discovered her only after I became an adult. I had gone to church all my life and learned about the men of the Bible as well as the church fathers. I did learn about the Marys, and a bit about Ruth and Esther, but the focus was mainly on male heroes, leaders, and teachers. Deborah, and many others, was not reinforced as a role model for girls or women during my Sunday school days. I remember reading about Deborah in the book of Judges when I was about twenty-seven and was fascinated because she contradicts much that I have learned about women and leadership. Here was an active woman who was the judge of Israel, essentially both a prophet and a leader in the days before the kings. Judges 4:5 tells us, "And she used to sit under the palm tree of Deborah between Ramah and Bethel in the hill country of Ephraim; and the sons of Israel came up to her for judgment." There was no apology made for her, no explanation of why this female seemed to interrupt the flow of the text, of the male pattern of authority.

Discovering Deborah and her role in God's story came at a crucial time in my life—I had begun graduate school in literary studies and was also serving in a staff position as lay pastor of youth at my church. Deborah interested me because she is multifaceted. According to Judges

4:4, "Deborah, a prophetess, the wife of Lappidoth, was judging Israel at that time." Within this short verse, there are three positions laid out for Deborah: prophetess, wife, and judge. In Judges 5, another role, that of mother, is added to Deborah's accomplishments as she proclaims herself a "mother in Israel." These positions are combined with the power to commission and lead Barak, the captain of the Israelite army, and later write a hymn of victory (Judges 5) praising God for the battle outcome, including the killing of the Canaanite king, Sisera, by another woman, Jael, making Deborah a remarkably active woman.

I began to study Deborah to investigate the ways in which theologians and Bible commentators deal with her various offices. Within the historical framework of medieval and early modern Europe, the era whose literature I now teach at the college level, I found that, more often than not, Deborah was considered an anathema. Medieval commentators usually referred to her as a prophet only, not as a judge. This meant that, although she could serve as a vessel of God to transmit his messages to Israel, she could not hold the same position of leadership in civil authority in deciding legal cases and enforcing the laws that the rest of the judges held. While the calling of prophet is certainly a worthy office, Deborah is unique in scripture insofar as she is a female who holds the post of judge, the precursor to the office of king in ancient Israel. Judges 4:5 tells us "the sons of Israel came up to her for judgment."

In the early modern era, celebrations of Queen Elizabeth use Deborah as an apology to allow for female authority, but commentary on the English monarch reinforced the idea that she, like Deborah, was an exceptional woman, not to be looked at as a precedent for other women to follow. Queen Elizabeth was often viewed by male commentators as a prince in female attire.

Studying Deborah in contemporary contexts, I find that not a great deal has changed in perceptions of the female judge, that her positions of power continue to cause discomfort. Many students to whom I mention Deborah as example either have never heard of her or have an incomplete knowledge about her, although they could recite 1 Timothy 2:12 from memory, admonishing women that they "are to keep silent within the church."

The more I studied this strong woman, the more I found my own belief system changing. The clearly restricted hierarchy of male over female, which within my church background meant males as pastors, females as pastors' wives; males as adult Sunday school teachers, females as nursery workers; males as ushers, females as coffee-servers; males as leaders, females as followers; males as prophets, females as listeners; and so on, began to blur and even crumble. Here was a woman as a leader, a wise prophet, an administrator and legislator, a writer, one who could speak the Word of God, thwart enemies, hold authority over a male, and even be a mother. Deborah led me on a pilgrimage to try to discover more about other women in church history, to consider the place and position of women in today's church, and to become a mentor of young women seeking to know more about themselves as created in God's image.

Part of developing my spiritual journey has been coming to see how women relate to God, to look not only at male models in the Bible, in church history, or in current life, and try to transfer male stories into female ones in order to be able to relate to them, but also to seek out female models/mentors. I now reexamine Scripture with an eye to the women of the text. Sometimes they have active roles, sometimes they are reticent, and sometimes they are silenced. Sometimes they are not mentioned, or if they are, they often go unnamed. Yet I know they are present, that they have names and lives, that they too share a thirst for God, a desire for the living water. These include the Samaritan woman at the well in John 4:7–30; the woman about to be stoned to death in John 8:1–11; the Old Testament women victimized by misogyny (such as the Levite's concubine who was raped, killed, and cut into pieces in Judges 19); the bleeding woman who dared touch Christ's garment in Luke 8:43–48; the prophesying daughters of Philip in Acts 21:8–9; the women Phoebe and Priscilla in Romans 16:1–3 who had leadership skills; the virgin Mary who bore and wept for her son at his crucifixion; Mary Magdalene, who first proclaimed his resurrection in John 20:18; and the great multitude of scriptural females who continue to prophesy the truth of the new birth.

There is also a deep, vibrant cloud of female witnesses in church history, from ancient Christianity onward. These are women who have written, preached, ministered, fought injustice, and provided models for the rich variety of roles women have played and can continue to play in building the Kingdom of God. Julian of Norwich is one of my favorites, an anchoress and mystical writer from fifteenth-century England who expresses her view of Christ and God in terms of love. Going to her cell in a little church was a spiritual pilgrimage I was able to complete one summer. Her God-inspired reassurance that "All will be well, all shall be well, and all manner of things shall be well" comes to me gently, in difficult times. She teaches me to share this message with others who so desperately need it in this age of anxiety.

Julian of Norwich is most renowned for her development of the idea of the second person of the Trinity as being female and maternal, and much discussion of her proto-feminist ideology has come from this point. Julian portrays Christ as our spiritual mother, in whom we are reborn and are nourished. For this image, she draws upon both the domestic and bodily spheres, as she vividly depicts Christ feeding his children as a mother breastfeeds her children:

> The human mother will suckle her child with her own milk, but our beloved Mother, Jesus, feeds us with himself, and, with the most tender courtesy, does it by means of the Blessed Sacrament, the precious food of all true life. . . . The human mother may put her child tenderly to her breast, but our tender Mother Jesus simply leads us into his blessed breast through his open side, and there gives us a glimpse of the Godhead and heavenly joy—the inner certainty of eternal bliss. (170)

This most primordial of all instincts, to find nourishment, to nurse, is used here to truly represent the most homely, or intimate, of relationships. At the same time, it invokes both the suffering of Christ, through the blood in his side, and the Church, through the sacrament which symbolizes that blood. It is a complex rhetorical construct, but what it conveys most directly to the reader is the archetypal idea of comfort.

In this analogy, Julian draws directly from two maternal images Christ used in the scriptures. The first, found in Matthew 23:37, portrays Christ as longing to gather his children of Israel the way that a hen would gather her chicks, snuggling them under her wings. More related to the body of motherhood is the John 3:5 image of being born again, of reentering the birth canal, only this time of the spiritual and not the physical realm. Christ embraced the feminine as he embraces his followers. In her portrayal of the love of God and God's desire for closeness to her and to the rest of his people, it is fitting that Julian would choose the closest of human relationships, of mother and child, in her analogy. Home, family, and the body are all central to this, the strongest of Julian's images.

Unashamed of the domestic, of the everyday, of the concrete, she crafts images appealing to women and men. Julian is thus important to teach, to read, for not only her feminist theology, for her display of medieval Catholic and mystical thought, for her contributions to the genre of Middle English prose, but also for her demonstration that literature need not consist of worlds removed from the realm of women. Her very "otherness" presents a challenge to both more traditional standards of aesthetics as well as patriarchal views of God. As feminist theorists advocate "reading against the grain" and "reading as a site of resistance," so Julian reads her visions of God in ways that are female, unorthodox, and even disturbing to some. Her works call us to question our views of the divine, of art, and of what should be contained in the literary canon.

Deborah helped me grow and reexamine my image of God, gender roles, and myself. As one of my spiritual mothers, she has helped give birth to me and introduced me to other spiritual mothers, such as Julian of Norwich. My studies have led me to other women, such as Christine de Pizan, late medieval defender of women against misogyny in her utopian *Book of the City of Ladies*; Aemilia Lanyer, the first British female to publish a sustained biblical commentary on Christ's passion; Margaret Fell Fox, the seventeenth-century Quaker leader who wrote the first treatise promoting women's right to preach; Mary Astell, who wrote the first proposal for a women's Protestant college; Susanna Wesley, mother and mentor of John and Charles Wesley; and Mary Fletcher and Mary Tooth, women who worked in early Methodist ministry.

Studying these strong women of faith has provided me with role models to reimagine women in Christian leadership. Sharing this knowledge in literature classes has created a more gender-balanced view of earlier centuries than traditional canons have allowed. Sometimes I begin a class with a meditation from Julian of Norwich, and she has become a favorite medieval writer of students. The early feminism of Christine de Pizan surprises many, as does the strength of Margaret Fell Fox in creating an apologia for women to speak out in the church. Others are impressed by the intellectual prowess of Mary Astell in a time when Reason seemed an exclusively male domain. The purpose of teaching is to enlarge and reconfigure entrenched thinking patterns created through lack of information. Through researching, publishing essays upon, and teaching others about these women who have nurtured me, I hope that I in turn have nurtured and will continue to guide others in their journey toward wholeness in Christ.

Suggested Works on Women in the Bible and Church History

Blessing, Carol. "'Most Blessed Daughters of Jerusalem': Aemilia Lanyer's *Salve Deus Rex Judeorum* and Elizabethan and Jacobean Bible Commentary." *Ben Jonson Journal*, Vol. 15, no. 2, Winter 2008.

Brown, Ann. *Apology to Women: Christian Images of the Female Sex.* Leicester: InterVarsity Press, 1991.

Chilcote, Paul. *She Offered Them Christ: The Legacy of Women Preachers in Early Methodism.* Wipf and Stock, 2001.

Hancock, E. Lee, ed. *The Book of Women's Sermons: Hearing God in Each Other's Voices.* New York: Riverhead Books, 1999.

Jule, Allyson and Bettina Pedersen, eds. *Being Feminist, Being Christian.* NY: Palgrave, 2006.

Julian of Norwich. *Showings.* Trans. Edmund Colledge and James Walsh. New York: Paulist Press. 1978.

LeClerc, Diane, ed. *I Am Not Ashamed: Sermons by Wesleyan-Holiness Women.* San Diego: Point Loma Press, 2005.

MacHaffie, Barbara J. *Readings in Her Story: Women in Christian Tradition.* Minneapolis: Augsburg Fortress, 1992.

McKenna, Megan. *Not Counting Women and Children: Neglected Stories From the Bible.* Maryknoll, NY: Orbis, 1994.

Norris, Kathleen. *The Quotidian Mysteries: Laundry, Liturgy and "Women's Work."* Mahweh, NJ: Paulist Press, 1998.

Stanley, Susie. *Holy Boldness: Women Preachers' Autobiographies and the Sanctified Self.* Knoxville : University of Tennessee Press, 2002.

Toriesen, Karen Jo. *When Women Were Priests.* San Francisco: Harper, 1995.

Primary Feathers: Learning to Discern God's Direction

Rebecca Laird

Thus says the Lord: Stand at the crossroads, and look, and ask for the ancient paths, where the good way lies; and walk in it, and find rest for your souls.

—Jeremiah 6:16

I have a penchant for watching raptors and water birds in flight. When I need perspective, I head for the hills or a high place, looking for a wider horizon. Inevitably, in such places, there are hawks and falcons or seagulls or pelicans winging across the sky. Even though they are small creatures, they seem to know how to get from one place to another by following some interior mapping system. Watching them helps me trust in the great winged dove of the Trinity—the Holy Spirit—that helps creatures like me find my way, too.

As my senior year of college waned, that awful question: What are you going to do after graduation? began to stare me down. One afternoon, when I could do nothing but stare back mutely at that question, I headed to the highest point on campus—the roof of the science building. I climbed the external stairs on the ocean side of the building and stopped only when I could find no further foothold. It was a glorious day to sit and gaze at the gray-blue ocean set against the white-blue sky, watching the gulls (and the surfer dudes) in the distance. The beauty of it all calmed me, and in time, I pulled my journal out of my backpack. Slowly I began to make a list of all the things I hoped I might do in my life.

My list was pretty long, and I didn't know how to put things in chronological order. I am not a "this one thing I do" kind of person. Some of the dreams on my list seemed more likely to occur sooner than later, like going to graduate school. But others, like working as an editor and writing books, seemed like things I'd do when I was old and gray and wise. I wrote down that I wanted to travel and live in Paris to learn more French (and be more chic and eat great food) and one day be bilingual. I also wanted to live in San Francisco. When I stepped into the City by the Bay for the first time at the age of eleven, I'd vowed that one day, it would be my home. I thought I might like to be a college chaplain. I'd so loved the chaplain who taught us to move beyond an individualistic faith and embrace our need for one another. At that juncture, I couldn't even imagine becoming an ordained minister or college professor—I'd not seen nor heard women in those roles to imagine that I was holy enough or smart enough for them to be options for me.

I cryptically wrote at the bottom of my list, "Maybe get married. Maybe have kids." I remember the hesitation I felt in writing down those hopes, for they were predicated on being loved by someone who would value my other dreams, too. I didn't want to hitch my life onto someone else's dreams, putting all my energies into another's hopes. I wanted a full life and real love. Was that too much to ask? I was deeply afraid that it was. I finished my list as the sun was setting. I put my journal away, feeling relieved. I did have some ideas on what I could do after graduation. I didn't have any multi-year plan or detailed outline, but I did know what interested me and what I seemed to be good at doing, and which environments and tasks motivated me.

Now that I look back at that moment from the vantage point of three decades past college, I see the order and precise way in which my dreams would come true varied in ways I could not control. But the remarkable realization is how many of the things on that list seem to have been God's dreams for me, too. God's plan and my list were connected. The one who created and called me led me in a life that fulfills me and benefits others. It would be years before I came across Frederick Buechner's confirming definition of vocation: "The place God calls you to is the place where your deep gladness and the world's deep hunger meet."[1]

I realize now that it was not my job to figure out the future; it was my task to be honest before God about my hopes and then to let God lead. To do that, I had to learn to flap my little untested wings in the direction I knew, trusting I'd see where to go next once I got there.

Discernment was not a word I remember hearing much in my college classes or in my home. More often, the concept of getting direction from

---

1   Frederick Buechner, *Wishful Thinking: A Seeker's Theological ABC* (HarperOne, 1993).

God was communicated in a phrase like, "God has told me to . . ." or "Listen to what the Word says." It all sounded pretty direct, like a mother saying firmly: "Go clean your room, and don't come out until it's done." As my post-college years unfolded, I did not hear God like that. I sensed God through nudges, reverberations in scripture, unexpected open doors accompanied by a thumb in the back, closed doors that I had tried vainly to open, divine encounters when someone said something that just opened my eyes. Discernment also came through active ministry. Serving through student ministries on campus (I had been the student director of campus ministries) and later through my local church helped me see that I could actually be God's answer in some small way for another person in trouble or pain. Ministry also showed me my limits. I tried to be Mother Teresa and found I wasn't her. Discernment, I was learning, is a lifelong spiritual discipline.

So when graduation day arrived, I had come up with a short-term plan. I had been selected to go to Paris for a summer mission project. Yes! Off I flew for the summer with three very tall college students—one of our assignments was to offer a summer children's basketball program in the park. I was a foot too short to help with that, so I did puppets and storytelling and learned to talk to the moms and kids when the basketball portions were going on. We were assigned to work mainly in an Algerian immigrant community, so the food was great—more couscous than croissants—and I needed to learn more about Islam than French culture to converse with folks who were recent immigrants from North Africa. It was not what I expected, but it opened new worlds for me.

When summer ended, I was moving to San Francisco. I had led a student mission team to work in a church plant in the Haight-Ashbury neighborhood during spring break of our senior year. Much to my surprise, just before graduation, the staff of that funky mission church had asked if I would be willing to join them. They had two job opportunities for me to consider: The first was self-supporting and all about ministry; the second had ministry responsibilities, too, and came with a modest salary, office work, and bookkeeping. I opted for the latter—even though the first job description was more to my liking and office work would be a stretch. My brand new B.A. degree was in literature/speech communications. I did not know a thing about bookkeeping. But I didn't want to fundraise. Even bookkeeping was better than asking people to support me. I wanted a job and to be able to pay my own bills and I really wanted to live in San Francisco. Review the list—Paris and San Francisco—Check! Check!

So I moved to San Francisco on Labor Day. All the staff had plans and had left the city, so I was alone in a new place for the first time in my life. My inner homing device propelled me to the end of Fulton Street to Ocean Beach. I climbed up on a cement barrier wall that holds back the waves in stormy times and looked out at the gray ocean and matching skies. Was I up to this? Was my dad right when he had said I'd never find a (straight) man in San Francisco? Should I have done what my parents would have preferred—go to seminary in the Midwest, or come home and look for work there? The waves and the wind and the water birds calmed me in time. Nope, this was the life I wanted. I was in the right place.

Those first few years out of college were amazingly wonderful and hard. I had my first paycheck stolen along with my wallet, but friends and family took pity when they heard the story and the checks they sent rather miraculously added up to exactly what I had lost. The church I worked for was always short on money and full of homeless and addicted people. I had to learn about boundaries, lived-out ethics, and recovery processes. I learned that God's healing work in people's lives (including mine) was usually very slow and not guaranteed. Love is always available, but my expectation that each person who came to our church would embrace faith and find healing, as if life were an escalator heading only upward, is a myth. Despair and depression and violence are as real in the city as are glitz and glamour and success. I had wanted to live out my faith in a place where it was not expected nor assumed, and in doing so, I learned quickly that my new neighbors had their own belief systems—New Age, Sufi, eclectic, agnostic—and that challenged me to learn from others' search for meaning and belonging rather than run in fear of difference. I struggled to find words and actions to witness to the love and grace of God in Jesus upon which I staked my very life. God helped me find new teachers, books, and friends to keep me growing in faith and maturity.

Within my first year out of college, I met the man I would eventually marry (a few years and several break-ups and reconnections later). He was my boss, and when we went out for dinner one night to a restaurant called "Friends" (I'm not making this up), as various members of our all-single staff often did together, it was just the two of us. We both noticed and acknowledged that our relationship was shifting to more-than-friends, which was both thrilling and troubling. We liked working together and did so rather well—his visionary skills were a good balance to my people-orientation. But how could we explore the relationship and work as colleagues? He was clergy, and I was both a staff and congregation member.

He'd told other women who had been interested in him that he did not date women in his congregation. How would we do this? I started looking for another job. I knew the future of the relationship was more important than that particular job—they could find a better bookkeeper and did.

Soon I got a phone call from the editor of a local publishing company. I had done an informational interview with him while still in college as I tried to sort out my after-college plans. The company had not been hiring at the time, but now they were looking for an editorial assistant in the religious books division. He had remembered me. Would I come in for an interview? I did. While my typing test wasn't great, the fact that I could interact easily with Christian authors and those from other religious groups (I'd been learning from my neighbors) meant I was hired. Check the list. Two more dreams—a gifted, complex guy loved me, and I had an editorial job (with high prestige and low pay) that required me to read and evaluate religious books all day. Check. Check.

Working in publishing was something I had imagined I might do later in life after graduate school, but I guessed that chronology wrong. In fact, it was my editorial position that allowed me to go back to school. The company's tuition reimbursement plan let me take one class at a time, as long as my boss vouched that the course would help me in my work. I began to pursue a master's degree in religion. I loved my job and going to school, but it was challenging. The program that I was pursuing required frequent travel across the Bay Bridge, often in traffic. And while I could leave work early to take a late-afternoon class, I had to make up the hours. The flexibility did not mean less work, it meant more. It took me six years to finish that degree.

In one of the first classes I took, on the History of Christian Spirituality, I began to notice how often the word discernment was used by Christian spiritual teachers. John Cassian, a 4th-century monk who founded a French monastery for men and women, talked of putting all thoughts on the scale of the heart (the inner place of choice and volition, not just emotion) in order to distinguish those that honored God and would result in good action from those that were freighted with pride and desires to be original and noticed. Ignatius of Loyola, the early 16th-century Spanish founder of the Jesuits, wrote his *Spiritual Exercises* to help his priests pause at least twice a day to review the day through prayer while paying attention to the ways present activities and interactions are leading toward (consolation) or away (disconsolation) from an awareness of God's presence and purposes. John Calvin, the French Protestant Reformer who lived in Geneva during the same time as Ignatius did in Spain, taught that the early Protestants were to take a daily account that started not with a list of wrongdoing but an awareness of being in the intimacy of Christ's love. He urged them to review the day, looking for moments and actions of God's presence and confessing areas in need of grace and forgiveness.

John Wesley, the English 18th-century Anglican and co-founder of the Methodist movement, offered a well-ordered way for persons to discern the work of the spirit through regular interaction with other members of small classes, or bands. Each week, members were to have an honest conversation about known sins, temptations, doubts, and spiritual victories. Band members were encouraged to ask and to allow others to tell them what they saw and heard in the lives of the others so all could cultivate more perfect love toward God, self, and others.

Oh my. From that class forward, I had a new vision of life. I wanted to be more intentionally led by the Holy Spirit. I now knew that would mean cultivating spiritual friendships and continually ordering my life by regular prayer, Bible reading, retreats, and active service. I would also need to allow others to look over my shoulder at any checklist I might manufacture and help me listen for God's guidance. I soon sought out a spiritual director with whom I met monthly—a practice I've engaged in for much of my adult life.

The first time I sought out a spiritual director during a time of acute confusion, she helped me with a question: Who told you that? She pushed me to articulate the faith assumptions and values that I had uncritically picked up in childhood that no longer held or helped in adulthood. Years later, another spiritual director made me stop talking long enough to learn to sit still in prayer so I might become familiar with God's "voice" that is beyond words. When I was not seeing a spiritual director regularly I was a part of a prayer group, much like a band, where friends mutually shared, cared, carried, challenged, and prayed each other through life's ups and downs.

As I neared thirty years of age, I finished seminary and gave birth to the first of my two daughters, who are the lights of my life. We moved across the country and began a long career shift from publishing to ministry. Now, with children in tow, my family travelled only wherever we could afford tickets. I went on fewer retreats but still sought out teachers and companions who could help me learn how to discern for myself and prayerfully be present with others. Discernment was not all about my finding my way. We are all mixed up together. We all have lists of dreams that God cares about, and few people I've ever met can read God's road map in isolation.

Recently, when perplexed by an intractable situation, a friend sent me these words via email: "God 'will cover you with his pinions, and under his wings you will find refuge' (Psalm 91:4)." This friend was clearly nudged by the Spirit—for God knows "bird talk" will get my attention in a time of disconsolation or confusion. These words from the Psalms were a confirmation of God's continued care and guidance for me. I pulled out my Bible and read the Psalm slowly and repeatedly, and the phrase "Cover you with his pinions" caught my attention, so I stayed there, praying those words as they moved from my head to my heart. The pinions are the primary feathers, those long wing or tail feathers that provide thrust, tilt, and lift. Without them, birds can't lift off the ground or soar. God covers me with the primary feathers of the spirit's care and will bear me up and guide when God's timing is sure.

Thirty years have flown by since my college graduation. I'm grateful that several checkmarks indicate the fulfillment of hoped-for accomplishments and adventures. I'm even more thankful for the ways some of those early dreams have been salvaged from missteps or diverted by Godly dreams that better fit my gifts and limits. In so many ways my heart's desires have been fulfilled. I will keep heading for the high places to discern God's direction and timing all the days of my life. I trust the updraft of the spirit; the leading is sure.

Fear Not

Sylvia Cortez

The view of the northwest face of Half Dome in Yosemite National Park naturally evokes awe and wonder, and when it is wrapped in per- fect light it leaves me speechless. The first time I saw Half Dome, I felt a sense of insignificance as I stood in the shadow of that huge rock. Yet I also felt acutely aware of the strength of my own existence and of the grandeur of life itself. Half Dome stopped me in my tracks and yet mysteriously propelled me forward, drawing me in to consider the summit no matter how long the journey.

That is a strong picture of how I felt in my early twenties. I would soon be graduating and was anxious for the experiences and the beautiful and exciting life I imagined for myself. I had not spoken with anyone about life after college and so didn't really know what to expect, but I had many assumptions about the ways I thought my life would generally turn out. Somehow I felt confident that my life would be beautiful, adventurous and spectacular. I remember feeling that I had a good grasp of how to face challenges and for the most part felt in control of my future. When you're young and you stand before something like the north face of Half Dome, it has the power to reveal the raw beauty of the world and to inspire courage to live life to the fullest. That's how my friends and I felt as we approached graduation and what we suspected was "real life" outside those university walls.

As our senior year was coming to a close, we wanted to savor our last days in college by spending one last long weekend together. So on a Friday afternoon we piled all of our camping gear into my tiny 1989 blue Toyota hatchback and headed for Yosemite. By the time we arrived well past midnight the full campground was quiet, our fellow campers asleep for hours. We tiptoed our way to our campsite, carrying the least amount of gear possible, and quietly unrolled our sleeping bags, exhausted from the long eight-hour drive and our own non-stop chatter. I remember settling under the quiet starlit sky, content and at peace with life and the company of friends.

Though my friends were seasoned campers, it was my first time camping, which meant my first time experiencing the enormous stillness of sleeping un- der the stars, the comfort of campfire conversations and satisfying laughter as we teased one another and shared stories. Acutely aware of my inexperience, I made sure to pay close attention, following their every move as we hiked, built campfires, and cooked our meals.

As a soon-to-be college graduate, I knew as much about life as I did about camping. Like any young person on the verge of adulthood, I was right to be excited about what lay before me, but I had no idea about the many amazing opportunities, difficult choices, consequences, events, and breathless moments I would experience. Like that early experience of standing before Half Dome, there have been times when I have felt a sense of insignificance in the space of this large world. Other moments have made me acutely aware of the strength of my own existence, and of the fleeting but beautiful present moments. I spent many of the years that followed doing what I learned to do on that camping trip—paying close attention to what my friends were doing and acting like I knew what I was doing. What I didn't realize was how little I knew of what to expect of the various turns and detours that I might encounter and of the many situations and seasons that would impact my perceptions and practice of faith.

It's been twenty years since that first trip to Yosemite. And while my love of the outdoors, of camping and hiking steadily grew, surprisingly it is only in recent years that I returned to Yosemite. Standing before Half Dome again, I contemplated my life as it was almost twenty years before. While Half Dome remained virtually unchanged, so much about my own life had changed, and I struggled to remember and recognize the person I was when I last stood there. And yet I recognized a stillness within me that matched the still and seemingly eternal presence of Half Dome. I felt very much at rest, still excited about the years ahead, knowing that in so many ways there has been adventure, and beauty, and that my life has been spectacular because of the people I have shared it with, and in many ways, nothing like what I had imagined.

In his book *Praying the Psalms*, Walter Brueggemann describes three phases he recognizes in the Christian life and the movement of many biblical stories. Brueggemann asserts that throughout life we are always moving through: orientation, disorientation, and reorientation. We all experience moments of orientation, when we have a clear sense of direction and when life seems whole and balanced; the ground beneath us seems fairly sturdy—we're excited about the road ahead and approach it with great optimism. We all experience moments of disorientation, when life throws us a curve ball and we find that we're no longer on stable ground. Questions, doubts, and fears abound in this phase. Reorientation is when we're able to move beyond the chaotic experiences to find ourselves on stronger footing; we have survived a time of dislocation and re-ground our lives in an altered way.

Orientation

When I think of the first phase, orientation, I often think of the first line of the 23rd Psalm: "The Lord is my Shepherd; I shall lack nothing." I also recall the season at the end of my college career when I felt invincible, confident, and assured. Moments of orientation are necessary and good because they offer us respite and the assurance of hope, joy, redemption, and direction. But as we all learn, times of orientation last only for a season. We rarely are able to stay in this state of awe and wonder, of rest and assurance. Instead, we move in and out of disorienting and reorienting stages as well. I had no idea of this in my early twenties. It made sense to me then that moments of orientation were the goal; they were, in fact, what most people were trying to achieve. I suppose I believed I would somehow arrive at a place in my life where I had no doubts, and felt no fear or sense of insecurity about life, myself, God, and the world. Intuitively I must have known there would be setbacks, but I felt very confident that I would be able to handle whatever scenarios came my way. Unfamiliar yet with the power of disorientation, I was unaware of the effect that obstacles, disappointment, broken dreams, loss, and failure would play in my life.

On my wall hangs a quote by Frederick Buechner that I return to again and again:

"Here is the world.
Beautiful and terrible things will happen.
Don't be afraid!"[1]

---

1   Frederick Buechner, *Wishful Thinking: A Seeker's ABC* (New York: HarperCollins, 1993), 39.

This is such a beautiful and powerful proclamation. I recite it to graduates and newlyweds; they are words I have prayed over newborn children. In the midst of all that I would want to share with others about life in general and about the Christian journey in particular, it would be this age-old message to "Fear not!"

Reflecting on 1 John 4:18, Buechner reasons that if perfect love casts out all fear, then perhaps it is also true that fear can cast out perfect love. My own journey has been riddled with moments of examination where I have had to identify and name my fears in order to adequately face the road before me. Past experiences can make us cautious; and fear itself can be paralyzing. But these words, "Fear not," form a running theme throughout scripture that testify to God's faithful presence and call us, with God's help, to live our lives with steady faithful courage in the face of the unknown.

So it is that sometimes we find ourselves on this steady ground of orientation where the call to fear not is a bit easier than at other times. Moments of orientation can be so steady, or so exciting as we await the future with no real sense of fear, that we are often unaware of how rare these moments are when we are in the midst of them.

Disorientation

We all experience moments of disorientation. While our immediate temptation may be to pass through this phase as quickly as possible, it has been helpful for me to remember that "Lost is a place too."[2]

I once ran a half marathon that I knew would be somewhat difficult and challenging, but I was completely surprised by the elevation change of the climb and the rain that pounded us at the beginning of the race. The adjustment I had to make during those first two miles to the rhythm of my breathing and running took some time because I was simply disoriented mostly by the rain. In much the same way, disorientation almost always begins with an element of surprise, and it may take some time to acclimate to the various changes that disorientation brings.

When I reflect on what I thought I knew about God and faith in my early twenties, I realize how linked those thoughts were with the many expectations I had about life in general. In all the best ways, living out my faith was closely linked to what I believed I would be doing vocationally, specifically, as a mis- sionary outside the United States. It was linked also to the friends I imagined I would share my life with—linked to the

---

2   Christina Crawford, *Survivor* (Boston: Dutton Adult, 1988), 17.

expectation that I would someday share in ministry with a husband, and know the beauty of raising a family, not to mention the achievements or opportunities I imagined for myself.

Twenty years later I find myself in a job that I love and am deeply grateful for, but that I never imagined for myself in my early twenties. Some of the friends I imagined would always be a part of my life have fallen away, and many other amazing and wonderful friends have been knit into my life. One of the most unexpected realities has been to not yet know the challenges and joys that come with marriage and motherhood. Even more surprising has been my evolving perspectives on marriage and motherhood as I grew older having more fully embraced the deeply rich life I live without these things. Though none of these areas turned out to be what I expected, each circumstance has carried with it elements of surprise, both positive and negative, and joys that stretched and challenged the perceptions I had about God and my place in this world. Though I look back now with the clarity of hindsight, there were many moments during the last twenty years when the unexpected wrapped in the not-yet caused anxiety within me and forced me to engage in questions of identity and self-worth. Who am I if not married and without children? How can I flourish as a single person? Do I really believe that I am loved and loveable if not in the most traditional manner? Vocationally, disorientation forced me to engage in questions about my calling. Despite my experience and training, as doors closed for the mission field, I found myself questioning whether I had accurately heard God's voice all those years earlier. Where was God leading me if not to the mission field? Such doubts and fears about things I had previously taken for granted forced me to consider whether I would ultimately trust in God's guidance, protection, and provision amid the many unanswered questions.

When things don't go the way we thought they would, or the way we think they should, there's a strong sense that something is wrong and terribly broken in our lives, and the future seems daunting. Disorientation is the awareness that life is no longer whole. It can be difficult not to allow the present circumstances (of which we can see only in part) to define our life's meaning. I might have been spared some anxiety if I had rightly understood the gift of disorientation, of being shoved into reflection about my present circumstances and unmet desires. I wish someone had asked me in my early twenties to consider and imagine all the many ways my life could be full and rich, deep with meaning, if only some or even none of my expectations had been met. Early on in my life I imagined fulfillment, joy, and happiness with very specific things in mind. This is not altogether bad. It's important to set specific goals and to envision certain hopes and dreams; knowing what we desire often gives us a sense of direction. However, when our imagination is limited only to those realities we imagine for ourselves, it makes it difficult to adequately embrace all that God is offering us.

Despite our optimistic theologies, our relentless expectations for happiness in our own image, our futile attempts at "effortless perfection," we all experience the pain of loss, rejection, deception, grief, shattered dreams, false hopes, difficult transitions, and death. I have been witness to disorienting experiences within my own community and the wider world again and again in the form of failed marriages, miscarriages, a sudden disease, broken dreams, bad choices, rejection, barrenness, injustice, death, accidents, poverty, and world disasters. And of course disorientation sometimes comes as a result of our own actions. I have been surprised to discover that being rooted in Christian faith was not an automatic, foolproof protection against the strong cultural norms or unhealthy practices we adopt for our lives. Cultural liturgies have a way of taking root in our lives, and it is precisely in moments of disorientation that we're able to examine our belief systems and our practice of Christian discipleship.

The questions I am forced to ask in the detours seem threatening as I realize that the foundations known and understood in the period of orientation are no longer enough. Though I can remember times when I trusted in God's provision, disorientation can thrust me into despair or make me frantic to make things happen on my own. Eventually I learn that in seasons of disori- entation it's quite normal to ask the question, "Why?" and, if I'm honest, even times when I've asked, "Why me?" No matter how acquainted we are with the biblical stories or the testimonies from within our own faith communities, we're often still surprised by our own experiences of disorientation. During these times I am most acutely aware of my own homesickness for God. When our pastors and spiritual mentors are faithful to the scriptures, they teach us stories of faith tested and lives gone terribly wrong but redeemed by God. They tell us not about God's faithfulness to always bless or provide for us, but of God's gracious mercy and saving love, of God's forgiveness and redemption, of God's faithful presence even in the midst of our greatest sorrows, even though we walk through the valley of the shadow of death.

As mentioned earlier, some of my most painful times of disorientation have revolved around my identity as a single woman. I am for the most part wonderfully content with my life. In my twenties I once heard musician Rich

Mullins say, "If you're happy being single you'll probably be happy being married. And if you're miserable being single you'll probably be miserable being married." As a young woman I internalized that message and so have been acutely aware that marriage was never going to solve any surface issues of happiness. I have been witness to the many expectations others have had for their own marriages and the journeys of disorientation in the face of those expectations. I have tried to be faithful to find contentment whether or not I was dating someone. I have learned that there are joys and sorrows in being single just as there are joys and sorrows in being married, and the point is to embrace it all, wherever I find myself at the present moment. Learning to be content has allowed me to manage hope and loneliness, to name all the ways hope, joy, and wholeness abound in my life with or without a spouse, especially as I remember my place in the story of God.

But the systems of this world and the status markers we use do not make it easy to flourish as a single person. As one friend often reminds me, we live in a married world. At times even faith communities have been slow to fully incorporate and embrace single adults into their community. Much like in the workplace, people in the church might sometimes expect more volunteer time from singles because of the false perception that surely we must have extra time on our hands without the demands of a family. Sometimes people within the church have seemed more consumed with finding me a husband than with asking me about my spiritual well-being and calling. Faith communities have been one of the most difficult places to find good, strong friendships. Many married men in the church community are cautious to develop friendships with single women for fear of "what might happen." Sadly, it has been equally difficult to form friendships with married women in the church because they have seen me as a threat. As one friend graciously observed, "Sylvia, you are beautiful, smart, funny, confident, and single, which is a huge threat to married women in the church." While the reality of extramarital affairs abound in our day, I do not believe we have found adequate ways to engage in conversations about sexuality within the Christian community that would help us discern healthy ways of interacting with one another, ways that do not alienate those who are single, and without dispersing our community into groups based on age or marital status. I long for a church committed to inter-generational practices, where societal labels are diminished and where we find unity and identity in the Kingdom of God, not by labels or status markers the world sets for us. We are all created for love, and love is present in the body of Christ. Instead of waiting to start a family,

I remember that I have already been set in a community of brothers and sisters in Christ, and that we are children of one God. In each disorienting phase, despite my sometimes stubborn prayers that I most certainly need specific things or people in my life, one of the most acute lessons I have learned is that I haven't needed any of these things to be assured of God's presence in my life, or of my own strong presence and place in the story of God. More importantly, I have also had to wrestle with the harsh realities of men, women, and children I have met around the world who do not have even the most basic needs. I remember Kanta in India, Mary in Nairobi, Solomon in India. My own aspirations and assumptions about what I have a right to are stretched by the encounters I have had with the wider body of Christ to which I belong. Their faces and their most basic needs challenge the way that I ultimately pray about my own needs and longings.

Once, keenly aware that I was entering a season of darkness, I found myself resisting it because I was afraid of what I would discover. At the time I feared that God would surely ask me to sacrifice that which I most desired, and I couldn't bear the pain of what I expected that particular dark night of the soul might bring. When I shared this with Mark, a close and trusted spiritual friend, he said to me, "Sylvia, the purpose of the darkness is that we don't know what we'll encounter." There it was again, the message hidden in my present disorienting experience, "Fear not!"

As I learn to set aside my conventional coping mechanisms during these vulnerable disorienting times, I approach and engage God in honest conversations that teach me about what I most deeply desire, and what I believe about myself and about God. Only when I have dared to draw near with all of my brokenness do I most fully encounter the One who knows my deepest longings, hurts, desires, and joys. As fearful an act as it may be, it is crucial to face the dark night, to examine my fears and the deaths I must die in order to grow. This forces me to remember and proclaim my true identity in this world, and the God in whom all hope and rest is found. Each of us is so much more than our wounds, our joys, our triumphs, our successes. We are beloved of God, above all things.

Reorientation

Brueggemann suggests that praying the Psalms is a way to move through disorientation into reorientation. He asserts that most of the Psalms can be appropriately prayed only by people who are living at the edge of their lives, sensitive to the raw hurts, the primitive passions, and the naïve elations that are at the bottom of our lives. For most of us, liturgical or devotional entry into the Psalms requires a real change of pace. It asks us to depart from the closely managed world of public survival, to move into the open, frightening, healing world of speech with the Holy One.[3]

What has most allowed me to move from disorientation to reorientation has been the healing reality of time coupled with transforming honest moments of prayer before the Lord, especially as I learn to pray as the Psalmist. Unlike the sacrifices I guessed that God would require of me, these times often offered freedom and a deep sense of joy as I have been assured of God's presence and deep love, and of my place in the story of God.

The movement from disorientation to reorientation is about emerging from a situation with a renewed sense of hope. It is a sort of resting place or landing after a turbulent time. But it is not a return to the way things were. As Brueggemann notes, "Nor is it a return to the old form, a return to normalcy as though nothing had happened. It is rather 'all things new.' And when it happens, it is always a surprise, always a gift of graciousness, and always an experience that evokes gratitude."[4] I am able to emerge with a renewed sense of hope because I emerge with a different perspective or a deeper awareness of God and of God's movement in the world. Reorientation may involve a changed set of attitudes or beliefs about my circumstance, or it may involve a deeper awareness of identity in Christ. It almost always involves knowledge of and relationship with God at a deeper level. As Christians, we continually engage in practices of renewal. The Christian life is not immune to the raw realities of struggle and pain and death. But at the core of our faith is always the promise of new life. To live out our lives in the context of Christian discipleship is to be vigilantly involved in the work of proclaiming and practicing resurrection.

Resurrection work is about bringing to life that which was once dead. It is the continual work of reconciling our lived experiences with the truth of the gospel and to Kingdom ways of imagining and living. My community, my work, the way that I spend my money, the dreams I cultivate, the possessions I accumulate (or don't accumulate), the way in which I sustain relationships, all of these are re-imagined out of my understanding of and place in the Kingdom of God.

Bursting forth in the message of Christ's life, death, and resurrection is the radical proclamation that sin and injustice, pain and sorrow, loss and

---

3   Walter Brueggemann, *Praying the Psalms* (Eugene, OR: Cascade Books, 2007), 8.

4   Walter Brueggemann, *Praying the Psalms* (Eugene, OR: Cascade Books, 2007), 11.

death, can be overcome. There in the message of life-death-resurrection is the reality that God in Christ has been and is present with us in pain, struggle, and mourning. Disorientation never seems to lose its sting, but it has been important for me to remember that it is a natural part of life, and that this season will pass. Knowing that there is movement beyond present experiences, especially times of disorientation, helps me to endure the struggle and not allow myself to be defined by it. Instead I can live into the various movements and anticipate reorientation and renewal.

To anticipate and engage in this transformative work requires that I pay attention to my experiences, or as Lauren Winner says, to pay "theological attention"[5] to all that is happening in and around me. In my work as a campus pastor I engage in exegetical work, examining the historical and literary con- text of the biblical texts, searching for scriptures' meaning and trusting that the Holy Spirit will continue to guide and give us a fresh word for our day. It has been helpful to use these same tools to exegete my own life and the world around me. Identifying the recurring themes in my own life allows me to name those places that God wants to transform, stretching the boundaries for me of what it means to be a part of God's Kingdom here on earth. It also allows me to ask the question, "What story is God trying to tell through my life?"

I cannot rush through the various phases, but I have become better able to identify ways to move through each season, trusting that my faithfulness to specific Christian practices will see me through. These spiritual practices change and evolve as I change and evolve, but I am keenly aware that I need certain practices to stay awake to the work of life and faith. Faith is no longer merely a set of beliefs in my head, but now is a living, dynamic process of allowing experience to inform faith, and faith to inform my practices, the ways I live and act in the world.

Christian Practice

Trusting in the various seasons and phases of life allows me to embrace the more important work of entering into the seasons of the Church. Throughout the world, many faith communities are committed to ordering time around the seasons of the Christian calendar. By honoring the various events surrounding the life, death, and resurrection of Jesus Christ, the Christian calendar leads the body of Christ through rhythmic reflections meant to continually direct our gaze on Christ and his ways. Learning

---

5   Lauren Winner, Mudhouse Sabbath (Orleans, MA: Paraclete Press, 2003.), 75.

to live in this Christian time challenges the ever-present temptation to structure time by my own agenda, experiences, or by cultural norms and rituals. Instead I learn to mark the days and seasons by God's time with the church, seeking to continuously encounter the story of God and deepening my faith in its message.

The season of Advent, which marks the New Year for Christians, invites me to a season of anticipation, waiting, and hope found in the birth of Christ. Christmas is the fullness of that hope, joy, and new birth. The season of Epiphany invites me to reflect and respond to the Revelation message, and reminds me to proclaim this gift to all. Ash Wednesday centers me in my humanity and forces me to acknowledge the sin in my life, and the need for God's forgiveness. The season of Lent invites me to enter into Christ's journey to the cross, giving me the opportunity to reflect on and practice sacrifice, prayer, giving, and self-discipline. Holy Week and Easter continue the journey through grief, death, and finally resurrection. Pentecost is joy and celebration for ministry, a gift of the Holy Spirit. And Ordinary time is a season of growth and continued renewal until we return again to the season of Advent. These seasons allow us to enter into the joy and sorrow that are wrapped in the story of God, and yet remind us of the ultimate hope we have in Christ's life, death, and resurrection. Throughout the year I catch myself anticipating the next season of reflection, as I am learning to continually approach and receive the message of Christ in these ways.

The lectionary, a series of biblical readings on a three-year cycle, accompanies the seasons of the Christian calendar. These readings provide for me a rhythmic steady diet of scripture that help me remain rooted in the story of God. Left to my own devices I might habitually read those books or passages of scripture that repeatedly bring comfort to me and my various circumstances. Instead, the lectionary focuses on all of scripture, offering daily readings in the Torah, Psalms, the Epistles, and the Gospels. In these readings I discover, again and again, the character of God at work in the lives of people who were lost and broken; God at work in the lives of people who were sinful but redeemed; God among those trying to faithfully follow God's leading and commands. I see the world and see myself in those pages and am often reminded of Barbara Brown Taylor's commentary regarding the scriptures: "The Bible interprets me faster than I can interpret it."[6] These scriptures reveal to me the work of God's mercy, grace, love, and discipline, and the movement of God reconciling the world to himself (2 Corinthians 5:19). They call me out of the fog of my circumstances, reminding me of my

---

6   Barbara Brown Taylor, *The Preaching Life* (Cambridge, MA: Cowley, 1993), 52.

place in the story of God and the call to be a faithful witness and a minster of reconciliation in the world.

The lectionary also allows me to examine all of the opposing liturgies I encounter in daily life. These various scripts that call for my attention and have the power to influence life practices and beliefs abound in society, economics, books, magazines, media, conversations, and even in our own imaginations. As I encounter these liturgies, the task is not to dismiss blindly all things that seem secular. Rather I hold close and am led by the liturgy of the Church, and the presence of Christ, the Word made flesh.

While no faith community is perfect, and church has at times been a source of pain and even disorientation, it has also consistently been a place where I encounter God in the liturgy, in the corporate reading of the scriptures, and in the participation of the Eucharist with those who faithfully gather. It is in this community that I have discovered myself, those sides I don't have to face when I'm by myself. In community I'm confronted with my neediness, but also discover that I am deeply needed by others and so am continuously reminded that our humanity is bound up in others. In this community that is the Body of Christ, I learn how to speak, how to think, how to act, how to be in Christ. So, I continue to pay careful attention to what those around me are doing as we gather to praise, thank, plead with, trust, and partner with Christ. Together we are witnesses to the continuing work of new resurrection stories within our communities. Together we mourn and celebrate, give and receive, live and die. Buechner suggests that we return to church again and again be- cause we desire to be reminded that the story of God really is true. In the midst of mundane moments, in the face of the brokenness in our world, in the deeply disorientating ways we might experience life at times, I believe we return to the Body of Christ to hear echoes of God saying to us, "Fear not!"

As we embrace this message again and again, we gain strength and courage to experience resurrection in our own lives. Resurrection is happening all the time. Each small act of faith is an act of courage, the practice of resurrection.

Whatever awe and wonder I felt at the site of Half Dome has paled in comparison to the continuous echoes of God's guiding presence throughout my life. And it is the humbling reality of God's presence at work in and through me that allows me to embrace the strength and power of my own existence in this wide world. I am so grateful that life has been and is full of mystery, joy, sorrow and even detours that often open surprising new experiences and opportunities. I am grateful that we serve a

God whose proclamation and call to us over the centuries has been, "Fear Not!" May our deepest prayers of longing, hope, and thanksgiving finally and forevermore find their full rest in God.

> For all that has been,
> Thank you.
> For all that is to come,
> Yes!

–Dag Hammarskjöld

Discussion Questions

§

I.   Love, Laughter, and Loss: Living in Relationships

Making, Breaking, and Keeping Friendships
Melissa Tucker

1. What does it mean to hold our friendships with open hands? Why is this often difficult?

2. Have you ever had to break a friendship deliberately? What was the result of this decision?

3. What do you hope the presence of friends in your life will look like five years from now?

Three Strikes and You're . . . In: Learning to Date
Coleen Montgomery

1. What does it mean to be "datable"? Is this a quality to strive for?

2. What are your essential and negotiable qualities for potential or current relationships? Why are these important?

3. Coleen makes a decision to date actively. To what extent should dating be an active pursuit?

Singleness: More Than a Holding Pattern
Jamie Noling

1.   How do you balance work and relationships? Should the demands of one influence the other?

2.   What has God called you to do? Do you feel outside pressure to define or modify your calling?

3.   What has been the church's treatment of single people, in your experience? How could this be modeled or improved?

4.   Are there situations in your life that make you feel as if you are in a holding pattern? What have you learned in the process?

Beyond Picture Perfect
Linda Beail

1.   If you desire marriage either now or in the future, what are your reasons? What is at the core of those desires?

2.   Can you imagine being content and fulfilled as a single person?

3. Have you ever bought into the notions that certain symbols of success or specific types of relationships and/or emotions would make you whole? Why do you think it is so difficult to "play the cards we are dealt?"

4. Do you believe that the twists and turns life offers might in fact be the richest parts of our journey?

A Foreign Affair: The Adaptive Journey of Intercultural Marriage
Melissa Gentzkow Lázaro

1. When have you had to navigate the intricacies of intercultural inter- actions? What strategies did you develop?

2. How has the opinion of your family affected your past or current relationships? How do you balance the voices of your loved ones with the voice of God in your life?

3. In what ways could considering the intention of a message first before the actual words be helpful in relationships?

Sailing On: A Mid-Life Look at a Medical Marriage
Allyson Jule

1. In what ways have you, like Allyson, relied on a socialized persona? If it has ever proven to be insufficient, how have you tried to adjust your actions?

2. Should one spouse's career ever take prominence over the other's in a marriage relationship?

3. Why do we often expect our lives to be smooth sailing once we meet that perfect person or land that perfect job? How can we live so that we are honest about our expectations and realities?

"Equal Opportunity Kitchen": A Dual-Career Family in Christian Ministry
Mary Rearick Paul

1. How does your parents' relationship affect your expectations and aims for marriage? How should areas such as name changes, meals, household decor and management, and careers be managed between two people in a marriage relationship?

2. Do you agree with Mary's interpretation of biblical passages such as Ephesians 5? Why? How can we allow space for honest conversations about the equality of women, especially in the church? What does equality in the church look like?

3. Mary asserts that cultural norms about the roles wives and husbands should play are so pervasive that we are often unaware of how much they affect us. Do you agree?

4. What do you sense God calling you to do with your life?

Negotiating Identity: Retaining a Sense of Self in Marriage and Motherhood
Melissa Burt-Gracik

1. How might conversations with a significant other regarding choice of last names impact that relationship?

2. If you have children or plan to have them, how do you perceive a healthy division of household and childcare responsibilities to be present in your life?

3. To what extent should a person's identity be determined by factors such as relationship status, family roles, or vocational positions?

What Does a Woman Look Like? Reflections on the Multiple, Messy, and Mutating
Bettina Tate Pedersen

1. What does being a woman look like to you?

2. Do you know women who encapsulate what you see as "ideal?" What do you admire?

3. How can women stop comparing themselves unfavorably to one another, or having unrealistic expectations of themselves? Does telling the truth about our flaws and struggles, and our accomplishments, help us to better appreciate ourselves and God's grace at work in our lives?

4. How is your own life messy, multiple, or mutating?

Choosing Motherhood: Adoption and the Single Life
Rebecca Flietstra

1. If you want to have children, would you consider raising them as a single parent? Why or why not?

2. Have you experienced situations that have not worked out according to your ideal plan or expectation? Did they turn out to be better or worse than your initial plan?

3. How does the practice of adoption relate to our calling as Christians?

Shaped by Motherhood: Cultivating Reverence and Irreverence in the Face of Social Roles
Ivy George
1. Do you see gender inequality as a thing of the past? In what ways is it still present?
2. What does it mean to be a female? How does motherhood impact this?
3. Has there ever been a time when you felt identified more as a woman than as a human being?
4. In what ways can both men and women participate in "giv[ing] life a chance," as Ivy describes?

II.   Between Calling and Commerce: Living in Faithful Vocation

The Importance of Ambition for Christian Women: Participating in God's Gracious Work in the World
Linda Beail
1. As a child, what did you want to be when you grew up? What do you want to be now?
2. How do you view ambition? Would you consider yourself ambitious? Does your fear of balancing work and family temper your ambition?
3. What kind of work is God calling you to do in the world?
4. Do you recognize any tendencies in your own life to self-efface, set impossibly high standards or internalize failure? Do you have a difficult time owning your accomplishments and receiving praise for them? Why do you think this is?
5. Have you experienced or been witness to the trap of performing tasks with "effortless perfection"? How can we combat this?
6. Is it surprising to you that both women and men need meaningful work and meaningful relationships?

Ambition and Vocation: Threads of Our Lives
Maxine Walker
1. What do your clothes say about you, your ambition, and your vocation?
2. Does ambition equate to pride? Who or what in your life has caused you to think this way?

3. Maxine says that women are often stumbling blocks, to themselves or to others. In what ways have you found this to be true?

Two in a Million: The Gifts of Work and Adoption
Melanie Springer Mock
1. How are being a professor/writer and being a mother both compelling parts of Melanie's identity? Do you see these as compatible, or in competition with one another? Why?
2. In what ways does the idea of biblical equality come into play in determining career and childcare responsibilities in a relationship?
3. In what practical ways can the church welcome and value working parents?

Riding the Third Wave: Gender Inequity in the Workplace
LeAnn Wiley Burton
1. Do you have or want to have children? How do you think this decision will affect your career?
2. How do you think your experiences (or lack thereof) of gender discrimination have shaped your perception of equality in the workplace?
3. Do you perceive women who work and have children differently than women who work and do not have children? How are your assumptions helpful or harmful?

Twists in the Path
Lindsey Lupo
1. In contemplating your vocation, do you find it helpful to think in five- or ten-year chunks of time rather than a one-time career decision? What do you see in your next ten years?
2. What fears or concerns do you have about taking a new path?
3. Who are the role models you look to for inspiration, wisdom and courage?

The Price of Independence: Paying for Life after College
Kelli McCoy
1. What has your family of origin taught you explicitly about money? What have they taught you implicitly? How have these lessons shaped your own attitudes toward finances?

2.   Are you anxious or excited about being financially responsible for yourself? How are you planning for your own financial independence?

3.   Who should pay on a date? How are the power dynamics affected by who pays?

A Husband is Not a Financial Plan
Becky Havens

1. What are some practical ways in which you can plan for your financial future?

2. How are historical and economic trends affecting women today?

3. In what ways has God called you to use your financial resources, currently or in the future? What does the concept of stewardship mean to you?

Loving God With All Our Hearts, Minds, Souls. . . and Money
Melissa Tucker

1. What are your financial priorities? Do Christians have a responsibility to direct their finances in particular ways? How?

2. Are you proactive in managing your finances? What are some financial strategies you employ or would like to employ?

3. What is the significance of tithing? How does this manifest in your own life?

III.   Wholeness and Holiness: Living an Embodied Life

Wonderfully Made or Wonderfully Made Up?
Kristina LaCelle-Peterson

1.   How has your sense of worth been shaped by influences from culture and the media?

2.   Kristina lists this question as one that changed her perceptions: "Why is it a given that women should always try to take up less space in this world?" What do you think?

3.   How does the concept of embodiment influence your understanding of Christian life and practice?

Gratuitous Sex within the Reign of God: A Gift That Grounds and Transcends
Heather Ross

1. What does it mean to have "Christian sex"? Is this a helpful term?

2. When is sex not a gift? How can we seek to preserve its gratuitous nature?

3. How can sex be re-imagined by the church to avoid the fetishization and psychological taboo that Heather describes?

Sheep among Wolves
Jenell Williams Paris

1.   Should Sarah have spoken out against Kevin? Why or why not?

2.   Have you witnessed these kinds of power imbalances being used improperly in the church? How might our notions of Christian femininity make us vulnerable to being taken advantage of? How does our Christian faith give us strength and discernment to combat abusive actions?

3.   Does this essay expand your conception of purity? How can we be both innocent as doves and wise as serpents?

Nurturing Body and Soul
Janell Lundgren

1. In what ways do you seek to live holistically?

2. What is your relationship with food like? How has it shifted over time?

3. Which areas of your life seem over- or under-developed right now?

Moving Beyond Balance to Fullness in Christ
Jennifer Lang

1.   Is balance a worthy goal to aim for? Why or why not? How does fullness differ from balance?

2.   Jennifer observes that women often are expected to take care of others before themselves. Is this true in your own experience? In what ways should we approach the competing demands of the people around us and ourselves?

3.   How do emotions play a role in your perception of yourself and in your interactions with others? How should they?

Transitions and Change: Finding the Still Point
Lois Wagner

1. What have been some significant times of transition in your life?

2. Are you currently in a position of uncertainty? How can you simply make the next move that you can see?

3. What are some ways right now that you can take care of yourself physically, emotionally, mentally, and spiritually?

Learning to Embrace the Mystery of Faith
Cassie Lewis
1.   Cassie describes three stages through which her faith has moved. Can you identify a similar progression in your own faith journey?
2.   How do you understand miracles in relation to God's presence in the world?
3.   In what ways does mystery inform your practice of Christianity?

In Search of Spiritual Mothers
Carol Blessing
1. How have biblical women and church mothers been discussed in the churches you have attended?
2. In what ways do the maternal images of God influence your faith?
3. What should leadership positions in the church for women look like?

Primary Feathers: Learning to Discern God's Direction
Rebecca Laird
1. What do you hope for?
2. What does it mean to discern?
3. Few people "can read God's road map in isolation," according to Rebecca. Who shares the process of reading with you?

Fear Not
Sylvia Cortez
1. What moments of your life have been ones of orientation, disorientation, and reorientation?
2. How might your life be rich and full of meaning, even if your expectations are never met?
3. What are some of the liturgies of the world that Sylvia describes? How are these countered in the liturgy of Christianity?

About the Contributors

Linda Beail is professor of political science and director of the Margaret Stevenson Center for Women's Studies at Point Loma Nazarene University in San Diego. She is the author of several articles and book chapters on feminism in popular culture, motherhood as a political identity, and evangelical political behavior. She recently completed work on a book entitled *Framing Sarah Palin: Pitbulls, Puritans and Politics* (Routledge, November 2012) about feminism and femininity in American politics. She loves pitching a baseball to her son in the backyard, dreaming about a trip to Paris with her daughter, and watching *Mad Men*.

Carol Blessing, Ph.D., is professor of literature at Point Loma Nazarene University, where she has taught since 1993 after earning her doctorate at the University of California, Riverside. Her publications include "Speaking Out: Feminist Theology and Women's Proclamation in the Wesleyan Tradition," co-written with Lisa Bernal in *Being Feminist, Being Christian*, "Queen Elizabeth I as Deborah the Queen: Exceptional Women of Power" in *Goddesses and Queens: The Iconography of Elizabeth I*, "The Trials of Mary Stuart: Anxious Circulations in John Webster's Drama," in *Women, Justice, and Power in English Renaissance Drama*, "'Most Blessed Daughters of Jerusalem': Aemilia Lanyer's Salve Deus Rex Judeorum and Elizabethan and Jacobean Bible Commentary" in *Ben Jonson Journal*, "Gilbert and Gubar's Daughters: The Madwoman in the Attic's Spectre in Milton Studies" in *The Madwoman in the Attic After Thirty Years*, "Exile and Maternal Loss in the Poems of Patricia Jabbeh Wesley" in *Exile and the Narrative/Poetic Imagination*, "'But Julian of Norwich said Jesus was a Girl!': Teaching the Mystics at a Conservative Protestant University" in *Studies in Medieval and Renaissance Teaching*, and the volume *John Milton* in Bloom's Classic Criticism series.

Melissa Burt-Gracik holds an M.A. in higher education from Geneva College and an M.Div. from Princeton Theological Seminary. She currently mentors student leaders as director of community life at Point Loma Nazarene University. Melissa enjoys writing, exercising on the cliffs of the Southern California coast, serving in her local church, and playing with her family.

LeAnn Wiley Burton is a business development consultant, responsible for strategic company branding that is dedicated to supporting new sales and client retention and providing in-depth research and analysis. Previously, she served as director of marketing and enrollment for a study abroad company and was an admissions counselor at her alma mater for two years. LeAnn received a bachelor's degree in political science from Point Loma Nazarene University. She lives in downtown San Diego with her husband, Zach, and pup, Lucy. They are in constant search of the best breakfast in the city and enjoy trying new places every chance they get—to date, more than 100!

Sylvia Cortez Masyuk is a graduate of Point Loma Nazarene University and Nazarene Theological Seminary. She worked as Director of Discipleship Ministries at Point Loma Nazarene University for eleven years where she thrived in collaborating with faculty and staff to develop creative programs for students in the area of Christian formation. Sylvia currently lives in the beautiful and ancient city of Kyiv (Kiev), Ukraine where she and her husband are enjoying their first year of marriage together. Sylvia loves to travel off the beaten path, the sight of piles of books, hiking, running half marathons, and giggling with her nieces and nephew. Her most consistent daily rituals include coffee and prayer.

Rebecca Flietstra is currently a biology professor at Point Loma Nazarene University, where she teaches vertebrate physiology, human anatomy and physiology, and neuroscience. Her scholarly work has focused on the intersecting issues from science and faith. She is the mother of two adopted sons, ages five and nine.

Ivy George, chair of the department of sociology and social work at Gordon College, was trained at the Universities of Madras (India) where she earned her B.A. in economics and M.A. in social work. She received a Ph.D. in social policy from Brandeis University and an M.T.S. at Harvard University. She has been at Gordon since 1983 and teaches in the areas of social change, international development, diversity, and gender studies, and she is presently working on a project studying the transformation of mothers of international adoptees. Ivy is vivacious, curious, cosmopolitan, and a loyal friend. She revels in truth, beauty, and peace. As a Christian, she does not suffer simple solutions to life's dark and persistent questions.

She thinks that outside of Jesus, great literature and good sociology have salvific powers. She knits with cotton and wool, kneads flour, cans, and lives by impulse much of the time. She line-dries her laundry and uses handkerchiefs. She tries to swim for exercise. She loves a guffaw, and hence is a liability to sit next to in the theatre!

Becky Havens is professor of economics at Point Loma Nazarene University, where she has been professor for twenty-five years and was a college dean for eleven years. She holds a Ph.D. in economics, and her areas of study are women and globalization, the feminization of poverty, and the economics of education. She teaches quantitative methods and statistics in the MBA program and a variety of economics courses in the undergraduate program. A student once described her as a teacher by saying, "Dr. Havens can teach statistics to a rock!" She loves tennis and communing with God during long walks on the bay.

Allyson Jule, PhD, is Professor of Education and Co-Director of the Gender Studies Institute at Trinity Western University in Langley, BC, Canada. She earned her PhD in London, England, at the Roehampton Institute (now the University of Roehampton). She taught in the UK for six years before returning home to Canada in 2008. Allyson Jule has particular research interests in the area of gender in the classroom as well as gender alongside religious identity. She is the author of *A Beginner's Guide to Language and Gender* and *Gender, Participation and Silence in the Language Classroom: Sh-shushing the Girls* and is the editor of two collections of sociolinguistic scholarship: *Gender and the Language of Religion* and *Language and Religious Identity*. Along with Bettina Tate Pedersen, she co-edited *Being Feminist, Being Christian: Essays from Academia*. Allyson Jule also is the media reviews editor for *Women and Language* journal and serves on the advisory council for the International Gender and Language Association (IGALA). She is a mother of two grown children and lives in the Vancouver area with her husband of over 27 years.

Kristina LaCelle-Peterson is an associate professor of religion at Houghton College and lives in scenic western New York with her spouse, son, daughter, and various pets. Despite the rural nature of her current setting, she has enjoyed living in or near Boston, New York, Washington, D.C., and Frankfurt, Germany. She is an ordained elder in the Free Methodist Church and worked in a church before starting her college teaching career. A few years ago she wrote a book, *Liberating Tradition*, to encourage people to embrace the full wonder of who God created us to be.

Rebecca Laird is on her third career and is still seeking to use both wings of her vocational call to pastoral ministry and teaching/writing. She spent her twenties in San Francisco as a developmental editor for religious books and as a staff member of a urban mission church, her thirties finishing seminary and being ordained while the bi-vocational mother of two small children and the spouse of a frequent-flyer husband, and her forties as a pastor focused on spiritual development ministries and pursuing a doctorate. Now, fully primed, she moved from her position as director of ministerial formation at the Theological School of Drew University and has joined the faculty of Point Loma Nazarene University as associate professor of Christian ministry and practice. One of her favorite pastimes is watching water birds—they seem to understand that it takes both wings to soar.

Jennifer Lang, MA, LPC, has 14 years experience in the counseling field. She practices at Hope Crossing Christian Counseling and facilitates expressive therapy for pediatric patients in the BJC Wings Hospice program in St. Louis, Missouri. Jennifer counsels people of all ages and particularly enjoys treating children and adolescents. She has a passion for the field of neurobiology and for healing people from the effects of trauma. She is trained in EMDR. Jennifer resides with her husband Fred and dog Cody. They have two grown daughters who also reside in Missouri. She is active in her local church and teaches children's church for 4 and 5 year olds. In her spare time, Jennifer enjoys reading, drawing, painting, calligraphy, photography, and piano.

Melissa Gentzkow Lázaro is assistant professor of communication and theatre and assistant director of Point Loma Nazarene University's forensics team. She has studied in three continents and has an M.A. in communication, a B.A. in speech, and a diploma in Spanish language and culture from the University of Acala de Heneres, Madrid, Spain. It was during this international coursework that she met her husband. They have been married for 11 years and have two children. Melissa is a keynote speaker for both business and Christian conferences. While her speaking venues allow her to share her expertise on various topics, her research focus has been nonverbal and intercultural communication. She has been a communication teacher, author, and consultant for the past fifteen years.

Cassie Lewis serves as the social worker in a supportive housing program run by St. Vincent de Paul Village in San Diego, helping those who have spent a lifetime on the streets adjust to life in an apartment setting. In this capacity she gets to organize game nights, movie nights, and dance parties (among other less entertaining tasks) with some of the most delightful people on this planet. She also serves as Health & Wellness Program Manager to provide opportunities for residents to develop habits of life-giving nutrition and exercise as well as artistic expression. Cassie holds a master's degree in Religious Education from Boston College plus a master's in Social Work from San Diego State University. An avid gardener and supporter of food justice and environmental sustainability, Cassie serves on the board of her local church as well as a special nonprofit called Bartimaeus Cooperative Ministries, operated by her favorite theologian, Ched Myers. She can be found most often on the tennis court or cruising around town on her bike, but she is at her very happiest when wielding a ping-pong paddle.

Janell Lundgren graduated from Point Loma Nazarene University in 2000 with a B.A. in philosophy/theology. A few years (and many temp jobs) later, she fortuitously discovered the Institute for Integrative Nutrition® and became a Certified Holistic Health Counselor, coaching clients in personal healing, cooking, and self-care. After a short stint as a nomad, Janell became the Kitchen Manager at the Occidental Arts and Ecology Center in 2007, where she rocked people's worlds with farm-fresh organic meals. Recently, she struck out once more for a life of adventure and can be found around the cookfires and kitchen tables of the world. Her highest food praise came from a six-year-old who, after tasting Janell's kale chips, declared, "This kale is better than chocolate cake!"

Lindsey Lupo is associate professor of political science at Point Loma Nazarene University, where she teaches American and comparative politics. Her research interests include urban politics, contentious political action, race and ethnicity, and social movements, and she has published a variety of journal articles and book chapters in these fields. Her book, *Flak-Catchers: One Hundred Years of Riot Commission Politics*, looks at the political and social implications of instituting post-violence riot commissions. She lives with her husband and two young daughters in Carlsbad, California, where she's always on the search for a good new restaurant.

Kelli McCoy is an assistant professor of history at Point Loma Nazarene University, where she teaches U.S. history, world civilizations, and women's history. She received her Ph.D. from the University of California, San Diego, after writing a dissertation examining the interaction between the law, gender, and class in the early twentieth-century United States. Kelli has made San Diego her home for most of her adult life and absolutely loves the beautiful ocean and the sunshine. She and her husband travel as often as they can, but always enjoy coming home again. Kelli recently gave birth to their first son, Caleb.

Melanie Springer Mock has two ten-year-old sons, Benjamin and Samuel, and two adult stepchildren. Her first grandchild was born last year. She is a professor of English at George Fox University and has written for a number of publications, including *The Chronicle of Higher Education*, *Adoptive Families*, *Mennonite Weekly Review*, and *Christian Feminism Today*, among others. Her most recent book, *Just Moms: Conveying Justice in an Unjust World*, was published by Barclay in 2011. Melanie enjoys running marathons, hanging out in the sunshine, and watching bad reality television. Though her kids stopped naps five years ago, Melanie still takes one every afternoon, even at her office.

Coleen Montgomery is a Point Loma Nazarene University grad who teaches high school English part-time and tries not to feel guilty about her piles of ungraded essays and unwashed laundry (among other things). She's happiest in the classroom when her students transition from Point Mongers to Critical Thinkers, and the California Association of Teachers of English published her article with that title. She's happiest at home when she hears her kids giggling and when she and her husband have plans for a night out that doesn't involve Target.

Jamie Noling is an associate campus pastor at Azusa Pacific University, where she has the joy of working with undergraduate students as they encounter God during their college years. Jamie is also an adjunct professor for APU and has taught courses in biblical studies, practical theology, and communication. Jamie has a doctor of ministry degree, with special emphasis on women's studies in the Christian church, from Gordon-Conwell Theological Seminary; an M.A. in theology from Fuller Theological Seminary; and a B.A. in communication from Pepperdine University. In the time since Jamie contributed her essay, she got engaged to John Auth and five months later, they were married at the church where her parents were married thirty-nine years before. She now is exploring a new chapter in her own life—marriage as a context for discipleship.

Jenell Williams Paris is professor of anthropology at Messiah College in Grantham, PA. She is the author, most recently, of *The End of Sexual Identity: Why Sex is too Important to Tell Us Who We Are* (IVP, 2010) and *Introducing Cultural Anthropology: A Christian Perspective* (co-authored with Brian Howell, Baker Academic, 2010). She and her husband, James, live in Grantham with their three sons.

Mary Rearick Paul is vice president for spiritual development at Point Loma Nazarene University. Previously she was associate professor at Olivet Nazarene University. She also served for more than eighteen years as a senior/co-pastor in several Nazarene churches. She received her B.A. in social work from Eastern Nazarene College, a master of divinity from Boston University, and a doctorate of ministry from Asbury Theological Seminary in 2005. She has been married for more than twenty-five years to Bruce Paul. Together they have had the great joy of raising two sons and working in multiple ministry opportunities.

Bettina Tate Pedersen is professor of literature at Point Loma Nazarene University and teaches nineteenth- and twentieth-century British literature, women writers, literary theory, and composition. She also teaches in the interdisciplinary women's studies minor program and serves on the women's studies steering board. She earned her Ph. D. at the University of Illinois, Urbana-Champaign. She is co-author/editor, with Allyson Jule, of *Being Feminist, Being Christian* and has published essays on British and Canadian women writers, feminism, and teaching. She is currently working on a book, *Why Feminism Still Matters*, and two personal memoirs. She shares life with her spouse of twenty-six years, Dr. Keith Pedersen, and sons, Kai and Soren.

Heather Ross is a philosopher, a Southerner, a mother, a teacher, a wife, a picker, a grinner, a lover, and a sinner. Oh, and she loves very ripe tomatoes. She is also an associate professor of philosophy at Point Loma Nazarene University. She is married to Brent, a United Methodist pastor, and has two children, Ian and Amelia. She is a lifelong Nazarene, and grew up in Nashville, Tennessee. She still speaks with a bit of an accent.

Melissa Tucker is an associate director of international ministries at Point Loma Nazarene University who spends much of her time crossing the U.S.-México border. Her job involves connecting people and opportunities, mediating cross-cultural relationships, paying attention to border issues, and mentoring college students. Not being able to choose between graduate education in theology or nonprofit management, she decided to pursue both – and recently became a licensed minister in the Church of the Nazarene. She adores San Diego (also home to an amazing net of family and friends), can't help but dance when good '70s funk comes on, and obsesses over theme party details.

Lois Wagner has pursued a career in nursing, psychology, and education for the past fifty years. She has functioned as a nurse in the hospital and community as well as nurse educator at four educational institutions. The focus of her career has been to serve and advocate for those who are underserved and marginalized in our society. She enjoys learning a great deal from her three children and six granddaughters. Living with the changes in her own life and supporting others as they go through changes (birth, illness, divorce, and death) has taught her a great deal about "letting go" of the past, dwelling in the present, and caring for oneself in the process. Whether it's the ocean of San Diego or the mountains of Montana (where she currently lives), being in nature is a healing place for her body, mind, and soul as she observes the changes and renewal that occur.

Maxine Walker is professor emerita of literature at Point Loma Nazarene University, where she also served as the director of the Wesleyan Center for 21st Century Studies for many years. Since retiring from teaching, she and her husband have enjoyed traveling extensively in the United Kingdom and Eastern Europe. She remains deeply in engaged in theological scholarship.